TOURISM AND BUDDHIST MONASTERIES OF LADAKH HIMALAYA

TOURISM AND BUDDHIST MONASTERIES OF LADAKH HIMALAYA

Dr. Prem Singh Jina

Publications

KALPAZ PUBLICATIONS
DELHI-110 052

Tourism and Buddhist Monastries of Ladakh Himalaya

Rs. 720

ISBN : 81-7835-518-3

Published in 2007 in India by
Kalpaz Publications,
C-30, Satyawati Nagar,
Delhi-110 052
Phone: 9212729499
E-mail : kalpaz@hotmail.com

Laser Type setting by: Tact Computer Graphics, Delhi
Printed at: Salasar Imaging System, Delhi

Dedicated to
Mrs. Manju Jina

Contents

Preface

Ladakh is today's Tibet. This land of mountains and picturesque situation of monasteries, the rich beauty of other ancient Buddhist monuments, the beat and rythm of musical instruments that accompany the chanting of Buddhist monks, the traditional folk songs and folk dances that have come down through the ages almost unchanged, the colourful masked dances of monastic festivals, the grandeur of snow-capped mountains around small and narrow river basins the simplicity, charm and hospitality of the Ladakhis all help to create this unique mountain abode of man a great attraction for tourists of all categories and economic status.

Keeping in view the above facts and the traditional cultural beauty of Ladakh the present book has covered thirty two chapters on various Buddhist monasteries and famous lamas of the concerned *gonpas*. In recent past tourism is a growing industry in Ladakh. Therefore, three chapters are based on it. Today state Government has given equal chance for the economic development of Ladakh, as a result Ladakh Autonomous Hill Development Councils Leh and Kargil are constituted. This caused political awareness in Leh and Kargil districts. Hence, two chapters on politics of this region are included. By and large this work is a balance approach for teachers and students who are interested on Ladakh Flora and Fauna tradition and Buddhist culture.

granite born of the immense heat generated by the friction between the two plates. In Ladakh, the suture zone between the continental masses runs a little to the south of the Indus valley. The drift continues, and is the cause of the frequent earthquakes in the Himalayan region. However, there appears to the much less geological activity in Ladakh than elsewhere in the Himalayan and the Karakoram. In 8th October 2005, killer earthquake came in Pak occupied Kashmir and at the border areas of Kashmir, i.e., in Uri Sector in which more than 50,000 people died. But Ladakh was uneffected from this earthquake as Ladakh lies beyond the high sensitive earthquake zone[2].

Ladakh has poor soil fertility with sandy character, but attracts Botanical experts to explore more than 500 herbs and shrubs species. Bushes of yellow and pink roses throughout along the Leh-Srinagar road particularly near the banks of rivers during summers attract every one. Besides, we can find scattered poplars with green fields in the settlement areas. However, white yellow and other Ice aromatic plants are found in the high passes. The edges of the fields and water courses are adored with yellow members of the ran-unaillaceae vetches, purple representatives of the scrophulariaceae species of milkwart, wild parsley and mint, and even dandelions. Belladonna is plentiful to the verge of nuisance, and lucerne crop up everywhere. Edelweiss grows in broad patches, but nature's most wonderful show is reserved, like the people's little box gardens, for the roof of her world[3].

Ladakh as said earlier is a place of Buddhist monasteries[4], but the question is that why these are so much popular? They are the rich cultural heritage of Ladakh, have beautiful wall paintings, statues, chortens and religious books. The paintings and sculptures of these monasteries are classified in the following major categories[5]:

1. Enlightened beings Buddhas, Bodhisattvas, Arhats, Gurus etc.
2. Ishtadevas.
3. Yi-dam, personal deities, deities of tantric systems.
4. Dharmapalas (choskyong, mgon-po, guardians of the doctrine);
5. Lokapalas (rgyal chen bzhi), "four great kings", guardians of the four directions.
6. Mandalas (dkyil khor).
7. Illustrations of the teachings (srid-pa'i'khor lo, the wheel of existence).

Since last couple of years Ladakh received highest number of tourists, i.e., more than 30,000 per year maximum of them visit country sides, some of them visit to Tsomoriri and other neighbouring lakes, thus disturb the wild habitat as well as the activities of black-necked cranes. Therefore, while making plans and projects for tourism development necessary arrangements should be undertaken to keep Ladakh free from environment pollution and other ecological problems.

References

1. Jina, Prem Singh : *Tourism in Ladakh Himalaya*; Indus Publication Company, New Delhi ; 1994.
2. *Ibid.*
3. Heber, Adolph Reeve, and Heber, Mrs. Kathleen Mary : In *Himalayan Tibet*, London, Seeley Service, 1926.
4. Jina, Prem Singh : *Tourism in Ladakh Himalaya*; *op. cit.*
5. Finegan, Jack : *Tibet : A Dreamt of Image*, Tibet House, New Delhi, 1986 : 128.

1
Geology of Ladakh

According to Geologists—Ladakh was once under sea stretched up to China at one direction and the other side to the Mediterranean. The whole region is later centuries subsiding continuously due to internal changes of the earth and finally elevated. Till tertiary period sea of this region was transforming into tremendous sedimentary deposits. Today ruin rocks with huge talus slopes at their feet are the results of such changes. For details the following papers/books should be consulted.

1. Baud Aymon et. al. (n.d.)

   Geological observation in SE Zanskar and adjacent Lahul area (N.W. Himalaya). *Eclogal ge'ol.* Halv. Vol. 77, No : 171-97.

2. Bhandari, L.L. ; Venkatachalu, B.S. and Singh, P.; 1974 : Stratigraphy, Polynology and palaeontology of Ladakh Molase Group in Kargil Area. In : Venkatachala, B.S. (et.al.), Proc. IV *Collq. Indian Micropolacont* and Start: 127-33.

3. Bose, M.N., Sah, S.C.D.; Sharma K.K. and Banerji, Jayasri; n.d. Mesozoic plant remains from Fukche, Ladakh; In: *GISL:* 157-72.

4. Choudhuri, B.K.; n.d. Structure, metamorphism and deformational history of the Pangong Tso area, Eastern Ladakh, In: *GISL:* 107-16.

5. Colchen, M.; 1977: Sure La Flyshe et. al. Molassede : Indus Himalaya due Ladakh-5; *Renu Ann Terre*: 60.

6. Crook, John and Osmaston, Henry (eds.); '1988: Geology, Geomorphology and Quaternary History of Zangskar; In: *Himalayan Buddhist Villages : Environment, Resources Society and Religious Life in Zangskar, Ladakh, Warminster Aris and Phillips.*

7. De Terra, H.; 1932: Geolgische Erforsehung in Westlichen Khen Lun and Karakoram Himalaya, Der Wissenschaftlich Ergebinisse der Dr. Trinklerschen Zentralasien Ekspendition Band 2, Berlin.

8. De Terra, H.; 1994: Investigation in Kashmir and Western Tibet, *RGST,* V : 44, Pt. 1.

9. De Terra, H.; 1934: Physiographic results of recent survey in Little Tibet, Geographical Review, New York; V. 24: 12-14.

10. De Terra, H. and Hutchinson, C.E.: 1934: Evidence of recent climatic changes shown by Tibetan Highland lakes; *Geographical Journal,* V. 84:311.

11. Dev, Sukh; Thakur, V.C.; Misras, D.K., and Bose, M.N.; n.d.: On some cladophledris-like ponds from koyul, Easter Ladakh In: *G.I.S.L:* 173-77.

12. Dixit, D.C.; Kachroo, R.K.; Rai, H. and Sharma, N.L.; 1971: Discovery of vertebrate fossils from the Kargil Basin, Ladakh (J&K), *Curr. Sci.* 40, 33:633-34.

13. Fort, M.; 1978: Observations Sur la geomorphology due Ladakh; *Bull. Assoc. Geogr, France.*

1982: Geomorphological observation in the Ladakh area (Himalayas) : Quaternary evolution and present dynamis; Delhi. Hindustan Pub. 29-58.

14. Frank, W.; Ganssers; A. and Trommsdorft, V.; 1977: Geological observations in the Ladakh area (Himalaya) - A preliminary report; *Schweiz Mineral Petrogr, Mith.* 57 : 87-183.

15. Gergan, J.T. and Pant, P.C.; n.d. Geology and Stratigraphy of Eastern Karakoram, Ladakh; In: *GISL*: 99-106.

16. Glociers Holland T.H.; 1907: 'A Preliminary survey of certain glaciers in the North-West Himalaya, *RGSI*; V : 35:123-26

17. Godwin, Austern H.; 1866: 'Notes on the Pangong Lake district of Ladakh from a journey made during a survey in 1863, *JRGS*, V : 37 : 343-63.

18. Gupta, K.R. and Sharma, K.K. 1978 : Nubra-Gartang Superlineament, Ladakh–Some geological observations and implications; *Photonirachak NF* 4(5), 221-32, 6, 15-21.

19. Herson, A.M.; 1934: Sketch of the geography and geology of the Himalayan mountain and Tibet ; Dehradun, Pt. 4.

20. Honegger, K.; Dietrich, V.; Frank, W.; Gansser, A.; Thoni, M. and Trommsdorff, U.; 1982: Magmatism and metramophism in Ladakh Himalayas (The Indus Tragpo Sutre Zone); *Earth Plant, Sci Lett.* 60(2): 253-93.

21. Lakhanpal, R.N.; Sah, S.C.D.; Sharma, K.K. and Guleria, J.S.; 1983 : 'Occurence of Livistona in Hemis Coglomirate bed of Ladakh'; In: *Geology of Indus Suture Zone of Ladakh,* V.C. Thakur and Sharma, K.K. (ed).

22. Lakhanpal, R.N.; Gyan Prakash, Thussu; J.L. and Guleria, J.S.; 1983 : A fossil fan palm from the Liyan Formation of Ladakh (J&K); *Palaechotanist,* 31(3).

23. La Touche, T.H.D.; 1888 : Rediscovery of Nummulitics in Zanskar; *RGSI,* V. 21:160–62

24. Lydekker, R.D.; 1880 : 'Geology of Ladakh and neighbouring district'; *RGSI,* V.13; 26: 26-59.

25. Mason, K.M.; 1922 : 'High climbs in the Himalayas prior to the Everest Expedition' *RGSI,* 107-08.

26. Mason, K.M.; 1930 : 'The Glaciers of the Karakoram and Neighbourhood'; *RGSI,* V 63, Pt. 2:214-73.

27. Mathur, N.S.; n.d. : 'The Indus formation of the Ladakh Himalaya : Its bio-zonation Correlation and faunal provincialism; In: *GISL*: 127-44.

28. Mathur, N.S. ; n.d. : Age of Kargil Formation Ladakh Himalaya, In: *GISL:* 145-50.

29. Mathur, N.S. and Pant, P.C.; n.d. : 'Early Ecocene for forminifera from Singhe La area, Zanskar region, Ladakh Himalaya', In : *GISL:* 151-56.

30. Mc. Mohan, C.A. ; 1901: 'Petrological notes on some peridotities serpentinites, gebhros and associated rocks from Ladakh, northwest Himalaya', *Mem Geol Gurv India,* Vol. 31(3): 303-29.

31. Oliver, DRG ; 1912 : 'Notes recorded in August 1911 on some of the lakes of Ladakh', *RGSI,* V. 42, Pt. 2: 127-32.

32. Pal, A.K. and Chatterjee, A.K.; 1978 : 'Fossil algael from the Indus Flysch of Ladakh'; *Geophytology,* 3(1): 62-78.

33. Pande, I.C.; Tewari, B.S.; Gupta, V.T.; Bisaria, P.C.; Chandha, D.K.; Mahajan, G.; Kumar, R.; Kumar, S. ; Kashyab, S.R. ; Kochher, N. and Virdi, N.S. ; 1964 : On the age of Indus Flysch, Ladakh ; *Bull. Indian Geol. Ass.* 2(1-2): 72-74.

34. Rai, H. ; 1982 : 'Geological evidence against the Shoyok Palaeo Suture, Ladakh', *Nature,* 297: 142-144.

35. Raiverman, V. and Mishra, V.N.; 1914: 'Suru tectonic axis Kargil Area, Ladakh', *Geol. Min. Met. Soc. Ind.* Golden Jubilee Symp. (Abst.).

36. Raiverman, V. and Mishra, V.N.; 1914 : Suru tactonic axis Kargil Area, Ladakh' *Bull. Geol. Min. Met. Soc. India* 48 : 1-16.

37. Sah, S.C.D. and Sharma, K. K. ; 1980 : 'Fossil palm from Hemis Conglomerate to Ladakh and significance in the age of the beds'; 11 *Him. Geol. Sem.* Dehradun, 22 (Abst.).
38. Sahni, M.R. and Bhatnagar, N.C.; 1962 : 'Fresh Water Mollusca and plant remains from the Territories of Kargil, *Rec. Geol. Surv. India,* 87(3) : 467-76.
39. Shah, S.K.; Sharma, M.L.; Gargan, J.T. and Tara, C.S.; 1976 : 'Stratigraphy and stractura of western part of the Indus Suture Belt Ladakh, North West Himalaya, *Him. Geol.* 6 : 523-56.
40. Sharma, K.K. and Gupta, K.R.; 1978 : 'Some observation on the Geology of the Indus and Shyok Valley between Leh and Panamik; Distt. Ladakh, J&K ; India', *Rec. Res. Geol.* 7 : 133–42.
41. Sharma, K.K. ; Sinha, A.K.; Bagdasarian, G.D. and Gukasian, R.Ch.; 1978: 'Potassium Argon dating of Dras Valcanics, Shyok Valcanics and Ladakh granite, Ladakh, N.W. Himalayas'; *Him. Geol.* 8(1) : 288-95.
42. Sharma, K.K.; Sharma, O.P. and Nagpaul, K.K. n.d. 'Distribution of Uth and K in granitic rocks of Ladakh batholith Indus Sutur Zone'; 61-69.
43. Sharma, K.K. and Gupta, K.R.: n.d. 'Calcalkaline Island area valcanism in India-Tsangpo suture zone'; In: *GISL*: 71-78.
44. Sharma, K.K. and Choubey, V.M.; n.d. 'Petrology Geochemistry and geochronology of the southern margin of the Ladakh batholith between Upshi and Chumathangr'; : 41-60.
45. Sharma, K.K.; 1982 : 'Deosai bothlith and its surrounding rocks contrib'; *Him. Geol.* 2 : 180-87.
46. Sharma, K.K. and Gupta, K.R.; 1982 : 'Northern Ladakh a scene of explosive volcanic activity

in early cenozic contribution; *Him. Geol.* 22 : 85-87.

47. Sharma, K.K. and Gupta, K.R.; 1983 : 'Calalkaliner zone Ladakh': In: *Geology of Indus Sutre Zone of Ladakh;* Thakur, V.C. and Sharma, K.K. (ed.).
48. Sharma, K.K.; Sharma, O.P. and Nagpaul, K.K.; 1983 : 'Distribution of radioelements Uth and K in granitic rocks of Ladakh batholith, Indus Suture Zone'; In : *Geology of Indus Şcultur Ladakh;* Thakur, V.C. and Sharma, K.K. (ed.)
49. Sharma, K.K.; n.d. : 'Transhimalayan granitoids of Ladakh and Karakoram Ranges Ladakh Himalaya'; Shams, F.A. (ed.), *Granites of Himalaya, Karakorum and Hindukush.*
50. Sharma, O.P.; Sharma, K.K. and Nagpaul, K.K.; 1981 : 'Fission Track geochronology of Ladakh Granite Complex N.W. Himalaya' (Abst.).

    In: *Seminar-cum-workshop on Geological Records and contemporary fluxes of Energetic changed particles Ahmedabad:* pp. 70-81.
51. Stoliczka, F.; 1866 : 'Summary of Geological observation during a visit to the provinces—Rupshu, Karnag, South Ladakh, Zanskar, Suroo, Dras and Western Tibet'; *Memoirs of Geological Survey of India,* Vol. 5(3) : 337-54.
52. Thakur, V.C.; Virdi, N.S.; Rai, H. and Gupta, K.R. ; 1980 : 'A note on the geology of Nubra-Shyok area of Ladakh, Kashmir Himalaya'; *Jour.Geol. Soc. India,* 72: 46-50.
53. Thakur, V.C.; 1981 : 'Regional framework and geodynamic evolution of the Indus-Trangpo Suture Zone in the Ladakh Himalaya Trans'; *Royal Soc. Edin. Earth. Sci.* 72: 89-97.
54. Thakur, V.C.; 1983 : 'Palaectectonic evolution of Indus Tsangpo Suture Zone in Ladakh and South Tibet' In: *Geology of Indus Suture Zone of Ladakh;* Thakur, V.C.; Sharma, K.K. (ed.)1: 195-204.

55. Thakur, V.C. and Sharma, K.K. (eds.); 1983 : 'Geology of Indus Suture Zone of Ladakh', Wadia Institute of Himalayan Geology, Dehradun, p. 205.

56. Thakur, V.C. and Mishra, D.K.; 1984 : 'Tectonic Framework of Ladakh and Shyok Suture zone in Eastern Ladakh, Northwest Himalaya Tectonophysis'.

57. Thakur, V.C. and Bagati, T.N.; n.d. : 'Indus formation: An arc-trech gap sediments. Details may be taken from Wadia Institute of Himalayan Geology, Dehradun (Uttranchal)

58. Thakur, V.C. and Mishra, D.K.; n.d. : 'Ophiolotic melanges in the Indus Suture Zone : Lithological descriptions and structural descriptions and structural features; In: *GISL* : 33-40.

59. Tewari, B.S. and Kumar, R. ; 1970 : 'Cretaceous fossiliferous limestone from Ladakh'; *Pub. Centre Adv. Stud. Geol. Chandigarh.* 7: 197-200.

60. Tewari, B.S. and Sharma, S.P.; 1972 : 'Charipbytes from Wakha river formation, Kargil, Ladakh', *Bill. Indian Geol. Assoc.* 5(3-4), 62-63.

2
Sindhu : A Great Trans-Himalayan River

Introduction

The Sindhu called Indus River is a great Trans-Himalayan River. It is one of the longest rivers in the world with a length of 1,800 miles (i.e., Approx. 2,900 km.).

The source of Sindhu River lies to the North-west of the Holy Mansarovar Lake in the south-western slopes of the Kailas Mountain, in north lat. 31°21′ and east long. 80°30′ at an estimated height of 17,000 feet. Near its source it bears the name of *Singe Khabab* or "Lion's mouth". It first takes a north-westerly direction to Tashigong, about 120 miles from the place of its reputed source.[1]

Clear Source

In 1812 Moorcroft went to Manasarovar and Mount Kailas insearch of Sindhu River source. He found, it had clear and broad source from which water rushing out. According to him :

"During summer Indus (Sindhu) after flowing 8 or 10 miles of its source, it was 240 feet broad and 2.6 feet deep, and it Garo, about 50 miles from its source, it was a clear, broad, rapid, but not deep, river"[2].

Singe Khabab

Among Tibetans and Ladakhis, Sindhu was popularly known as Singe Khabab. Before entering

Ladakh it is united by many streams. As I said earlier that:

"There is, however, another branch, Singe Chu, of the Sindhu which rises in Singi Tot in Nari Khorsum, on the northern slopes of the Kailas, and sunning north 100 miles then turns west under the mountain of Aling Kangu, 23,000 feet above the sea, and after the Gartok River at Tashigang, having itself received a considerable feeder called the Lung Chu, about 20 miles above the junction. The elevation of the country through which these streams flow varies from 15,000 to 18,000 feet. Thus Singe Khabab rises in south-western Tibet now under China at an altitude of 16,000 feet, and flows about 200 miles in a north-westerly direction, before entering Ladakh of Jammu and Kashmir at an elevation of about 15,000 feet, united many streams now bears the name of the northern confluent Sindhu"[3].

Enters at Demchok in India

In Indian territory, the Sindhu enters at Demchok, 14,000 feet above the sea level. It, here leaves the table land through which it has previously flowed and enters the deep gorges between the Himalayas and Kailas. At the junction of the Hanle River, above 60 miles below Tashigong, an elevation of 13,800 feet ; it is muddy torpid stream, without any apparent current, about 4 feet deep and 20 or 25 feet wide. Thomson says:

"It would appear to have a rocky and rugged channel. Such at least was the description given to us by our guides, and as the mountains on the south-west appeared to close in very abruptly within a very short distance of the junction of the Hanle, we could not doubt that the open and level plain which we found on this portion of the river's course was of limited extent and quite an exceptional feature in the character of the country through which Sindhu flows. From the great elevation and abrupt slope of the range which runs parallel to the Hanle River on the east, there can be no doubt that the spurs which it sends down on its north-east slope towards the Dindhu must be hold and rocky ; and though the hills on the left bank of the Hanle River are much less elevated, yet they ruse as they advance to the eastward"[4].

At the junction of the Hanle River to the next junction of the Puga rivulet Thomson followed the Sindhu River and describes :

"The River varies much in width, being seldom less than 25 yards, and sometimes as much as 80 yards, the stream very gentle, not exceeding 2 miles an hour, except in a few rapids, and it was in most places fordable. It then gradually assumes a more northerly course, the mountains on either side approach much more closely than formerly, and those on the right continue extremely lofty ; the river now flows more rapidly, but is often wider and shallow, one rapid being not less than 150 yards in width."[5]

In 1991, I visited Chaga village, later came to Nyoma which is the headquarter of Chang- Thang sub-division of Leh district, noticed that Sindhu while entering in Ladakh at Demchok flowed with less velocity and had a few feet in depth. Cunninghan who visited to this part of Ladakh in 1847 also experienced the same, as he remarks:

"At the junction of the Puga rivulet the Indus River here 240 feet broad, mean depth of 1.7916 feet, and an extreme depth of only 3 feet. The greatest surface velocity was 3.658 feet per second, or 2.5 miles per hour, and its mean surface velocity was 2.727 feet per second or nearly 1 mile and 7 furlongs per hour. From this data the discharge of Indus would only be 774 cubic feet per second. The stream at this point was quite clear between grassy banks, half sand and half mud. Below this the character of the stream becomes quite changed, the waters rushing impetuously down a narrow channel full of huge boulders and enormous rocks."[6]

Drew gives the following description about Sindhu River near the junction of the Hanle stream.

"We find ourselves in a level plain, of an average width of 2 miles, which stretches far to the south-east; near where flows the (Sindhu) river is a thin growth of grass which makes the plain by far the most important pasture-ground in Rupshu. The mountains which bound the valley on both sides rise to 19,000 and 20,000 feet that is to say, they are about 6000 feet above the flat. On the north-east the erect of the ridge is about 8 miles distant. Below the junction of the Hanle stream the river takes the north-westerly direction, and widens into a plain some 4 miles across, sandy at the outer portions, but covered about with pasture where the river flows through it. There are some small isolated rocks here projecting up the plain."[7]

Sindhu River when arrives at Upshi it flows in a wide, smooth stream :

"To the narrow defile or gorge called Rong, which confines the river south of Upshi, the Valley in again open. The Indus (Sindhu) flow in a wide, smooth stream, between banks of alluvial gravel with a depth that makes it just fordable ; the hills rise in some parts smooth and with a gentle slope, in others bold and steep, on both sides reaching, within a few miles to a height of 5,000 feet above the river. The river flows in a north-westerly direction as far as the village of Upshi at the month of the Gya ravine, in narrow valley called Rong, where the river flows between rocks, along which it is difficult to find a practicable path; still there are also villages in the side valleys and a small population finds just enough of cultivable land to get a subsistence from.[8]"

Sindhu with Varied Widths

Sindhu River after Upshi village flows swiftly with varied widths. Thomson says :

"The Indus River width from 30 and 40 to 100 feet, at it was flowing swiftly over large boulders, and quite unfordable. Platforms of alluvium almost level-topped, and often attaining a thickness of 100 feet are here interposed between the river and the mountains, which, still composed of highly-inclined strata of conglomerate and associated rocks, advanced in a succession of spurs to the centre of the Valley. Just above Marsalong (or Marshelong) the Indus is crossed by a wooden bridge, and from this place the direction of the valley becomes more westerly, and the mountains on both sides recede considerably from the river, leaving an open space of 5 or 6 miles in width[9]."

Sindhu flows through Largest Cultivated Tract near Leh

After Upshi village, Sindhu flows the banks of important villages viz. Stagna, Shey, Chushot, and Choglamsar. Drew remarks:

"Before reaching Leh, the principal village in the river bank is Chushot, where the alluvial flat is half a mile wide and several miles long ; this is therefore, the largest cultivated tract in Ladakh. The village has over 200 houses, not concentrated into a village scattered over the plain, single or in twos and threes, at intervals of hundred yard or so."[10]

Sindhu joins Zanskar River near Nimo

From Ranak to Pitak (Spituk), the distance is 130 miles, and the direction generally north-west. The fall of the river is 3,200 feet, or 24.6 feet per mile. Above Ranak the Indus (Sindhu) is generally fordable, but from thence to Leh it can, as a rule, in summer only, be crossed by bridges. The bed of the Indus at Pitak has an elevation of about 10,500 feet. The river is here a tranquil but somewhat rapid stream, divided into several branches by gravelly islands generally swampy and covered with scrub. Holding its course still north-west, it is joined about eleven miles beyond Leh, near the village of Nimo, by its first tributary, the Zanskar, which helps green the Zanskar valley. Many interesting mountain trails beckon to the Zanskar valley. The Zanskar river flowing in a direction from south to north, it is here a very rapid, turbid stream, and contributes more than half the amount of water to the main stream below. The valley, where the two rivers unite, is very rocky and precipitous and bends a long way to the south. Thus, Indus, which rises from an altitude of 16,000 feet at Nimo discended to about 10,000 feet in Jammu Kashmir State".

Sindhu near Khalsi meet wanla torrent

About 30 miles below Nimo at Khalsi the Sindhu is about 10,000 feet high, and is joined by the Wanla torrent. The valley is generally very barren, with sugged mountains on both sides, but there is a large strip of cultivated land watered from a side stream on the plateau on which the village is situated, and which is 250 feet above the river bed. The river is here crossed by a wooden bridge, now has been replaced by Iron made bridge, and is only about 50 feet wide. The small size of the river, after a course of nearly 400 miles, can only be accounted for by the excessive aridity of the elevated tract through which it flows.[12]

Later Sindhu River flows towards Dumkhar, Skrubuchan etc. Here it becomes narrow, however at the bank I have noticed small patches of cultivated lands of both sides. I visted Bima in 1998 and Dumkhar in 2003, both these villages are located at the bank of Sindhu. Drew remarks :

"Besides the villages which are seen along the Indus valley there are several in the side valleys which join from right and left. At the mouth of these valleys on sees but a narrow opening, from this they often stretch up for miles, and contain cultivated land and small hamlets."[13]

Sindhu joins Hanu stream below Achinathang

At Achinathang village the valley narrows considerably. Below this village the Hanu streams flows in from the north by a narrow defile and joined Sindhu River. Here follows the details :

"Below the junction of Hanu stream with Sindhu, the botton of the Indus valley is a narrow rock bound gorge. The river flows in it with an eddied but not uneven surface; its depth must be great to allow the body of water to pass along such a narrow channel, for the width is in one place 65 feet and in another but 46 feet. The walls of this gorge are nearly vertical, above them rise other steep but more broken cliffs; above these the granite retires, but there are greater heights behind. All this is granitic rock. Over this rocky ground the path is a difficult one; a laden horse cannot go along it, and with difficulty can an unladen pony be led. It is the same on both sides of the river. This difficulty of the road isolates the villages of this part of the valley, cuts them off greatly from inter-course and it prevents the traffic between Ladakh and Baltistan from taking this route, which at first one would think to be its natural one. The level of the river is about 9,000 feet, summer time is hot."[14]

Sindhu joins Dras River

In 1998 from Bima when I was traveling towards Chigtan village, I was informed that Dras River also joins Sindhu River. Here follows the details :

"Between 70 and 80 miles below Khalsi in a north-westerly direction receives from the south the river of Dras which has a discharge of not less than 500 cubic feet. The valley here is more open, the mountains without any diminution of elevation receding considerably from the river. It now takes a turn to the north as far as the village of Kartaksho where it becomes confined within steep and precipitous cliffs and continues so as far as Tolti, or indeed to Kiris"[15].

General description of Sindhu in Indian Territory

The Sindhu River, thus flows from Demchok to Batalik flows through Ladakh in India, later enters in Pakistan. In Ladakh it passes through great rugged mountains and pretty villages. Here follows the details:

"The path is along the river, sometimes in a piece of sandy alluvium, sometimes over the great rugged blocks of a talus and sometimes on the face of a cliff, washed at the base by the river, the road being carried on precarious-looking timbered galleries fixed into small projections of the rocks. The scenery is always of stony expanse and rugged rocks; only at every few miles a pretty village at the opening of a ravine pleases one by its thick crops and the foliage of its fruit-trees which here as we desend the valley, more and more flourish"[16].

Sindhu in Pakistan first joins with Shyok

In Pakistan Sindhu River after flowing about 150 miles, joins Shyok which also through Ladakh in Nubra Valley enters in Pakistan. Here follows the details :

"The village of Kiris is 40 miles below that of Marol, and is the point where the Shyok joins the Indus. The Shyok Valley seems nearly parallel to and at levels corresponding with, the Indus valley and has much the same general character.

At their junction the Shyok is considerably wider and more rapid than the Indus, being 150 yards wide, while the Indus is but 80 yards. The Indus, however, is much deeper, so that neither river so decidedly preponderates over the other as to enable their relative sizes to be determined at a glance. Probably the discharge to the two is nearly equal. The direction of the united streams, which are now known by the name of Aba' Sin, becomes nearly due north, and it flows for many miles through a narrow ravine to the plain of Skardu, about 30 miles below Kiris. Skardu is the chief place of Baltistan and here the Shigar valley joins the united streams of the Indus and the Shyok. At the meeting of the waters the valley widens considerably. There is seen between the mountains and the river a curving crescent-shaped plain 20 miles in length, and varying from 1 to 5 miles in width. In the widest part are two isolated hills about 1,000 feet in height. Between these flows the Indus, and immediately below the Indus receives the water of the Shigar and becomes a river of great volume and speed"[17].

Sindhu and Shyok River Junction

At the junction of Shyok River, the Sindhu River had 520 feet broad with 7.11 feet depth. Thomson remarks:

"The Indus here was found 520 feet broad, with a mean depth of 7.11 feet and an extreme depth of 7¼ feet. The mean surface velocity was 2.128 feet per second, or about 1½ miles per hour. The greatest surface velocity was 2.586 feet per second, or rather more than 1¾ per hour."[18]

Water Discharge of Sindhu River

At the junction of Shyok River, Sindhu has water discharge 4,525 cubic feet per second during winter and just double during summer. Here follows the details :

"The water discharge 4,525 cubic feet per second in the winter. Of this amount about 2,000 cubic feet are probably supplied by the Shyok River, and the remaining 2,500 cubic feet by the Indus proper."

Sindhus Flows Gently

Near Skardu a small branch of stream joined Sindhu, which later flows gently but more wide. Here follows the details :

"The Indus here traverses the open valley of skardu in an extremely winding course. At one time it wishes the base of the cliffs which terminate the projecting spurs, at another it flows between high banks of alluvial conglomerate or of fine clay. Not unfrequently these clay cliffs recede to a considerable distance from the river, in which case the intervening space is generally sandy. A small branch of the stream, at times little more than a chain of pools, often runs close to the cliffs, indicating a former channel of the river; and when this is the case the low ground between the two channels is often swampy and grassy. The bed of the Indus at this point of its course is very little inclined, the stream flowing in general very gently over a sandy bed, its surface quite smooth and tranquil, occasionally only a little rippled in turning round a projecting rocky spur where its bottom is gravelly and the inclination perhaps a little greater. Opposite Skardu the Indus, even in the depth of winter, is a noble stream, often more than 500 feet wide and 9 or 10 feet deep in the centre"[20].

Sindhu Contracts and Velocity Increased

Beyond Kamar village Sindhu contracts suddenly, therefore, its velocity increased considerably. Here follows the details:

"About 1 mile beyond Kamar, which is the last village on the north side, and to the west of the Skardu plain, the valley of the Indus contracts very suddenly, the mountains closing upon the river, and at the point where it passes from the open plain into the narrow ravine the inclination of its bed seems to increase and the rapidity of its flow to become much greater. This result is quite in accordance with what has been observed in the Nubra plain. Indeed, narrow valley are so generally steeply sloping and wide valleys so generally nearly level, that it can scarcely be doubled that the inclination of the surface is in some way connected with the width or amount of excavation of the valley"[21].

Sindhu Flows through Narrow Space

Sindhu remains to flow through a narrow ravine beyond the end of Skardu plain. As cited below:

"For a mile or two beyond the end of the Skardu plain, the mountains are sufficiently far apart to allow of the interposition of a narrow platform of conglomerate. Soon, however, even this disappears, and thenceforward for nearly 50 miles from Skardu the Indus runs through a narrow ravine of a very uniform character. The mountains on both sides of the river are extremely steep, and almost uniformly rocky and precipitous. At distant intervals a small platform of alluvium is interposed between the cliffs and the river, but march more frequently precipies directly overhang the stream or steep bare rocks, only not absolutely precipitous"[22].

1000 Feet Sindhu Fall

At Rondu, the Sindhu flows 500 feet below the level of the village. And the height of the village is almost half from the height of its source that is 6,700 feet from the sea level. Here follows the details:

"About 40 miles down the river from Skardu is the village of Rondu or Mandi which has an elevation of 6,700 feet. The river flows past some 500 feet below the level of the village between perpendicular rocks of massive gueiss. In a narrow part it is spanned by a rope bridge made of birch twigs, which is 370 feet long in the curve with a fall in it of some 80 feet, the lowest part being about 50 feet above the stream. The approach to the bridge is over slippery rocks; the path to it is so narrow and difficult that one's steps have to be aided in places by ladders. For a long distance the river flows in a narrow gorge, the verticle rocks that form it being over 600 feet high. The elevation of the river here would indicate a fall of about 1,000 feet since leaving Skardu, or the river flows very tranquilly till it leaves the Skardu plain from the village of Kamar, a distance by the road of 29 miles, but not more than 20 miles along the course of the river. This is equivalent to a fall of about 50 feet per mile which, for a stream discharging so long a volume of water, is very considerable indeed, but not more than is indicated by the general turbulent course of the river. Just below Rondu, the Indus is crossed by a good twig suspension bridge, at the village of Shuot. The valley continues to narrow and the mountains to become more precipitous. From the village of Sapser, a short way below the junction of the Tak valley, to Sasil in Haramosh, the Indus valley is without any village. The river rushes widely through a gloomy gorge whose sides consist of precipitous mountains coming down to the very edge of the torrent. In a few places the water, although rapid, is unbroken and can be crossed on skin rafts, but these breaks are few and always and in a roaring cataract"[23].

Confuence with Gilgit River

Sindhu flows the right banks of the high up mountains and passed through Sasil and Sai villages. Before reaching to Sai, Gilgit river joins it. Aylmer says:

"The road, which follows the right bank, is constantly forced high up the mountain side only to re-descend at the next side valley. It is with great difficulty that even a lightly-laden coolie can pass along this road. The left bank is absolutely impassable. The heat in this gorge is very great in summer at Sasil, where the river makes its great bend to the south; it is crossed by an extremely shaky twig suspension bridge, which none but the local men will cross. Below Sasil there are a few small hamlets on the above the right bank, but there are none on the left, which is waterless tract of country. The road on the left bank is very bad, but that on the right is said to be better. Just above the junction of the great Gilgit river, the stony, barren plain of Bunji is reached, which lies along the left bank for a dozen miles. At the Sai ferry the width of the Indus in flood is quite 300 yards, and it flows at the rate of 6 or 7 miles an hour. The passage is difficult and sometimes dangerous. For particulars vide Bunji"[24].

Sindhu Flows 1200 Feet above the Sea Level

Sindhu River now rushing through a 6-7 miles wide valley downwards to Atak, where it flows only 1,200 feet above the sea level. Vigne remarks:

"There as a vast torrent, rushing through a valley 6 to 7 miles wide, and holding a south - westerly course which might be traced downwards for at least 40 miles"[25].

Sindhu-Kohistan Region

At the well known Naga Parbat, Astor River after emerging from the east part of the glacier joins the Sindhu. Later flows between Swat and Hazara areas before entering Punjab. Biddulph says :

"In no other part of the world, probably, is there to be found such a large number of lofty mountains within so confined a space. This immense mass of mountain is intersected by numerous deep valleys, and these, owing to some peculiar geographical formation which I have not remarked in other parts of the Himalayas, are generally narrower at their mouths than higher up. It is not unusual to see among them valleys of from 10 to 30 miles in length, supporting a population, varying from 500 to 5,000 souls, with an embouchure so narrow that it is difficult to find a pathway beside the torrent, which issues between overhanging rocks. In addition to this, the enormous such of water during the summer months from numerous and extensive glaciers and snow-fields impedes communication. Several valleys exist into and out of which cattle and horses can only pass during two months of the year, and in which the continual falling of huge masses of rock from the steep mountain sides under the action of frost, snow, and sun frequently sweeps away the narrow and frail pathways. The roads are of the rudest kind, and necessity has made the inhabitants intrepid cragsmen"[26].

Upper Sindhu

From Bunji to the village of Gor Sindhu meets Paro stream and small rivulet called Gies, then it flows in a westerly direction and again joins with a small Talpin stream. Finally near Kalabagh it enters into the Punjub Plains. Thus, Sindhu before entering Punjab Plains joins with mostly glacial melted streams, and known Upper Sindhu"[27].

Lower Sindhu

In the lower part of Sindhu it receives five tributaries—the Jhelum, Chenab, Ravi, Beas and Sutlej, give the name Punjab. Thereafter it becomes much larger and flows at an elevation of 259 feet. Gradually its speed becomes slow, and soil being deposited on its bed, which result to fertile the Punjab region".[28]

Sindhu merges into Sea

Near Tatta the Sindhu River begins its deltaic stage and breaks into distributaries that join the sea at various point south-southeast of Karachi. Here Sindhu delta covers an area of 3,000 square miles".[29]

Historical background of Sindhu River

In Rig Veda of 1500 B.C. The name of Sindhu River refers as a roaring river of power:

"Sindhu might surpasses all streams that flow. His roar is lifted up to heaven above the earth; he puts forth endless vigour with a flash of light........ Even as cows with milk rush to their calves, so other rivers roar into the Sindhu. As a warrior king leads other warriors, so does Sindhu leads other rivers......... Rich is good steeds in Sindhu, rich in gold, nobly fashioned, rich in ample wealth. Sindhu is too alive and too divine to be 'it' and so Sindhu is 'he' ! When the Vedic seer invokes heaven and earth, he also invokes the Sindhu. The Veda refers to the Ganga only twice ; but it makes as many as thirty reference to the Sindhu"[30].

In Rig Veda Sindhu's roar is considered as the thunderstorm:

"The Rig Veda compares the sound of the flowing Sindhu to the roar of thunderstorm, indicating the sense of awe inspired by the river in the minds of Aryans"[31].

The Aryan or Indus civilisation popularly knows Harappa and Mahenjodaro; was very well flourished along the banks of Sindhu. Therefore, under the said civilisation Sindhu symbolises the power and strength. Later during Vedic period the Sindhu denoted 'vastness' as sea has. In Ramayana, Sindhu is seen to be the given the title 'Mahanadi' means 'the mighty river'. In Mahabharat, Sindhu is mentioned along with Ganga and Saraswati and was expressed as important as Ganga. Kalidas and Panini the famous Sanskrit scholar of 5th century had praised Sindhu and denoted as a powerful river[32]".

In Raghuvansha Kalidas says that on the advice of his maternal uncle Yudhajat, Rama conferred Sindh on Bharata. Rama's ancestor Raghu's triumphant had relaxed on the banks of the Sindhu[33].

It is said that Bhasa play was based on the romance of Prince Avimark and Kurangadi Princess kurangadi was of Sindhu-Sauvira[34].

According to Bhavishya Puran, Maharaja Vikramaditya had Sindhusthan, a state at the border of Sindhu River[35].

Jain scholars believe that the eleventh Jain Tirthankar was from Sindhi State and called Anshnath. During eighth century A.D. Sindhis had good affection for their country and they often sang song, music and performed dance in the honour of Sindhu River[36].

Under the legend it is said that Buddha permitted the 'Bhikshus' to wear shoes in Sindhudesh as the area has extreme cold, dry and dusty climate.[37]

In Kapilavastu when Sthavirtis, the Price of Rorik became his disciple the four auspicious houses of lotus colour, had come from Sindhudesh[38].

During Buddha period, Roruka of Sindh competing with the capital of the Magadha empire. When Bimbisar was the king of Magadha empire, he sent Rudrayan, the king of Sindhu-Sauvira, a rare portrait of the Buddha. The two powerful ministers of Sindh at the time were Hiroo and Beru, their names still common amongst the Sindhis[39].

Chandragupta was the first Maurya king who won Sindh and displaced the Nandas, occupied Pataliputra, later established the great Mauryan empire[40].

In Ramayana it is mentioned that Sindh state was under king Dasaratha's empire. When Kaikeyi asked Sulk, Dasaratha proclaimed:

The sun does not set on my empire, Sindh, Sauvira, Saurashtra, Anga, Vanga, Magadha, Kashi, Koshal. They are all mine[41].

When Sita was kidnapped by Ravana, Rama asked vanaras to go Sindh with their horses and search Sita there[42].

At the end but not least in the Kashmir history we have references of Sindhu. According to Rajatarangini Kuya's son Sindhu rose to lead the elephant brigade of Kashmir. He was the advisor of Queen Dida and honoured by 'Sindhu' Gaja[43].

Hydrology

The Upper Sindh has many snow fed tributaries, therefore does not have good discharge, during winter months it is at a minimum side. From the first week of June water rise, sometimes floods occur in Ladakh and Skardu regions during July or August when sun shines brightly, snow melts rapidly and caused floods.

However, it is a normal fashion during rainy season in the Lower Sindhu regions. Here, Sindhu annually carries about one half of the total supply of water, i.e. 144,283,000,000 cubic yards. The Jhelum and Chenab each one-fourth as much as the Sindhu; and the Ravi, Beas, and Satluj combined comprise about one-fifth of the total supply of the system, i.e., 271,316,000,000 cubic yards[44].

Climate

The Upper Sindh region receives less rainfall, because most of this region comes under Trans-Himalayan belt and lies more than 10,000 feet high from the sea level and surrounded by high Himalayan mountain peaks vary from 20,000 to 25,000 feet. In the lower Sindhu region the percentage of rainfall is comparatively higher and receives monsoon rains from July. The areas under high mountains through which Sindhu flows experiences temperature below freezing point on the north during January, while in July it reaches as maximum of about 38^0C. In Sindh and Punjab, Jacobabad, one of the hottest spots on earth, is situated west of the Sindhu River in Upper Sindh and often records summer maximum of 49°C[45].

Vegetation

Due to desert condition in Upper Sindhu vegetation is poor, however through irrigation by canals from Sindhu River and by Glacier melted water, permit cultivation. In the Lower Sindhu region, Sindhu River carries fertile soil, thus result good vegetation. But due to overpopulation, overgrazing etc. destruction of both trees and vegetation caused to mark deterioration in groundwater level. On the Sindh plains, there are thorn forests of open acacia, bush, undergrowth of poppies, vetch, thistles and chickwed. Near the Sindhu River are stretches tall pampa like grass, and streams and canals are often lined with tamarisk trees and some dense serub. Besides, cultivated areas close to the river have many trees.[46]

Animal Life

The Sindhu River is the source of rich palla variety fish. Between the Swat and Hazara area the river is noted for trout fishing. In recent years fish culture has been practiced in reservoirs of dams and barrages. Near Leh in Ladakh trouts are rearing in ponds.[47]

The Indus Water Treaty

In 1947, after the partition, the international boundary between India and Pakistan cut irrigation system of the Bari Doab and the Sutlej valley project, originally designed as one scheme, into two parts. The headwork fell to India while the canals ran through Pakistan. This led to a disruption in the water supply in some parts of Pakistan. The dispute that thus arose and continued for some years was resolved through the mediation of the world by a treaty between Pakistan and India in 1960, is known as the Indus Water Treaty. According to this agreement the flow of the three Western rivers of the Indus Basin—The Indus, Jhelum, and Chenab (except a small quantity used in Kashmir) will be utilized exclusively for Pakistan, whereas the entire flow of the three eastern rivers the Ravi, Beas, and Sutlej will be used by India. In accordance with the settlement, Pakistan was to build two storage dams, eight link canals, and five barrages and to operate a drainage schemes, using tubewells that make underground water available for surface irrigation. The Indus Basin projects are to be completed by 1975[48].

Dams

The Mangla Dam on the Jhelum River, near the town of Jhelum, was completed in 1967. The dam has a crest length of about 11000 feet and a maximum height of 380 feet and is one of the largest rolled earth-fill dams in the world. The Tarbela Dam was established in the early 1970 on Indus, 80 miles northwest of Rawalpindi. It is 9,000 feet long, 485 feet high, and enable to irrigate 350,000 acres of land and provide 2,100,000 kilowatts of electricity. Thus, by and large there are five important barrages on the Indus River, before it reaches the plain areas. In plain too there are important barrages viz. Jinnah, Taunsa etc. help to produce large quantity of electricity and irrigate land[49].

Sindhu Darshan and B.J.P. Government

Sindhu Darshan Abhiyan was started by B.J.P. President L.K. Advani in 1997. Later when B.J.P. Government came in power at Centre Sindhu Darshan Abhiyan turned into 'Sindhu Festival'. Normally L.K. Advani led the delegation of Ministers, Governors, actors, artists, reporters etc. for the inaguration of Sindhu Festival every year. In 2003 fortnately during Sindhu Darshan I also went at Shey, where Sindhu Festival was organised. I saw a group of state and Central Government Ministers at the stage, popular among them were Tourism and Cultural Minister Jagmohan,Union Urban Development Minister Ananth Kumar, Minister for State for Civil Aviation, Rajiv Pratap Rudy. Minister of State for Home Affairs Swami Chinmayannand and Minister of State for Tourism and Culture and Parliamentary Affairs Bhavanaben Chikalia. Besides there were many important dignitories such as Governor M.G.C. Sexena, Chief Minister Mufti Mohammad Sayeed, Minister for Finance and Ladakh Affairs Mr. Muzaffar Hussain Baig, Minister for Employment and Information Technology Mr. Nawang Rigzin, Chief Executive Councillor Mr. Thupstan Chhewang, Mr. Pinto Norboo MLA, D.G. Police Mr. Gopal Sharma, Shankaracharya of Kanchi Math, Swami Dayanand Tirath Jagadgura, Executive Councellors etc[50].

Sindhu Festival : A Symbol of National Integration

On the occasion of Sindhu Festival Advani said ; "I hope the Sindhu River becomes a symbol of International Unity and will strength the bonds of unity between various regions and communities probably then, people from Pakistan, China and India will be able to collect here and celebrate the festival"[51].

Peace Floats during Sindhu Darshan

Chief Minister J & K State Mufti Mohammad Sayeed referred to the great civilization Sindhu River represents and said that it is the oldest and the lasting identity of the area. He said this river carries a message of peace and love wherever it flows, and messengers of peace had climbed these high mountains and spread the message of non-violence, place and brotherhood. This message we are committed to carry forward he added[52].

Leh-Mansarovar Road

The Deputy Prime Minister L.K. Advani opened the 7th colourful Sindhu Darshan Festival amidst chanting of verses from Holy Scriptures in the presence of Jagadgura Shankarcharya of Kanchi Peeth. The holy water brought from various rivers from the country was immersed in the Sindhu River, symbolizing national unity. On this occasion he also unveild the idol of Kailas Mansarovar and a photo exhibition. Besides more than 5000 devotees attended the function. On this event, he said:

"I had told Fernandes (the Defence Minister) to tell the Chinese Government that they should open a passage to Kailas Mansarover from Leh. The journey to Mansarovar that otherwise takes 27 days will then be completed in four. He added Now I will tell the Prime Minister that when he visits China on June 22, he must formalise and cement these talks. He said that India's relations with China are improving and Sindhu whose source, Mount Kailas is in China, would further promote these relations"[53].

Sindhu Darshan and Tourism

Sindhu Darshan would helps to increase tourism in Ladakh. L.K. Advani said on the occasion of Sindhu Festival in 2003 that Union Tourism Ministry has accelerated its plan for transforming Sindhu Darshan into a major pilgrims as well as tourists of China and Pakistan would also come to Ladakh to participate in the event. He added that a Sindhu Darshan Bhawan would be established at New Delhi, which will be entrusted the task of organizing this festival in future. On this occasion Chief Minister Mufti Mohammad Sayeed said, Jammu and Kashmir is not only a paradise for tourist but also a famous destination for pilgrim tourism. Referring to Ladakh's grievances he added that his government would not allow any injustice to be meted out any region. Therefore, whatever has been done for Ladakh region in the last seven months to meet their aspirations was no concession as they have right to demand these. He further added that Sindhu River represents oldest and the lasting identity of the area[54].

Sindhu Darshan during Congress led Government

In 2004 Sindhu Darshan Festival was organised by Union Tourism Minister Renuka Chowdhury. This year (i.e. 2005) the festival was inaugurated by State Tourism Minister Ghulam Hasan Mir. The inauguration of the festival was low profile unlike on the past when some Central Ministers used to inaugurate it. As said earlier during NDA's rule, the festival used to be inaugurated by L.K. Advani. The inauguration was marked by a cultural programme representing traditional songs and dances of all three regions of the state. Colourfully attired artists presented 'Chabskyang' dance of Ladakh, 'Rauf' of Kashmir and 'Dogri' of Jammu[55].

In conclusion I would say Sindhu Darshan a good source to attract pilgrim tourists in Ladakh. Therefore, state Government should make all necessary arrangements in order to encourage pilgrim tourism like Amarnath and Vaishno Devi Darshan.

References

1. Gazetteer of Kashmir and Ladakh, First Pub. 1870, Reprinted in 1974 by Vivek Pub. House, Delhi, India.
2. Moorcroft, William : Travels in the Himalayan Provinces of Hindustan and the Punjab in Ladakh and Kashmir, in Peshawar, Kabul, Kunduz, and Bokhara ; By Moorcroft and Mr. George Trebeck from 1819 to 1825. Prepared for the press, from original journals and correspondence by Horace Hayman Wilson, London, John Murray, 1841, 2 Vol. and Gazeteer of Kashmir and Ladakh.
3. Jina, Prem Singh : Sindhu Abiyan (Sindhu Darshan), In : Development of Ladakh : Recent Researchers; 129-138.
4. Thomson is Gazetteer of Kashmir and Ladakh; *op. cit.*
5. *Ibid.*
6. Cunningham, Alexander : Ladakh, Physical statistical and historical, with notices of the surrounding countries, London, with Aller 1854, pp. 12(2), 485, map, plates and Gazetteer of Kashmir and Ladakh; *op. cit.*
7. Drew, Frederic : The Jammu and Kashmir territories, A Geographical account. London, Edward Standford, 1875, pp. 568. Illus. 3 maps. and Cf. Gazetteer of Kashmir and Ladakh; *op. cit.*
8. Gazeteer of Kashmir and Ladakh; *op. cit.*
9. Thomson in Gazetteer of Kashmir and Ladakh; *op. cit.*

10. Drew, Frederic : The Jammu and Kashmir territories; *op.cit.* and Gazetteer of Kashmir and Ladakh; *op.cit.*
11. Gazetteer of Kashmir and Ladakh; *op.cit.*
12. *Ibid.*
13. Drew, Frederic : The Jammu and Kashmir territories; *op. cit.* and Gazetteer of Kashmir and Ladakh; *op. cit.*
14. Gazetteer of Kashmir and Ladakh; *op. cit.*
15. *Ibid.*
16. *Ibid.*
17. *Ibid.*
18. Thomson in Gazetteer of Kashmir and Ladakh; *op.cit.*
19. Brittania-Encyclopaedia; 492-94.
20. Gazetteer of Kashmir and Ladakh; *op. cit.*
21. *Ibid.*
22. *Ibid.*
23. *Ibid.*
24. Aylmer in Gazetteer of Kashmir and Ladakh; *op.cit.*
25. Vigne, G.T. : Travels in Kashmir, Ladakh, Iskardo, the countries adjoining the mountain course of the Indus and the Himalaya, North of Punjab, London, Henrey colburn, 1842. Vols. and Gazetteer of Kashmir and Ladakh; *op. cit.*
26. Brittannica-Encyclopedia; 492-94.
27. *Ibid.*
28. *Ibid.*
29. *Ibid.*
30. Sindhu Darshan : A book-let, published by Deptt. of Tourism, Govt. of India.
31. *Ibid.*
32. *Ibid.*
33. *Ibid.*

34. *Ibid.*
35. *Ibid.*
36. *Ibid.*
37. *Ibid.*
38. *Ibid.*
39. *Ibid.*
40. *Ibid.*
41. *Ibid.*
42. *Ibid.*
43. *Ibid.*
44. Brittannica-Encyclopaedia; 492-94.
45. *Ibid.*
46. *Ibid.*
47. *Ibid.*
48. *Ibid.*
49. *Ibid.*
50. *Daily Excelsor*, Vol. 15, 116/03:3.
51. *The Indian Express*, June, 2003 : 4.
52. *Daily Excelsor*; Vol.15, June, 2003; *op.cit.*
53. *The Indian Express*, June, 2003; op. *cit.*
54. *Daily Excelsor*; Vol. 15. *op.cit.*
55. *Times of India*, Sunday, June 12, 2005 : 7.

3

Ornithological Study in Ladakh

Several Ornithologists made expedition in Ladakh since early days, however, among them notably Osmaston and Meinertzhagen made collecting visits to Ladakh in the 1920s and 1930s. They collected more than one hundred bird species. Today by increasing human pressure in the form of grazing, clearance for firewood, tourist traffic pressure in the form of trekking, increasing air and road traffic and fast changing infrastructure have been apparently altered the number and range of many bird species.

To study bird species in Ladakh we can divide the region in the following categories:

1. Around settlements.
2. Dense tree cover.
3. Cultivated habitat.
4. Away from cultivation.
5. At the river and lake banks.

Around Settlements: Here we can collect the following bird species:

1. House Sparrow.
2. Common Rosefinch.
3. Mountain Chiffchaff.
4. Black Redstart.
5. Grey Tit.

6. Pied.
7. Citrine Wagtails.
8. Hoopoe.
9. Magpie.

Dense tree cover: The following bird species are normally found in the dense tree cover and shrubs:

1. Rufous Turtle Dove
2. Cuckoo
3. Golden Oriole
4. Scaly-Bellied Green woodpecker
5. Greenish Warbler

Cultivated habitat: The bird species here found to pick insects, some of them are here follows :

1. Common Swifts
2. House and Crag Martins
3. Small Skylarks
4. Kestrel
5. Hobby
6. Rock and Hill pigeons and quails
7. Goldfinch

Away from cultivation: The birds species we can see away from cultivation or rugged mountain bird habitats are:

1. Golden Eagles
2. Bearded Vultures
3. Himalayan Griffons
4. Snow Pigeon
5. Chough
6. Alpine Chough
7. Raven
8. Black Redstart
9. Sulphur-bellied Warbler
10. Plain-coloured Mountain Finch

11. Brandt's Mountain Finch
12. Adamn's Snowfinch
13. Horned Lark
14. Wall Creeper

At the river and lake banks: Ducks and many migratory birds have the home of Ladakh. They migrated during summers and return before winters. Some of them are listed below :

1. Common Tern
2. Common Sandpiper
3. Ibis-bill
4. Brown Dipper
5. White-capped Redstart
6. Grey Wagtail
7. Kingfisher
8. Bar-headed Geese
9. Black-necked Cranes
10. Great Crested Grebe
11. Terns
12. Gulls
13. Ruddy Shelduck
14. Teals
15. Sand Plovers

Here follows a list of birds which is based on the Ornithological research conducted by Ornithologists time and again.

S.No	*Name*	*Scientific Name*
1.	Adam's Snowfinch	Montifringilla adamsi
2.	Alpine Chough	Pyrrhocorax graculus
3.	Alpine Swift	Apus melba
4.	Asio Owl sp.	Asio sp.

(*Contd.*)

(*Contd.*)

S.No	*Name*	*Scientific Name*
5.	Baillon's Crake	Porzana Pusilla
6.	Barred Warbler	Sylvia nisoria
7.	Bearded Vulture	Gypeatus barbatus
8.	Black Kite	Milvus migrans
9.	Black Redstart	Phoenicurus ochrurus
10.	Black throated Accentor	Prunella atrogularis
11.	Black throated Thrush	Turdus ruficollis
12.	Black winged stilt	Himantopus himantopus
13.	Blue Rock Pigeon	Columba livia
14.	Blue Rock Thrush	Monticola Solitarius
15.	Bluethroat	Luscinia svecica
16.	Blyth's Reed Warbler	Acrocephalus dumetorum
17.	Booted Eagle	Hieraaetus pennatus
18.	Brahminy Mynah	Sturnus pagodarum
19.	Brandt's Mountain Finch	Leucosticte brandti
20.	Brown Accentor	Prunella fulvescens
21.	Brown Dipper	Cinelus pallasi
22.	Brown-headed Gull	Larus brunnicephalus

(*Contd.*)

(*Contd.*)

S.No	*Name*	*Scientific Name*
23.	Carrion Crow	Corvus corone
24.	Chiffchaff	Phylloscopus Collybita
25.	Chough	Pyrrhocorax pyrrhoeorax
26.	Chukar	Alectoris chukar
27.	Citrine Wagtail	Motacilla citreola
28.	Collard Dove	Streptopelia decaocto
29.	Common Pochard	Aythya ferina
30.	Common Rosefinch	Carpodacus erythrinus
31.	Common Sandpiper	Tringa hypoleucos
32.	Common Snipe	Tringa hypoleucos
33.	Common Swift	Apus apus
34.	Common Tern	Sterna albifrons
35.	Coot	Fulica altra
36.	Cormorant	Phalacrocorax carbo
37.	Cuckoo	Cuculus canorus
38.	Curlew Sandpiper	Calidris testaceus
39.	Desert Wheatear	Oenanthe deserti
40.	Eastern Great Rosefinch	Carpodacus rubicilloides

(*Contd.*)

(*Contd.*)

S.No	*Name*	*Scientific Name*
41.	Gadwall	Anas strepera
42.	Garden Warbler	Sylvia borin
43.	Garganey	Anas querquedule
44.	Golden Eagle	Aquila Chrysaltors
45.	Golden Oriole	Oriolus oriolus
46.	Goldfinch	Carduelis
47.	Goosander	Mergus merganser
48.	Goshawk	Accipiter gentilis
49.	Great Black-headed Gull	Larus ichthyetus
50.	Green Sandpiper	Tringa ochropus
51.	Greenish Warbler	Phyllosocopus trochiloides
52.	Greenshank	Tringa nebularia
53.	Grey Heron	Ardea cinerea
54.	Greylag Goose	Anser anser
55.	Grey Plover	Pluvialis squatarola
56.	Grey Tit	Parus major
57.	Grey Wagtail	Motacilla cinerea
58.	Guldenstadt's Redstart	Phoenicurus erythrogaster
59.	Gull-billed Tern	Gelochelidon nilotica

(*Contd.*)

(Contd.)

S.No	Name	Scientific Name
60.	Hen-Harrier	Circus cyaneus
61.	Hill-Pigeon rupestris	Columba
62.	Himalayan Griffon	Gyps himalayensis
63.	Himalayan Snowcock	Tetraogallus Himalayensis
64.	Himalayan Rubythroat	Luscinia pectoralis
65.	Hobby	Falco subbuteo
66.	Honey Buzzard	Pernis apivorus
67.	Hoopoe	Upupa epops
68.	Horned Lark	Erempohila alpestris
69.	House Crow	Corvus splendens
70.	House Martin	Delichon urbica
71.	House sparrow	Passer domesticus
72.	Isabelline shrike	Lanius collurio
73.	Isabelline wheatear	Oenanthe isabellina
74.	Jungle Crow	Corvus macrorhynchos
75.	Kentish Plover	Charadrius alexandrinus
76.	Kestrel	Falco tinnunculus
77.	Kinglisher	Alcedo atthis

(Contd.)

(*Contd.*)

S.No	*Name*	*Scientific Name*
78.	Lapwing	Vanellus vanellus
79.	Large white-rumped Swift	Apus pacificus
80.	Lesser Golden Plover	Pluvialia dominica
81.	Lesser sandplover	Charadrius mongolus
82.	Lesser Whitethroat	Sylvia curruca
83.	Little Bunting	Emberiza Pusilla
84.	Little Gull	Larus minutus
85.	Little Owl	Athene noctua
86.	Little Ringed Plover	Charadrius dubius
87.	Little Stint	Calidris minutus
88.	Little Tern	Sterna albifrons
89.	Long-legged Buzzard	Buteo rufinus
90.	Magpie	Pica Pica
91.	Mallard	Anas platyrhynchos
92.	Marsh Harrier	Circus aeruginosus
93.	Merlin	Falco columbarius
94.	Montagu's Harrier	Circus pygargus
95.	Moorhen	Gallinula chloropus

(*Contd.*)

(*Contd.*)

S.No	*Name*	*Scientific Name*
96.	Mountain chiffchaff	Phylloscopus sindianus
97.	Night Heron	Nycticorax nycticorax
98.	Osprey	Pandion
99.	Paddyfield Warbler	Acrocephalus agricola
100.	Pallid Harrier	Circus macrourus
101.	Peregrine	Falco peregrinus
102.	Pheasant-tailed Jacana	Hydrophasianus Chirurgus
103.	Pied Wagtail	Motacilla alba
104.	Pintail	Anas acata
105.	Plain coloured Mountain	Leucosticte nemoricola
106.	Plain Sand Martin	Piparia paludicola
107.	Pleschankad's Wheatear	Oenanthe pleschanka
108.	Quail	Coturnix coturnix
109.	Raven	Corvus corax
110.	Red-breasted Rosefinch	Carpodacus puniceus
111.	Red-fronted Serin	Serinus pusillus
112.	Red-rumped Swallow daurica	Hirundo
113.	Redshank	Tringa totanus

(*Contd.*)

(*Contd.*)

S.No	*Name*	*Scientific Name*
114.	Robin Accentor	Prunella rubeculoides
115.	Rock Bunting	Emberiza pusilla
116.	Rose-breasted Pipit	Anthus roseatus
117.	Rose-coloured Starling	Sturnus roseus
118.	Ruddy Shelduck	Tadorna ferruginea
119.	Ruff	Philomachus pugnax
120.	Rufous-backed shrike	Lanius schach
121.	Rufous Turtle Dove	Streptopelia Orientalis
122.	Saker	Falco cherrug
123.	Sand Martin	Riparia riparia
124.	Scaly-bellied Green woodpecker	Picus squamatus
125.	Schrenck's Sedge	Aerocephalus bistrigiceps Warbler
126.	Short-toed Lark	Calandra cinerea
127.	Shoveler	Anas clypeata
128.	Small Skylark	Alauda gulgula
129.	Snipe sp.	Gallinago sp.
130.	Snow pigeon	Columba leuconota
131.	Solitary Snipe	Gallinago solitaria

(*Contd.*)

(Contd.)

S.No	Name	Scientific Name
132.	Sparrowhawk	Accipiter nisus
133.	Spotted Crake	Porzana porzana
134.	Starling	Sturnus vulgaris
135.	Stonechat	Saxicola torquata
136.	Sulphur-bellied Warbler	Phylloscopus griseolus
137.	Swallow	Hirundo rustica
138.	Teal	Anas crecca
139.	Temminck's Stint	Calidris temminckii
140.	Terek Sandipiper	Tringa terek
141.	Tickell's Leaf Warbler	Phylloscopus affinis
142.	Tree Pipit	Anthus trivialis
143.	Tufted Duck	Aythya fuligula
144.	Wall Creeper	Tichoedroma muraria
145.	Whiskered Tern	Chlidonias hybrida
146.	Whistling Thrush	Myiophunus caeruleus
147.	White-breasted Dipper	Cinclus cinclus
148.	White-capped Redstart	Chaimarrornis leucocephalus
149.	Wigeon	Anas penelope

(Contd.)

(*Contd.*)

S.No	*Name*	*Scientific Name*
150.	Wire-tailed Swallow	Hirundo smithii
151.	Wood Sandpiper	Tringa glareola
152.	Wren	Troglodytes troglodytes
153.	Wryneck	Jynx torquilla

Source: University of Southampton Ladakh Expedition, 1980, pp. 186-189.

For more details the following research papers and books on Ornithology may be studied:

1. Anon, (1): 1976: Study of black-necked crane, *Grus nigricollis Conservation* News South East Asia, 10 (3): 10-11. The rare species of the crane bird from Ladakh.
2. Anon, (2): 1977: Ornithology In: *Himalayan Expedition* 1977, University of Southampton England, pp. 38-67.

   It includes ornithological field work conducted by the members of expeditions is Ladakh.
3. Cordeaux, W.W.; 1894: List of birds observed in Dras and Suru. *Naturalist*: pp. 367-74. Various species of bird recorded from different regions of Ladakh are listed.
4. Delany, S. and C. Williams; 1979: 'The Summer Survey of Birds in the Suru Valley and the Autumn Migration Study in the Indus Valley' in Report of the University of Southampton Himalayan Expedition, 1977.
5. Denby, C. and A. Phillips; 1977: The Ornithology of the Upper Indus in Report of the University of Southampton Ladakh Expedition, 1976.
6. Gole, Prakash; 1978: A buzzard nest is Ladakh. *J. Bmy Nat. Hist. Soc.* 75 (1): 213-14.

   Reports about long-legged buzzard bird *Buteo rufinus rufinus* have been included.

7. Koelz, W.P.; 1940: Notes on the birds of Zanskar and Purig. *Papers of the Michigan Academy of Science, Arts and Letters*, 25: 292-322.

   Various species of birds are surveyed from Ladakh region.

8. La Personne, V. S., 1928: A collecting trip to Ladakh. Part 1. *Journal of the Bombay Natural History Society*, 32: 504-517.

9. Lapersonne, V. S.; 1928: A collecting trip to Ladakh. Part 2, *J. Bmy. Nat. Hist. Soc.*, 32 (4): 650-59. Various birds are studied from high altitude region of Ladakh.

10. Littledale, H.; 1889: Rough Notes of travel and sport (in 1888) is Kashmir and Little Tibet. *J. Bmy Nat. Hist. Soc.*, 4 (1): 98-118. Ornithological research studies from Ladakh is included.

11. Ludlow, F., 1920: Notes on the nidification of certain birds in Ladakh; *J. Bmy. Nat. Hist. Soc.*, 27(1): 141-47. Number of bird species have been studies from Tso-Moriri, Wakha and Suru valleys of Ladakh.

12. Meinertzhagen, R.; 1927 "Ladakh with special reference to its natural history". *Geographical J.*, Jo: 129-63.

    Investigated avi-fauna from Ladakh.

13. Meinertzhagen, R.; 1927 "Systematics results of birds collected at high latitudes in Ladakh and Sikkim. Parts 1 and 2. *J. Bmy. Nat. Hist. Soc.* 34: 363-422 and 571-633.

14. Osmaston, B.B.; 1925: The birds of Ladakh, *Bird Study*. 20: 663-719.

15. Osmaston, B.B.; 1926: Bird nesting in the Dras and Suru Valleys. *J. Bmy. Nat. Hist. Soc.* 31: 186-196. Different birds have been surveyed.

16. Osmaston, B.B.; 1927: Notes on the birds of Kashmir. Part 1. *J. Bmy. Nat. Hist. Soc.* 31: 975-99.

Details about bird species from Ladakh have been studied.

17. University of Southampton : Ladakh Expedition 1980, Report on Ornithology of Ladakh, August 1982; pp. 204-51 B and W plates. Detail study of birds from Suru and Indus Valleys have been made.

18. Wathen, M.L.; 1923: Ornithological notes trip to Ladakh *J. Bmy. Nat. Hist. Soc.* 29: 694-702.

4

Ladakh: A Home of Endangered Species

In Ladakh one can finds a variety of wild species. Before Dogra invasion Ladakh had large number of Ibex, Antelope, etc. thence, attracted many Himalayan tribes, e.g., Mons, Mongols, Baltis and Aryans. Time and again they migrated from the adjoining countries and settled down along the Indus River banks. Therefore, here they found the following three rich sources for their livelihood:

1. Fertile lands for agriculture purposes.
2. Pasturegrounds for their animal grazing.
3. Wild habitat for hunting.

Among others wild habitat was the easiest source for their livelihood. So, they killed them whenever needed and enjoyed their life. When they were able to kill any Ibex, then all together enjoyed; otherwise sat together and expressed grief. On such occasion they carved on stones and rocks. Many of such carvings particularly of Ibex images we can see in Lower Ladakh, i.e., is near Alchi, Dumkhar, Skrubucan, Tia, Timogang etc. From 10th century A.D. until the Dogra invasion Ladakh was under the Buddhist kings, hence wild habitat got enough preservation. However, during Dogra period these animals became the prey of Dogras. As a result the population of wild animals along the Indus and its adjoining areas reached to the lower limit. During British regime a large number of hunters were given hunting licences for hunting in Ladakh. By virtue of this the rest of wild animals who migrated to high mountains were also being suffered a lot. After 1947. Ladakh became a part of India, consequently under the wildlife preservation, Ladakh region was declared total ban for wildlife hunting. Thereafter, by the Government and locals co-operation we can understand that today Ladakh has become the harbour of endangered species. Here follows some of them.

Blue Sheep (Pseudois nayur)

It looks more like a wild sheep, but in behaviour more like to goat. In Ladakhi language we call it '*napo*'.

Tibetan Argali
(*Ovis ammon*)

It is rare wild sheep, finds in the high mountains.

Ladakh Urial
(*Ovis Orientalis Vignei*)

In Ladakh it is popularly known '*Shapo*', and normally we can see them along the edge of the mountains that bound the Indus Valley.

Tibetan Antelope

This animal often seen on the high mountains, popularly known 'Tsos' and famous for fine wool.

Asiatic Ibex

In Ladakh it is known '*Skyin*' and is a wild ungulate (hoofed animal). This animal normally seen along the high mountain edges.

Tibetan Gazelle

This endangered specie apparently restricted to the south of Indus River. A list of wild animals of Ladakh is given below:

1. Blue Sheep (Pseudois nayaur); Bharal or *Napo*
2. Tibetan Argali (Ovis ammon), *nyan*
3. Ladakh Urial (Ovis Orientalis) or *Shapo*
4. Asiatic Ibex (Capra Ibex Siberica) or *Skyin*
5. Tibetan Gazelle or *Goa*
6. Tibetan Antelope or *Tsos*
7. Wild horse or kyang (Equus hemionus)
8. Markor (Capra Falconeri)
9. Marmot (Arctomys hemachalanus)
10. Pallas Cat (Felis manul)
11. Snow Leopard or Tchan (Panthere Uncia)
12. Wild yak or Dong (Bos grenniens)
13. Wild Dog (Cuon alpinus)
14. Black Beer (*Haput*)
15. Wolf (Canislupus)
16. Hare (Ribong)

The following books and papers can be consulted for further study :

1. Anon; 1976: Wildlife Expedition in India. Tigerpaper 3(2): 22, Records of bird *Grus nigricollis* from Ladakh being studied.
2. Anon; 1977: Wildlife expedition is India. Tigerpaper 4(2): 15. Records of wildlife species from Ladakh had been studied.
3. Darrah, H.Z., 1898: Sports is Highlands of Kashmir, London, 8 vol. pp. xviii, 606. Illustrated studies on mammalian wildlife species from Ladakh have been taken.
4. Dar, M. and Gaur, R. (n.d.): *Ladakh* In: The wildlife of J & K; A Sanctuary Pub.; Srinagar: pp. 25-39.

5. Fox, J.L.; 1998: the Ri-daks of The Mountain (The 're not just deer) *Ladags Melong,* Leh: 36-37.
6. Fox J.L.; Norbu, Chering and Chundawat, R.S.; 1991: The Mountain Ungulates of Ladakh, India; *Biological Conservation* 58: 167-90.
7. Fox, J.L.; 1984: Population density of mountain goats in southeast Alaska. Procd Blenn. Symp. North Wild Sheep and Goat Coune. 4: 51-60.
8. Fox, J.L., Sinha, S., Chundawat, R.S. and Das, P.; 1991: Satus for Snow Leopard, Panthera Uncla is northwest India. *Biol. Conserv.* 55: 282-97.
9. Fox, J.L. and Norbu, C. (n-d.): Hemis: A National Park for snow leopard in Indian Trans Himalaya Int. Bed. Book, of Snow Leopards: 6.
10. Fox, J.L.; Norbu, C. and Chundawat, R.S. (n.d.): Tibetan argali (Ovis ammon hodgsoni) established a new population, *J. Mamm.*
11. Fox, J.L.; Sinha, S. and Chundawat, R.S. (n.d.): Ibex activity patterns and habitat use in the Himalaya Mountains of India, *J. Mamm.*
12. Fuller, T.; 1989: Population dynamis of wolves in north-central Mimesota Wildlife. Monoge. No. 105.
13. Ganhar, J.N.; 1980: The wildlife of Ladakh. Hamukh Pub. Srinagar. Kmr. Ind. p. 91. General account of the wildlife species from Ladakh had been studied.
14. Hartmann, H.; 1987: Pfianzengesell chafter vockepe standorte aur der pubalpinon und alpinen stuisim sudhehen und osthchen Ladakh. *Candollea* 42:277-326.
15. Jina, Prem Singh; 2002: The Ecology of wild life of Ladakh. In : *Development of Ladakh Himalaya: Recent Researchers,* Kalpaz Publications, Delhi.

16. Mallon, D.; 1983: The Status of Ladakh Urial Ovis orientalis vignei in Ladakh, India. *Biol. Conserv.* 27: 327-81.
17. Mallon, D.; 1991: Status and conservation of large mammals in Ladakh. *Biol Conserv.* 66: 104-19.
18. Mallon, D. and Prodon, Roger; 1995: Ecology and Conservation in Ladakh; In RROL 4 and 5: 109-114
19. Oshorne, B. Mallon, D. and Fraser, S.; 1983: Ladakh threat and strenghold of rare Himalayan mammals, *oryx.* 17:182-89.
20. Seikh, Abdul Gani; 2002: The wildlife of Ladakh; In: *Development of Ladakh Himalaya: Recent Researchers*; Kalpaz Pub, Delhi: 153-163.
21. Snow Leopard in Captivity; 1995: *Ladags Melong*, Leh; 27.

5
Fossils from Ladakh

The various ranges of mountains in Ladakh were from about 50 million years ago by buckling and folding of the landmasses. Consequently by squeezing landmasses together formed Ladakh, Zanskar and Greater Himalayan ranges. Now the question is how this was happend? We can answer this question in this way, when Indian plate ground its way under the Asian one, the land along the whole line of impact, thus lifted thousands metres high into the air. Hence, in Ladakh by virtue of the materials Great Himalaya was formed, while the Zanskar range consists of larger layers of sediment from the ocean floor, and the Ladakh range was emerged when the above said two plates got friction and immense heat as a result generated, therefore, Ladakh range has got granite presipitation. In Ladakh I have found many fossils in Stok, Kha-latse (Khalsi), Zanskar etc. which give the prove of the solid plates action. The following research papers/ books will give more details:

General Fossil Fauna

1. Bhandari, A.K.; Gupta, V.J.; Ahluwalia, A.D.; Srimal N. and Chakraborty, S.K.; 1982: Perminan fusulinids from Karakorum region, Ladakh Himalaya, India. *Contribution to Himalayan Geol.*, 2: 33-37.
2. Dungrakoti, B.D.; Das, B.K. and Sinha, P.K.; 1977: Record of additional fossils from the

formation of Zanskar, Ladakh district, Jammu and Kashmir. *Recd Geol Surv Ind,* 189(2) : 161-65.

3. Gupta, V.J.; 1973: Indian Palaeozoic stratigraphy. *Hindustan Pub. Corporation (Ind.)* G.U.B. Jawahar Nagar, Delhi, p. 207. This includes details of fossil collected from Ladakh.
4. Gupta, V.J.; 1977: Indian Palaeozoic fossils. Centre of Adv. Study in Geol. Panjab Univ. Chandigarh. 9: p.100. Discussed fossil-fauna found in the rocks of Ladakh.
5. Gupta, V.J.; 1978: A note on the Palaeozoic stratigraphy of the Luneak Valley with a description of a new species of Retichonetes from Surichun La. In: *Recent Researches in Geology*. Vol. 4 Ed. Gupta, V.J.: Hindustan Pub. Corp. (Ind.), Delhi: 37-45.
6. Gupta, V.J.; 1978: The stratigraphic position of syringothyris Limestone of Kashmir and its equivalent in the Himalaya. In: Himalayan Goel. Ed. Nautiyal, S.P. Vol. 8 (Part 1) Wdia Institute of Himalayan Geology, Dehradun, Ind. Hindustan Pub. Corp. (India), Delhi: 82-92. Discussed Stratiographic position of syringothyris Limestone of Ladakh.
7. Gupta, V.J. and Budurov, K.J.; 1980: A new species of *Neocavitella* from Ladakh, India. *Bull. Geol. Assoc.* 13(2): 143-44.
8. Gupta, V.J. and Kumar, S.; 1975: Geology of Ladakh, Lahaul and Spiti regions of the Himalaya, with special reference to the flysch deposits. *Geol. Rund.,* 64(2): 540-63.
9. Gupta, V.J.; Mahajan G. ; Kumar S.; Chadha, D.K.; Bisaria, P.C.; Virdi, N.S.; Kochar, N. and Kashyap, S.R.; 1970: Stratiography along the Manali-Leh Road Pub. *Cent. Advance Study Geol Panjab Univ. Chandigarh* 7: 77-84. General fossil study of Ladakh is included.

10. Gupta, V.J. and Kaul, Ravi; 1975: Lower Carboniferous fossils from Ladakh. Res. Bull. (*Sci*) Panjab Univ. Chandigarh, 26(1-4): 83-87.
11. Gupta, V.J. and Waterhouse, J.B.; 1978: Eurydesma from Lahaul and Ladakh. *Bull. Ind. Geol. Assoc.* 11(2): 141-52.
12. Joshi, V.K. and Arora, R.K.; 1976: On the palaentological finds in Zanskar area, Ladakh with reference to the Permo-Carboniferous and Triassic sequence. *Himalayan Geol. Smr.* Delhi, 1-9.
13. Pal, Devender and Mathur, N.S.; 1973: Some observations on stratigraphy of structure of Indus flysch, Ladakh. In: *Himalayas Geol*, Ed. Natulayal, S.P., Vol. 7, Wadia Institute of Himalaya, Geol. Hindustan Pub. Corp. (India). Described the details of fossil from Indus belt.
14. Pande, I.L. et. al.; 1969: On the age of Indus flysch. *Bull. Ind. Geol. Assoc.* 2: 72-74. Discussed about Indus flysch from Ladakh.

Invertebrate Fossil

1. Bhandari, L.L.; Venketachala, B.S. and Singh, H.; 1972: Stratigraphy, Palynology and Palaeontology of Ladakh Molasse Group is Kargil area. *Proc. Him. Geol. Smr.*, Roorkee (Abt.).
2. Desio, A.; 1962: Cretaceo fra in Karakorum at Hindu Kush (Asia Central). In: *Palaeontological Taxonomia Evolution. Int. Geol. Cong.* 20th (1956) 1958: 345-54. Cretaceous fossil molluscus studied from Ladakh.
3. Dungrakoti, B.D., Sinha, P.K. and Das, B.L.; 1971: Trilobites from the Zanskar Valley. Ladakh District, Jammu & Kashmir State *Ind. Miner*, 28(4): 18-29.
4. Fossa-Mancini, E.; 1928: Foraminifera de, calcare grigio di seiusciul (Lago Pancong), in

spedizione Itilian de Filippi Nell Himalaya Caracorum and Turchestan Cinese (1913-14). Series II-Sotto La Dlezion di (Giotto Dainelli)-6, Fossil del secondaria and del Terziana: 189-223.

Descriptions of formnifera from Ladakh are given.

5. Gupta, V.J.; 1974: Permian conodonts from Ladakh. *J. Geol. Soc. Ind.*, 15(3): 338. Described the permian Conodonts from the Ladakh.
6. Gupta, V.J.; 1980; Himalayellacl-A new Upper Triassic conodont genus from Ladakh, India, *Recd. Res. Geol.*, 8 : 269-70. Described the conodont genus from Ladakh.
7. Gupta, V.J.; 1982: Some contribution on the ophiolites of Ladakh and Nagaland. Proc. Symp. on Tibet plateau, Peking, China-1, 593-98. Described ophiolites of Ladakh.
8. Gupta, V.J. and Kachroo, P.K.; 1977: Carboniferous conodonts from the Luneak Valley of Zanskar Tehsil, Ladakh district, J & K. In: *Recent Researches in Geology*. Hindustan Pub. Corp. (India.) Delhi: 206-8. Checklist of conodonts recorded from Tanze area of Luneak valley of Leh district is provided.
9. Gupta, V.J. and Kumar, S.; 1978: Ophiolites in the tectonic framework of Ladakh In: Structural Geology of the Ladakh, Saklani, P.S. (Ed.): 265-72.
10. Gupta, V.J. and Prokop, R.J.; 1978: Kallimorphocrinus indicus sp. nov. (Cirnoidea) from the Lower Carboniferous of Himalayas, India. *Rivista Italiana de Palaentol and Stratigraphica,* 18(1): 57-62. Description of fossil echinodern-*K. Indicus* from Ladakh.
11. Gupta, V.J. and Sahni, A.; 1980: Upper Triassic Ostracodes from the Chharap Valley, Laheul/ Ladakh Himalaya, India. In : *Recent Researches in Geology*, Vol. 6, Hindustan Pub. Corporation

(India) Delhi: 687-94. Recorded Triasic Ostracodes from Ladakh.

12. Gupta, V.J. and Suneja, I.J.; 1973: Lower Palaeozoic trilobites from Ladakh Himalaya. In *Recent Researches in Geology*, Vol. 8. Hindustan Pub. Co. (India), Delhi : 54-65.

13. Gupta, V.J. and Waterhouse, J.B.; 1978: Eurydesma from Lahaul and Ladakh. *Bull. Ind. Geol. Assoc.* 11(2): 141-52.

    Systematics and palaeozoogeography of a molluscan fossil, *Eurydesma* from Ladakh are given.

14. Gupta, V.J. and Waterhouse, J.B.; 1978: Permian invertebrete fauna from zone of Spiti and Ladakh regions. In: *Contribution to Himalayan Geol*, 1: 5-19.

15. Gupta, V.J. and Waterhouse, J.B.; 1980: Early Permian Invertebrate faunas from the Ralakung Volcanies ; Ladakh Himalayas. In: *Recent Researches in Geology*, Vol. 5. Hindustan Pub. Corp. (India). Delhi : pp. 31-49.

16. Gupta, V.J. and Webester, G.D.; 1979; Palaeozic Crinoid from the Ladakh Himalaya, India. *Rivista Italina Palaeontol and Geologia*, 86(1): 137-50.

17. Imaura, T.; 1966: Discovery of a trilobite from the Shimoyana Limestone (Permian). Sakawa, Kochi Prefecture. *J. Geol. Soc. Japan.* 72(9): 451-52.

    Permian trilobite from Ladakh region is described.

18. Razdan, M.L. and Muthu, V.T.; 1976: Record of the fossils of Ladinic Stage of Middle Triassies in the Rusi La area of Kargil Tehsil Ladakh district, Jammu and Kashmir. *Indian Miner* 30(4): 63.

    Stratiographic distribution of various fossil trilobites collected from Zanskar range in Ladakh.

19. Sahni, M.R. and Bhatnagar, N.C.; 1962: Freshwater Mollusca and plant remains from the Tertiaries of Kargil, Kashmir. *Recd. Geol. Surv. Ind.*, 87: 467-76.

Freshwater Tertiary Molluscus from Kargil are studied.

20. Shah, S.K. and Sharma, M.; 1971: A preliminary report on the fauna is Rediolarites of ophiolite-melange zone around Mulbekh, Ladakh. *Curr. Sci.* 46(23): 817.

Gives report on planktonic foraminiferal and rediolarian from Ladakh.

21. Srivastava, D.K.; Bhandari, A.K., Srimal, N. and Radeliffe; 1980: A record of inchnogentus chondrites from Ladakh, Jammu & Kashmir, India and its significance. *J. Geol, Soc. Ind.* 21(a): 458-560.

22. Tewari, B.C.; Gupta, V.J.; Mahajan, G.; Kumar, S.; Chadha, D.K.; Bisaria, P.C; Virdi, N.S.; Kochhar, N. and Kashyap S.R.; 1969 (1970): Some forminifera from the Indus Flysch, *Ladakh Pub. Centre Adv. Stud. Geol.* Punjab Univ. Chandigarh. 7: 191-96. Description of various species of Foraminifora collected from the Indus flysch exposed near Gya (Ladakh) is presented.

23. Tewari, B.S. and Pande, I.C. 1970 (1974): Permian Fossiliferous Limestone from Lamayaru, Ladakh, Pub. *Centre Adv. Study Geol Panj Univ.*, Chandigarh No. 7: 188-90. Includes the study of fossil foraminifera (Orbitoline), fossil Radiolaria cretaceous age and Cryptosome Bryozoans, Sulcoretepora of permian age from Ladakh region of J & K state.

24. Tewari, B.S.; Pande, I.C. and Kumar, R.; 1970 (1974): Lower cretaceous fossiliferous

Limestone from Khalsi, Ladakh. Pub. *Centre Adv. Study Geol. Punj. Univ.* Chandigarh, 7: 197-200. It describes fossil foranimifera from Ladakh are being recorded.

25. Weller, J.M.; 1935: Permian Trilobites from the Central Himalayas (Ladakh). *Conn. Acad. Arts. Sci. Men,* Vol. 9. Article 3: pp. 31-35.

Vertebrate Fossils

1. Dixit, P.C.; Kachroo, R.K.; Rai, H. Sharma, N.C.; 1971: Discovery of Vertebrate from the Kargil Basin, Ladakh (J&K). *Curr. Sci.* 40(23): 633-34.

   Vertebrate fossils from Ladakh are described.

2. Gupta, V.J. and Janvier, P.H.; 1978: A review of Devonian Vertebrate localities of the Indian Himalaya (Kashmir, Ladakh and Kumaon), with remarks on their stratigraphic and palaeographic significance. *Contribution to Him. Geol.,* 1: 20-34.

3. Gupta, V.J. Janvier, P.H.; 1980: An Osteolepid fish from the Middle Devonian of Zanskar, Ladakh, India. *Recent Res. Geol.* 8: 66-88.

4. Gupta, V.J. Janvier, P.H.; 1981: Remarks on the Osteolepid fish from the Devonian of Zanskar, Ladakh. *Bull. Ind. Geol. Assos.* 14(1): 81.

5. [illegible] Pub. Cent. Adv. [illegible]

6
Flora of Ladakh

Despite many visitors, Dr. Moorcroft was the first Britisher to my knowledge during 1819 to 1825 collected many plant species and sent the same to Wallich for further classification.

In 1835, Vigne visited Ladakh. He collected ninety plants, later sent the same to Royal Botanical Society, but due to very bad condition, were not been identified. Falconer entered Dras in 1819 for the purpose of plant collection. However, nothing is known about his collection. Thomas Thomson visited Ladakh during 1847-48. He gave comparatively good information about plants.

Richard strachey of J.E. Winterbottom visited Mansarovar lake in 1848 via Ladakh. He collected many rare plant species.

In 1849, Henry explored some plant species from the Chang-Thang region of Leh district. During 1855-57, Sehlagintweit brothers also collected plants from this region.

Henderson and Hume visited Ladakh in 1873. They listed as many as seventy six plants. A. Meebold entered Ladakh in 1905. He collected plants from Suru, Kangi, Da and Khardong Valleys.

Ralph Randles Stewart conducted Botanical tour during 1912-13. He collected plants from Dras, Suru, Upshi and Rupshu areas. On 18th July 1912 Stewart entered Ladakh with three men for the first time. They crossed Zoji-la and finally came in Leh on 30th July; later on 2nd

August 1912 he climbed Khardong pass, but due to snowstorm he could not reach to the summit. Therefore, returned to Srinagar via Timisgam, Khalatse (Khalsi), Sa-pi la, Pakartse and Yarungshan la. In 1913 he once again made extensive tour and collected plants from Hemis, Upshi, Gya, Tsokar etc. In the same year returned to Shimla via Kyelong and Kulu in Himachal Pradesh.

In recent years the following scholars collected plants from the different parts of Ladakh.

1. Abrol : 1962
2. Rayunath : 1976
3. Dhar : 1980
4. Srivastava and Gupta : 1982
5. Kaul, Sharma and Singh : 1994.

M.K. Kaul made an extensive survey during 1975-90. He listed more than 350 plants ; later published a book based on these plants named 'Medicinal Plants of Kashmir and Ladakh: Temperate and Cold Arid Himalaya' in 1977 from Indus Publishing Co. New Delhi.

During 1994 Dr. Prem Singh Jina identified some plants from Chang-Thang region. He included a list of these plants with local names in his book 'High Pasturelands of Ladakh Himalaya' Published in 1995 from Indus Pub. Co., New Delhi.

In 1999 Dr. Prem Singh Jina again made extensive tour in Ladakh with Dr. Thinles Yangzor and collected sixty five medicinal plants which are used in Tibetan medicine. He had written a paper with Yangzor on them entitled 'Amchi system in Ladakh'. It was included in Development of Ladakh Himalaya : Recent Researchers ; published by Kalpaz Pub. New Delhi in 2000.

Today Field Research Laboratory, Leh scientists are doing remarkable job in the preservation and propagation of Medicinal plants. They visited

Zanskar, Nubra, Chang-Thang, Kargil etc. and collected many plants, later published the following volumes on them.

1. *Cold Desert Plants* -Vol. 1, Leh Valley.
2. *Cold Desert Plants* -Vol. 2, Nubra Valley.
3. *Cold Desert Plants* - Vol. 3, Chang-Thang Valley.
4. *Cold Desert Plants* - Vol. 4, Zanskar Valley.

Here follows a list of hurbs, shrubs and other plants for ready reference for research scholars on Ladakh.

List of Aromatic and Medicinal Plants

Acantholimon Lycopodioides

Achillea Millefolium

Aconitum Hetrophyllum

Aconitum Violaceum

Aconogonum Tortuosum

Adonis Chrysocyathus

Agropyron Repens

Alium Corolinianum

Allium Chrysocyathus

Allium Przewalskianum

Allium Schoenoprasum

Amaranthus Spinosus

Anaphalis Busua

Anaphalis Contorta

Anaphalis Triplinervis

Androsace Mucronifolia

Androsace Rotundifolia

Anemone Obtusiloba

Anemone Rivularis

Anemone Rupicola

Anthemis Cotula

Aquilegia Fragrans

Arabidopsis Thaliana
Arabidopsis Wailichi
Arabis Tribetica
Archillea Millefolium
Arctium Lappa
Arenaria Serpyllifolia
Arnebia Euchroma
Arnebia Guttata
Artemisia Absinthium
Artemisia Annua
Artemisia Bienis
Artemisia Brevifolia
Artemisia Dracunculus
Artemisia Gmelinii
Artemisia Maritima
Artelmisia Parviflora
Artemisia Persica
Artemisia Sacrorum
Artemisia Sieversiana
Artemisia Tournefortiana
Asperugo Procumbens
Aster Tibeticus
Astragalus Candolleanus
Astragalus Ciliolatus
Astragalus Himalayanus
Astragalus Rhizanthus
Astragalus Zanskariensis
Atriplex Hartiensis
Atriplex Hortensis
Avena Fatua
Barbarea Vulgaris
Barberis Pachyacantha

Berheris Ulicina
Bergenia Stracheyi
Betula Utilis
Biebersteinia Odora
Bulpleurum Longicaule
Bulpleurum Setaceum
Bulpleurum Thompsoni
Bunium Persicum
Bupleurum Falcatum
Campanula Colorata
Campanula Pallida
Capparis Spinosa
Capsella Bursa-Pastoris
Capsella Thomsoni
Caragana Versicolour
Carduus Nutans
Carum Carvi
Centaurea Depressa
Chaerophyllum Acuminatum
Chaerophyllum Aromaticumlinn
Chaserophyllum Villosum
Chenopodium Album
Chenopodium Botrys
Chenopodium Folliosum
Chloris Virgota
Christolea Crassifolia
Chrysanthemum Purethroides
Cicer Arietinum
Cicer Microphylum
Cichorium Intybus
Cirsium Arvense
Clematis Orientalis

Clematis Tibetana
Codonopsis Clematidea
Codonopsis Ovata
Colchicum Luteum
Convolvulus Arvesis
Corydalis Adiantifolia
Corydalis Flabellate
Corydalis Govaniana
Corydalis Meifolia
Cotoneaster Falconeri
Cotoneaster Nummularia
Cousinia Thomsoni
Cremanthodium Decaisnci
Cremanthodium Ellisil
Crepis Flexuosa
Cuscuta Capitata
Cuscuta Europaca
Cuscuta Reflexa
Cynoglossum Denticulatum
Cynoglossum Wallichii
Cynoglossum Zeylunicum
Dactylorhiza Hatagirea
Datura Stramoniaum
Deplphinium Bruonbianum
Deplphinium Cashmirianum
Dianthus Anatolicus
Dipsacus Mitis
Draba Setosa
Dracocephalum Heterophyllum
Dracocephalum Moldavica
Dracocephalum Stramineum
Echinochloa Colona

Echinops Cornigerous
Elaeagnus Angustifolium
Elsholtzia Densa
Elsholtzia Strobilifera
Ephedra Gerardiana
Ephedra Intermedia
Epilobium Angustifolium
Epilobium Palustre
Epilobium Roseum
Epilobium Royleanum
Epipactics Helleborine
Erigeron Alpinus
Erigeron Bellidioids
Erigeron Sublyratus
Eritrichium Canum
Eryngium Billardieri
Euphorbia Hispida
Euphorbia Stracheyi
Ephorbia Tibetica
Euphrasia Laxa
Euphrasia Officinalis
Euphrasia Platyphylla
Fagophyrum Cymosum
Fogopyrum Esculentum
Fogopyrum Tataricum
Ferula Jaeschkeana
Filaya Arvensis
Fritillaria Roylei
Galinsoga Parviflora
Galium Aparine
Galium Verum
Gentiana Algida

Gentiana Tianschanica
Gentianella Moorcrofitana
Gentianella Paludosa
Geranium Pratense
Geranium Sibiricum
Geranium Wallichianum
Gnaphalium Lutto -Album
Halogenton Glomeratus
Heraclecum Cachemiricum
Heraclecum Pinnatum
Herminium Monarchis
Hieracium Virosum
Hieracium Vulgatum
Hippophae Rhamnoides
Hippophae Tibetana
Hippuris Vulgaris
Hordeum Vulgare
Humulus Lupulus
Hyoscyamus Leptocarpum
Hyoscyamus Niger
Hyoscyamus Pusillus
Indigofera Heterantha
Inula Obtusifolia
Inula Racemose
Inula Royleana
Iris Ensuta
Juglans Regia
Juniperus Communis
Juniperus Micropode
Juniperus Recurva
Jurinear Ceratocarpa
KIochia Indica

Koelpinia Linearis
Krascheninnikovia Cerastoides
Lactuca Orientalis
Lactuca Serriola
Lactuca Tataraica
Lagotis Cashmeriana
Lamium Amplexicaule
Lancea Tibetica Lepidium Apetalum
Lepidium Capitatum
Lepidium Ruderale
Leontopodium Monocephalum
Lindelofia Longiflora
Lindelofia Stylosa
Lomatogonium Carinthiacum
Lonicera Gtlauca
Lonicera Spinosa
Lotus Corniculatus
Lychnis Apetala
Lycium Ruthenicum
Malva Verticillata
Mattiastrum Thomsonii
Meconopsis Aculeata
Medica Jacquemontii
Medicago Falcat
Medicago Lupulina
Medicago Media
Medicago Stiva
Melilotus Alba
Mehlotus Officinalis
Menthna Logifolia
Microula Tibetica
Morina Longiflora

Morus Alba
Myricaria Elegans
Myricaria Germanica
Nepeta Coerulascens
Nepeta Discolor
Nepeta Eriostachya
Nepeta Floccosa
Nepeta Glutinosa
Nepeta Longibracteata
Nepeta Podostachys
Nepeta Royleana
Onosma Hispidum
Oxyria digyna
Oxytropis Lapponica
Papaver Nudicaule
Pedicularis Cheilanthifoli
Pedicularis Longiflora
Pedicularis Pycnantha
Pedicularis Pyramidata
Perovskia Absotenoides
Perovskis Atiriplicifolia
Phragmites Karka
Physalis Alkekengi
Physchlaina Praealta
Pleurospermum Candollic
Podophyllum Hexandrum
Polygonum Affine
Polygonum Aviculare
Polygonum Glabrum
Polygonum Hydropiper
Polygonum Minus
Polygonum Paronychioides

Polygonum Persicaria
Polygonum Vaccinifolium
Polygonum Verticillatium
Polygonum Viviparum
Populus Alba
Populus Anserina
Populus Caspica
Populus Euphratia
Potentilla Anserina
Potentilla Argyrophylla
Potentilla Atrosanguinea
Potentilla Bifurca
Potentilla fulgeus
Poentilla Multifida
Potentilla Pabulariva
Potentilla Sericea
Prangos Pabularia
Primula Denticulata
Primula Rosea
Prunus Armeniaca
Psychrogeton Andryaloides
Pyrus Malus
Ranunculus Aquatilis
Ranunculus Diffusus
Ranunculus Histellus
Ranunculus Laetus
Rheum Spicifor me
Rheum Webbianum
Rhodiola Heterodonta
Rhodiola IMbricata
Ribes Alpestre
Ribes Orientale

Rosa Eqlanteria
Rosa Moschata
Rosa Webbiana
Rosularia Alpestris
Rubia cordifolia
Rubus Saxatilis
Rumex Acetosa
Rumex Nepalensis
Rumex Pateintia
Sagina Saginoides
Salix Alba Salix Daphmoides
Salix Elegans
Salix Pychnostachya
Salix Tetrasperma
Salvia Sclarea
Saponaria Vaccaria
Saussurea Albescens
Saussurea Bracteata
Saussusea Gossypiphora
Saussusea Jacea
Saussusea Obvallata
Saussusea Sacra
Saxifraga Stenophylla
Scorzonera Virgata
Scrophularia Koelzu
Scutellaia Heydei
Sedum Crassipes
Sedum Ewersil
Sedum Quuadrifidum
Sedum Tibeticum
Setaria Glauca
Setaria Viridis

Silene Moorcoftiana
Silene Vulgaris
Sisymbrium Loeseli
Sisymbrium Sophia Solanmum Nigrum
Sophora Moorcroftiana
Stachya Tibetia
Stellaria Media
Stipa Capillata
Stipa Sibirica
Swertia Petiolata
Swertia Thomsonu
Tamarix Gallica
Tanacetum Dolichophyllum
Tanacetum Fruticulosum
Tanacetum Gracile
Tanacetum Officinale
Taraxacum Sikkimensis
Thalictrum Alpinum
Thalictrum Minus
Thlaspi Arvense
Thymus Serpyllum
Trifolium Pratense
Trifolium Repens
Trigonella Corniculata
Trigonella Emode
Triticum Avestivum
Tussilago Fafara
Ulmus Wallichiana
Urtica Dioica
Urtica Hyperborea
Urtica Parviflora
Verbascum Thapsus

Veronica Anagallis
Veronica Beccabunga
Veronica Serpyllifolia
Vincetoxicum Hirundinaria
Viola Kunawarensis
Vitis Vinifra
Waldheima Glabra
Waldheima Stoliczkai
Waldheima Tomentosa

Other Plants

Aconitum Napellus multifidum
Agrostis Alba
Allardia Glabra
Allardia Nivea
Allardia Stoliczkai
Allardia Tomentosa
Alopecurus Hemalaicus
Anaphalis Nubigene
Anaphalis Virgata
Anadropogon Ischaemum
Androsace Villosa
Arctium Lappa
Artemisia Amygdalina
Artemisa Salsoloides
Astragalus Coluteocarpus
Astragalus Frigidus
Astragalus Melanostachys
Astragalus Rhizanthus
Astragalus Subulatus
Astragalus Tibetanus
Bryum Tibeticum
Buplcurum Falcatum

Campanula Aristala
Campanula Latfolia
Carex Rigida
Chaerophyllum Acuminatum
Chorispora Sabulosa
Chrysanthemum Richteria
Cicer Songaricum
Corydalis Gortschakovii
Cremanthodium Decaisnei
Delphinium Brunonianum
Dianthus Anatolicus
Draba Alpina
Draba Glacialis
Dracocephalum Nutans
Elymus Dahuricus
Epilobium Angustifolium
Epilobium Latifolum
Galium Boreal
Galium Verum
Gentiana Aurea
Gentiana Carinata
Gentiana Decumbens
Gentiana Tenella
Hedysarum Microcalyoc
Hypericum Perforatum
Impatiens Brachycentra
Impatiens Thomoni
Inula Barbata
Inula Rhizocephaloides
Juncus Membranaceus
Juniperus Macropoda
Jurinea Ceratocarpa

Lagotis Glauca
Lamium Album
Lavatera Kashmiriana
Leontopodium Alpinum
Lonicera Asperifolia
Lonicera Microphylla
Lychnis Himalayenis
Lychnis Nutanus
Myosotis Sylvatica
Nepeta Leucolaena
Origanum Vulgare
Pedicularis Bicornuta
Pedicularis Tenuirostris
Phleum Alpinum
Phlomis Bracteosa
Pleurospernum cadollii
Podophyllum Emodi
Podygonum Polystachyum
Polygonum Tortuosum
Potentilla Fruticosa Inglisic
Potentilla sibbaldi
Primula Stuortii
Salix Daphnoides
Saussurea Albescens
Saussurea Jacea
Saussurea Soracephala
Saxifraga Cernua
Saxifraga Flagellaris
Saxifraga Hirculus Indica
Saxifraga Jacquemontiana
Saxifraga Stracheyi
Scutellaria Prostrata

Sedum Asiaticum
Sedum Ewessii
Sedum Rhodiola
Sempervivum Acuminatum
Senecio Arnicoides Frigida
Senecio Chrysanthemoides
Silene Tenuis
Stellaria Graminca
Swertia Cordata
Tanucetum Artemisioides
Thermopsis Infeata
Trachydium Rojlei
Veronica Deltigera

For further details the following papers/ books may be consulted :

—Chaurasia, O.P. and Singh, B.; 1996 : Cold Desert Plant Vol. 1, Leh-Valley, FRL (DRDO), Leh.

—;1996: Cold Desert Plant,Vol. 2, Nubra Valley, F.R.L. (DRDO), Leh.

—;1997 : Cold Desert Plant, Vol. 3, Chang - Thang Valley ; F.R.L. (DRDO), Leh.

—;1998 : Cold Desert Plant, Vol. 4, Zanskar Valley ; FRL (DRDO), Leh.

Sing, B and Sareen, S.K. (1999) : Ethno-medicinal plants of arctic desert-Ladakh used in veterinary practices-JETB, Vol. 23; No.1: 16-66.

—;1999 : Ethno-medico-botanical Survey of Nubra Valley (Ladakh)-*JETB*, Vol. 23. No1: 167-72.

—and Bhatt, B.B. (1999) : Rare, endangered and threatened (RET) medical flora of Ladakh Himalaya and their conservation strategies. In: South-East Asian Seminar on herbs and herbal medicines, Patna (Bihar) : 16-19 Jan.

—and Singh, D.V. (1999) : Important Botanical Drugs of Ladakh In : *5th International Congress on Ethnopharmacology*, Lucknow 17-21 Nov. (Abstract).

—; Atrey, D.P. and Basant Ballabh (2000) : Propagation studies of some important medicinal plants of Cold Desert Himalaya Ladakh. In: *Asian Seminar on Indigeous system of medicine*, Rajgir (Bihar) : 8-10th April.

—and Singh, B. (2000) : Herbal Drugs of Ladakh Himalaya used in Amchi system of Medicine. In: *4th Colloquium on Ethnopharmacology*, Metz France, May. (Abstract).

—and Basant Ballabh; 2000 : Effect of Gibberelic acid (GA3) on Germination Behaviour of Important Medicinal Plants of Ladakh. In : *87th Indian Science Congress*, Pune, Jan. May.

—; Attrey, D.P. and Basant Ballabh, 2000 : Floral diversity of Ladakh Himalaya and its conservation strategies, In : National Consultation on conservation of High Altitude Wetlands, W.W. F. India, Leh-Ladakh, July.

—Bhatt, B.B. and Singh, D.V.; 2000 : Ethnobotany of Ladakh Himalya, In : *Ladakh: Past and Present*; Prem Singh Jina (ed.); Gyan Publishing House. : New Delhi, : 373-86.

—O.P. Brahma Singh and Basant Ballabh (2001), Potential Aromatic Flora of Himalayan Cold Desert: Ladakh and Lahul Spiti. *J. Eco. Taxon. Bot.* 25(1) : 91-97.

—and Gurmet (2003) : A check list on Medicinal and Aromatic Plants of Trans-Himalayan Cold Desert (Ladakh and Lahaul-Spiti); FRL and CCRAS, Leh. pp. 85, 20 Colour Plates and 1 Map.

—Chowdhery, H.J. and Agrawal, D. 1991: Ladakh: The Enigmatic World of Cold Desert Plants, Santuary 11(4) : 42-49.

—De Tesra, Helmut, 1993 : Scientific exploration of the Eastern Karakoram and Zanskar Himalayas; *Himalayan Journal*, Vol. 5 : 33-45 (A Herbarium of Ladakh Plants with 500 representative specimens was made during this period).

—Dhar, U., 1980 : Plants of Kargil-Znskar; In: *Ladakh: Integrated Survey* P. Kachroo (ed.) Kashmir Univ. Srinagar, India : 48-51.

—Dwivedi, S.K.; Attrey, D.P. and Eli Paljor 2000: Seabackthorn-A potential plant for conserving flora and fauna of Ladakh. In: National Consultation on conservation of High Altitude Wetlands. W.W. F, India, Leh-Ladakh, July.

—Fyson, P.F. 1918 : Notes on Botany, Proceed. of Indian Science Congress meeting held in Lahore in Jan. 1918. *Botanical Bulletin*, Presidency College, Madras, Aug. 1918 : 12-17 (contains notes on flora of Ladakh).

—Gohil, P.N. and M.A. Quardi ; 1992 : Ethnobotany of Kagil-Medicinal Plants used by Balti. Bard, Dokpa Races, *J. Eco. Taxon. Bot. Add. Ser.* 10 : 301-306.

—Gupta, O.P.; T.N. Srivastava, S.S. Gupta, and O.P. Badola (1980): An Ethnobotanical and Phytochemical Screening of High Altitude Plants of Ladakh, Part-2, *Bull. Medico-Ethnobotanical Research*, 2(1) : 67-88.

—Karchroo, P.; Sapru, B.L. and Dhar, U.; 1977 : Flora of Ladakh ; Bishen Singh, Mahendra Pal Singh; Dehradun, India; p. 172.

—Kashyap, Shiv Ram (1921) : Notes on the Distribution of liverworts in the Western Himalayas, Ladakh and Kashmir; *Journal of Indian Botany*, Vol. 2.

—Kaul, M.K.; Sharma.; P.K. and Singh, V.; 1975; Crude drugs of Zanskar used in Amchi system of medicine. In: *Glimpses of Indian*

Ethnopharmacology P. Pushpa nagaden, Ulf Nyamm and V. George (eds.). *TBGRI,* Trivadrum : 163-77.

—Kaul, M.K.; 1977 : *Medicinal Plants of Kashmir and Ladakh: Temperate and Cold Arid Himalaya,* Indus Pub. Co., New Delhi.

—Navchoo, I.A. and Buth, G.N. ; 1989 : Medicinal system of Ladakh, India; *Journal of Ethnopharmacology* 20: 137-46.

—Pugsly, H.W.; 1936 : Enumeration of the species of Euphrasia L. Sect semicalearata *Journal of Botany, Britis and Foreign,* London, V 75 : 273-88. (Description about flora of Ladakh is made).

—Raghunathan, K.; 1976 : *Preliminary Techno-economic survey of natural resources and herbal wealth of Ladakh,* CCRIMH Pub. New Delhi

—Singh, B. and Chaurasia, O.P. ; 1978 : Medicinal plants of cold desert of India. In : Golden Jubilee National syposium on species medicinal and aromatic plants biodiversity consevation and Utilization, Calicut, India:, pp. 10-12. August (Abstract); 15.

—Singh, B. and Chaurasia, O.P. (2000) : Medicinal flora of Indian cold desert; In : Proceed. of the 25 International Horticulture Congress, Brussels, Belgium Acta Horticulture, 523 part 13 : 65-72. and Dwivedi, S.K.; 1998 :

—Plant biotechnology and herbal flora of Ladakh. In : *National Symposium of Herbal Medicines.* SBS Postgraduate Institute of Biomedical Science and Research Dehradun; March 27-29, 1997; Proceed. 1-8.

—and Jadhav, K.L.; 1996 : Botanical Curiosities in the Alpine Flora of Khardung-la, *JETB,* Vol. 20, No.1; 135-42.

—1995 : An Ethnobotanical study of Indus Valley, *JETB,* Addl. Ser. 12:92-101.

—2000 : Medicinal and Aromatic Plant Resources of Cold Arid Zone, In: *Dynamics of Cold*

Arid Agricultural, J.P. Sharma and A.A. Mir (eds.) Kalyani Pub. Ludhiyana : 147-65.

—Stewart, J.L. ; 1870 : Notes on botanical tour in Ladakh or Western Tibet. Transactions and Proceedings of Edinburgh Botanical Society, V 10: 207-39.

—Stewart, R.R., 1916 : Flora of Ladakh and Western Tibet, *Bulletin of Torrey Botanical Club,* New York, V 43, 15 : 571-90 ; 625-59.

—Stewart, R.R. ; 1944 : Ferns of Gilgit Baltistan and Ladakh ; *Bulletin of Torrey Botanical Club,* V. 71, N6 : 660-62.

—;Ferns of Kashmir, *Bulletin of Torrey Botanical Club,* V. 72, N 72, N 4, 1995: 399-426.

—Suma, T.S. 1988; Medicinal Plants of Ladakh (J&K), Foundation for Revitalisation of local health tradition, 50, MSH Layout Anandnager, Banglore: 1-12.

—Vidyarthi, O.P.; 1997; Wild and Cultivated Plants of Jammu, Kashmir and Ladakh, Pub. by Dte. of Social Forestry Project JK Govt. 21.

Viswanathan, M.V. and Mankand, N.R.; 1984: Medicinal Plants of Ladakh (J&K), *Journal and Economic Taxonomic Botany,* Jodhpur, India, 5: 401-07.

Viswanathan, M.V.; 1999: Edible and Medicinal Plants of Ladakh (J&K), *J. Econ. Taxon. Bot.*, 23(1): 151-154.

7
First Hand Tibetan Manuscript on Shyang Monastery of Ladakh

Himalaya

Ladakh looks like the roof of the world with vast sandy desert full of dust and barren lofty mountains. It has two districts : Leh and Kargil. Leh is dominated by Buddhists, whereas Kargil by Shia Muslims. During 1981-82, I visited some lofty places of Ladakh for my research work. I found many Tibetan Inscriptions on stones and rocks in Leh district. The details have been included in my books *Tibetan Manuscripts and Inscriptions of Ladakh Himalaya (1998), and First hand Tibetan Inscriptions on Stones and Rocks of Ladakh Himalaya* (2003).

The following Tibetan manuscript has been collected from Shyang Monastery of Leh district, Ladakh. It is located about 13,000 feet from the sea level and is 65 km far away from the district headquarter, Leh.

Text

Classical and Orthography form

Aom sva sti

rdo rje' achang chen ti lli na ro dang

mar pa mi la chos rze sgam po pa.

Phag mo gru pa rgyal ba abri gung pa.

bka brgyud bla ma rnams la phyag 'atshal lo kye lags.

gling las mchog tu gyur pa 'adzan bu gling.

dge bcuai khaims ldan rgyal mo bsod nams rgyal mo khri lcam rgyal mo rnams.

sku tshe rtan cing mnga thang chyas par shog.

kye khong gi chab srid bzang poai mnga aog adir.

yul la dbang bai dri sku log ltar rgyu gnga yod bjengs.

gsung gi brtir du yig drug phyed gnyis stong. rin chen bcud bsus rdo rje bshag abum dang.

thugs rten dbyangs sgam bkra shis rin chen bsgrags rnam gsum bzhangs kye klegs.

phyi snod 'ajig rten abyung ba rlung gis btegs.

tang bcud sems can 'aod gsal lha nam 'achad.

gling bzhiai mchog gyud pa 'adzam bu gling.

bde chog gnas chen hi si gngas kyi nub.

se ngge kha 'ababs 'abrug pai gyas phyogs na.

bla mai gdang sa shang lvang chos rdzongs 'adir.

drung pa dbus pa sku tshe brtan gyud cig kye legs.

phu na gngas dkar ti si spung 'adra bzhir.

mdo na sprang char bsil ma rgyur 'ababs shing.

bar na sna tshogs 'abru bcur rtag tu smin.

gle zhes bya ba rgyal poai pho brang na.

mi dbang bla chen tshe dbang rnam rgyal ched bzhugs.

'ae ma ho.

sngon gyi bsod nams rgyu las legs 'akhrungs pa

chos blon chen po bum pa sde la bstod khyod kyi chab srid bzang poai mnga ’aog adir

tshe sngon tshogs bsags dle ’abyor mi lus thob.

phyi ma rjes su dran nas dan pai chos la mos.

mi rigs khung btsun spyung sgrung ’adzans pa ni.

yon gyi bdag mo bzang mo rin chen gyis tshe la ’adas ba no no tsang rin chen thar pa thob phyir du rin chen gser dang bzang rnas dang.

sgyu lus phung po mi tog la sogs la.

mdo nas brgyud pa ngan song sbyong rgyud bz hengs.

kye legs yon bdag spun mchog bso phyed rgya ra ni dang.

nam mkha bzang bo khu ’aun rnam gsum gyis.

gsung rab mthong ba don ldan ’adi bzhengs so.

yon gyi bdab mo bzang mo zhes bya yis.

dpon rnams mnyes pai zhabs togs legs par byas.

’ae ma ho.

bu moai mchog gyur chos skyong bzang mo dang.

dga skyid bde ba dang spal lcags la sogs tse ring nad med chos la dkar bar shog.

yi geai ’adu byed sor moai rtse las grug.

mkhas pai rjes ’abrangs ’agang nga gnyis kyis gris.

’adi yis dge bas yon chod gnyen ’abrel rnams.

bla med byang chub myur du thob par shog.

Roman Transliteration

Om sva sti.

do je chang chen ti li na ro dang.

mar pa mi la chos ze gam po pa.
phag mo du pa gyal va di gung pa.
ka gyud la ma nams la chag tshal lo.
kye leges.
ling las chog tu gyur pa dzam bu ling.
ge cu thim dan gyal mo sod nam gyal mo thi camgyal mo nams.
ku tshe tan cing nga thang gyas par shog.
kye khong gi chab srid zang poi nga aog dir.
yul la vang ve dri ku log tur gyu nga yod jing.
sung gi tir du yig tug cheed nyis fong.
rin chen cud dus do je shag bum dang.
thugs ten yang gam ta shis rin chen dags nam sum zhengs kye legs.
chi nod jig ten jung va lung gis tegs tang cud sems can od sal lha nam chad ling zhii chud gyud pa dzom bu ling.
de chog nas chen hi si gangs kyi nub.
seng ge khababs dug pe yas chogs na.
la me dang sa shang vang chos dzongs dir.
tung pa us pas ku tshe tang gyud cig.
kye legs.
phu na gangs kar ti si spung da zing do na dang char sil ma gyur babs shing.
bar na na tshog du cut tag tu smin.
le zhes ca va gyal po pho dang na.
mi vang lha chen tshe vang namgyal sku ches zhugs.
Ae ma ho.
ngon gyi sod namgyu las legs thungs pa chos lon chen po bun pa de la stod.
kyod kyi chab srid bzang poi ngog dir.
tshe ong tshog sags tal jor mi lus thob
chi ma jes su tan nas tan pe chos la mos.

mi rigs khung tsum cung tung dzams pa ni.
yon gyi dnag mo bzang mo rin chen gyis.
tshe la das pa no no tsang rin chen phar pa thob chir du.
rin chen ser dang bzang nas dang.
gyu lus phung po mi tog la sog la.
do nas gyud pa ngan song jong gyud zhengs.
kye legs yon dag pun chog so ced gya ra ni dang.
nam kha zngs po khu aun nam sum gyis.
sung rab thong va don dan di zhengs so.
yon gyi dab mo zang mo zhes ca yis.
pon nams nyes pe zhab togs legs par cas.
ae ma ho bu me chog gyur chos kyong zang mo tang.
ga kyid de va tang pal cags la sogs tse ring nad med chos la kar var shog.
yi ge du ced sor me tse las dug khas pe jes dang gang nga nyis kyis dis.
di yis ge vas yon chod ten dil nams la med cang chub myur du thob par shog.

Translation

Om Svasti

I salute to Tilo[1], Naro[2], Marpa[3], Mila[4], Chosze Gampopa[5], Phagmodu pa[6] and gyul va Drigung pa[7] of kargyud lama tradition kye legs.

Ladakh is situated in the North of India. kings and queens (of Ladakh) are (honest) and characterful.

I wish they may live long (for thousand years).

(By the blessings of king and queen) the citizens (of Ladakh) may become (happy) and prosper.

Religious kings and queens (of Ladakh) are (always ready) to do religious works.

The citizens (of Ladakh) are also to help in religious activities.

They ingraved many (Buddhist) images on stones, printed religious books and constructed chortens.

Shyang (monastery) which looks like heaven from the distance people of (Shyang) village[8] (also) have good character like god/goddess.

They are settled down at the right side of Sindhu River.

King Tsewang Namgyala is staying at Leh.

Under his (kind) regime. Tungpa Upa (Rinpoche) is doing (religious works) at Shyang village.

(Thus) many (welfare) and religious works had been carried out during his regime.

I salute to religious Minister Bum pa de.

He took birth (Under his regime) by his (previous) welfare works.

In his eastern kingdom I also got chance to live happily.

Zang mo Rinchen made statues, stupas and printed religious book in her house in the memory of Tsewang Rinchen.

Namka Zangpo and Chospon also sponsored (Zang mo Rinchen) in her religious works.

I wish sponsors, Chos kyong zang mo, Deskyit Deva, Paleak etc. may become healthy live happily and may have long life.

Tibetan alphabet used as

ka	kha	ga	nga
ca	cha	ja	nya
ta	tha	da	na
pa	pha	ba	ma
tsa	cha	dza	wa

zha	za	’a	ya
ra	la	sha	sa
ha	a		

Notes

1. **Tilo :** Tilopa, he was a famous Bengali Mahasiddha.
2. **Naro :** Naropa, he was the pupil of Tilopa, was born in Bengal, went at the age of eleven to Kashmir to study, was married for some years, afterward lived and wrote at phullahari near Nalanda, then joined the University at Nalanda where he was elected abbot *(upadhayaya)* but went off to find his personal guru in Tilopa, with whom he stayed for a dozen years. Tilopa subjected Naropa to severe disciplines, initiated him into the mysteries of Cakrasamvara and Kalacakra Tantras, communicated to him. The yogic system of the mahamudra (Tib. Phyag rgya chen mo, pron, Chhakgya Chhenmo), which Tilopa had received from Dorje Chang, and taught Naropa six major topics (Chos drug): mystic heat (gtum mo, pron. tum mo); illusory body (sgyu lus); dream state (rmi lam) ’radiant light(‘od gsal, pron. Osal); transference of consciousness (’pho ba’); and the after-death state (bar do, pron. bardo). CF. Finegan Jack: Tibet; A Dreamt of image ; Tibet House ; New Delhi ; 1986 : 91.
3. **Marpa.** Tib. Mar pa chos kyi blo gros (Pron. Marpa Chhökyi Lodrö) or Marpa for short, after earlier study with Drokmi, came as a pupil to Naropa, who was then himself a great mahasiddha and teaching at Phullahari. In all Marpa visited India three times and stayed with Naropa more than sixteen years under whom he studied with Naropa more than sixteen years, under whom he studied the

Guhyasamaja Tantra, the Vajra Tantra, "and the essence of all Mahamudra (the great seal or great symbol)". From another mahasiddha named Maitripa, Marpa also received the tradition of composing the *coha*, a type of verse or song spontaneously made up by tantric practitioners as the direct expression of their personal feelings and realizations. This tradition Marpa later transmitted to his disciple Milarepa, who became Tibet's probably most famous yogi and poet. Returning to Tibet in the manner of the mahasiddha for whom many different lifestyles were equally acceptable. Marpa chose to live the life of an ordinary householder, with a wife and spiritual companion whom he married at the age of forty-two, and whom he called Nairatmya (the consort of Hevajra). In line with his householder's manner of life, Marpa made it a point to be out plowing his fields when Milarepa first came looking for him. Yet Marpa also did a large work as collector and translator of texts and in the composition of *dohas*. Above all he brought back to Tibet the "Six topics of Naropa", and transmitted to Milarepa. "kindled the lamp of the Buddhist doctrine in the snowland of Tibet" Cf. Finegan. Jack; Tibet: A Dreamt of Image; *op. cit.*, : 91-92.

4. **Mila :** Mi-la-ras-pa Pron. Milarepa and was born in 1040 A.D. When Milarepa learned that in his absence his widowed mother and family had been enslaved by an evil uncle, and he went and took revenge by magical means. After that he turned to the life of a wandering yogin, and lived in many solitary places. By virtue of the inner mystic heat (gtum mo, pron. clothing) he was able to endure the coldest weather in only cotton clothing hence his familiar name Milarepa. "The cotton-clad Mila". Dwelling at Mount Kailash and

Lake Manasarovara, which were holy places of the Bon-po, he overcame them in magic contests and took possession in the name of Buddhism. Cf. Finegan, Jack : Tibet : A Dreamt of Image; *op. cit.* : 92.

5. **Chos ze Gampopa:** He was born in 1079 A.D. and was the chief disciple of Milarepa, and was originally known as Dwags po lha rje (Pron. Takpo Lha-je), i.e. Lha-je of the Takpo district in Eastern Tibet, but later from the name his hermitage and also as being a reincarnation of King Songtsen Gompo, he was called and Gam po pa (Pron. Gompopa), i.e., "the man of Gompo". In his earlier life Gam po pa learned medicine, married the daughter of a local Chieftain, and had children but, after his wife, son, and daughter all died of a pestilence, he became a monk of the Kadan-pa order. At the age of thirty-two he heard from three beggars of Milarepa, and made a long journey of find him and become his disciple. Under Milarepa Gampopa received the initiation of *vajra-guru* and ordained as a fully-qualified teacher of Tantra. Gampopa was the author of a number of works, notably the *Jewel Ornament of Liberation, and the Precious Rosary*. Cf. Finegan, Jack : Tibet : A Dreamt of Image; *op. cit.* : 92-93.

6. **Phagmo-du-pa :** Tib. Phag-mo-gru-pa pron. phakmotru-pa was the disciple of Gam-po-pa. In 1158, a few years after the death of Gampopa, he founded a monastery of m thel (Pron. Thil) as the head monastery (gDan-sa-Thel, Pron. Densa Thil) of his sect. Later his follower named his sect as Phakmotru-pa suborder. Cf. Finegan, Jack : A Tibet : Dreamt of Image, *op. cit* : 95.

7. **Gyal va Digung pa :** Tib. gyal ba 'bri gung pa (Pron. Gyalva Drigung-pa), a suborder of the Kagyu-pa. Jig rten mgon-pa (Pron. Jigten Gonpo)

was the founder of this sect. He was the disciple of Phakmotru-pa. In 1179 he established Drigung monastery 128 km north-east of Lhasa from which the sect took its name. Jigten Gompo was also himself known as Drigung Rimpoche. Cf. Finegan, Jack : Tibet : A Dreamt of Image, *op. cit.* 96.

8. **Shyang :** or Shang, Lat 33° 53′ Long. 77° 43′. In olden days this village was under the Kardari of Hemis. The stream flowing through shang joins the Indus River at Marsalang. A road leads up this stream to Gya, and was the one generally employed in summer in going to Kulu, when the bridges on the Gya stream were carried away. This road was extremely steep, going over a pass called to Getsechuk. Cf. Aylmer, in *Gazetteer of Kashmir and Ladakh*; First Pub. 1890, Reprinted in 1974 by Vivek Pub. House, Delhi : 732.

9. **Tsewang Namgyal :** Trashi Namgyal died childless, therefore, his elder brother Lhachen Lhawang Namgyal's elder son Tsewang Namgyal succeeded the throne of Ladakh. Religiously, he is called an incarnate king, and was supposed to be an incarnation of Phyag-na-rdo-rje (Pron. Chana Dorje), i.e. the Bodhisattva Vajrapani. The king declared that, after the pattern of Lhasa and Tholing, his ancestors had placed the bones of the Buddha as an elephant on the Namgyal Tsemo hill at Leh, but since people were not going there to worship he would himself build a monastery and establish the doctrine of the Buddha on a basis similar to what it had under his ancestor Ral-pa-can (Pron. Repachen), the third great religious king of the Yarlung Dynasty. "But', say the chronicles of the kings of Ladakh in conclusion of the section on Tshewang Namgyal "as his work on earth was finished he went to heaven." In spite of that unfulfilled work,

Tshewang Namgyal did build a Maitreya temple at Basgo, and in the paintings in this temple there is a portrait (on the entrance wall to the right) of himself together with his two younger brothers who successed him in turn as king. Cf.Finegan, Jack: Tibet: A Dreamt of Image; *op. cit.*, p. 176.

8

Ganglas Samstan Phug (Tib. sgan glas bsam gtan phug): A cave temple of Ganglas in Leh, Ladakh

Ganglas cave temple is located above Leh town[1] at the foot of Khardong pass[2]. It was famous meditation centre, lamas used to go there for meditation[3]. During seventeen century[4] it was developed under Geluk-pa tradition[5] and put under the Spituk Monastery[6]. Subsequently locals called it as Shankar Gonpa[7].

Statues

In this temple we can acknowledge the following main statues:

1. Tsong- Khapa[8]: The main statue.

   Tsong-Khapa was the founder of Geluk-pa order of Mahayana Buddhism. He was a great scholar and studied under famous teachers of Nyingma-pa, Sakya-pa, Jonang-pa, Kagyu-pa, Tshal-pa, Phakmotru-pa, Shalu-pa and Kadampa. He was especially influence by the Nyingma-pa Las kyi rdo-rje, the Sakya-pa Red mda'pa and Kadam-pa lamas chos-skyabs bzang po and dbu-ma-pa.

2. Gyal- chab-je[9]: At the right of Trong-khapa is standing posture.

3. Khas-dub-je[10]: At the left of Tsong-Khapa in standing posture.
4. Cuksikjal[11].
5. Sakyamuni Buddha[12].

Main Photographs

1. Gyalba
2. Panchen

Thankas

There are many Thankas in this monastery, however the following are important Thankas:

1. Sixteen Arhats (*Tib. gnas brtan beu drug*)[13]
2. Doljang (*Tib. sgrol ljang*)[14]

Wall Paintings

In the temple the following are the important frescoes:

1. Sangyas Smanla (*Tib. sangs rgyas smanbla*)[15]
2. Mithug pa (*Tib. mi/athrugva pa*)[16]
3. Tungyas (*Tib. ltung bshags*)
4. Sangyas (*Tib. sangs rgyas soldang*) or One thousand Buddhas
5. Nastan cu dug (*Tib. gnas brtan beu drug*)[17].
6. Gyan drug chog nyis (*Tib. gyan drug mchog gnyis*)[18]

Today the condition of the ganglas Samstan Phug temple is not satisfactory. At many locations the wall paintings have been destroyed by vandals. By and large paintings on walls are reasonably in fair condition. Morever, necessary steps should be taken in order to preserve the 17th century paintings and architectural structure. But, I never advise to the concern Gonpa authorities to renovate the temple. Renovation means loss of old cultural heritage and paintings.

Notes and References

1. **Leh town:** Lat 34°10′ Long 77°37′ Elev 11,538 ft. It is the district headquarter of Leh district, and lies about 1,000 feet above the Indus River and occupies the slope, and surrounds the base of a low spur on the last side of the valley, while the centre and west side are occupied by extensive tracts of cultivation. The fields rise in terraces and are watered by little rills drawn from a stream which flows down the centre of the valley Cf **Gazetteer of Kashmir & Ladakh**, Vivek Pub. 1974:582.
2. **Khardong pass:** It is the highest pass in the world lies at 18,380 ft. from the sea level and the gateway of Nubra valley.
3. It is said that in older days a big boulder slipped into the Ganglas village, fortunately it stopped upper side of the village and by virtue of this a cave was formed. During 16-17th century A.D. some lamas visited there and found it suitable for meditation. Thereafter, it became a tradition of Geluk-pa lamas, who during the course of their study in the monastery often go to the above temple for meditation.
4. In this temple I found a Tibetan inscription, which indicates that it was built during 17th century A.D. and put under Geluk-pa tradition.
5. **Geluk-pa tradition:** Tib dGe-lugs-pa (pron. Geluk pa) or order of the "*model of virtue*" is popularly known as the "*yellow hat*" (*or Zhwa ser, Pron. Chaser order*). Cf. Finegan, Jack: '*Tibet: A Dreamt of Image*' Tibet House, New Delhi; 1986: 98-99.
6. **Spituk monastery: Tib. dpe-thub** (Pron. Pitok or Spituk). It was founded by Drags-pa-Bum-de, the king of Ladakh during the beginning of 15th century A.D. Thereafter, was built on the slope and summit of an isolated rock about 8 km below Leh town and near Kushok Bakula Airport, on the Leh-Srinagar Highway. Cf. Finegan, Jack; *op. cit.*, 194.
7. **Shankar monastery: Tib. gSang-mkhar** (Pron. Sankar or Sankar or Shankar). It was earlier at

sgan-glas (pron. Ganglas) villager, later during 17th century A.D. A new monastery was built 3 km. north of Leh and named it also Shankar. It is under the control of Spituk monastery.

8. **Trongkhapa: Tib. tsong-kha-pa-blo-gros-grags-pa** (Pron. Tsongkhepa Lotro Trakpa), also known sJe *Rin-pr-che* (pron. Je Rinpoche) or the precious ruler, was born in the district of Tsongkha (meaning Onion valley in the vicinity of Kokonor lake is Amdo, Tibet; now under China) in 1340. He is also regarded as an incarnation of Manjusri, and was the founder of Ganden monastery. His strict monastic discipline is known with Geluk-pa order. Cf. Finegan, Jack, *op. cit.*, pp. 100-101.

9. **Gyal Chab je: Tib. rgyal tshyabrj-rje.** He was the another main disciple of Tsong-khapa.

10. **Khas-dub-je: Tib. Mkhas-grub- rje.** He was the another main disciple of Tsongkhapa.

11. **Cuksikjal: Tib. spyan-ras-gzigs.** Pron, Chenresik. The lord of compassion, is a manifestation of Amitabha, is shown in white colour; is commonly known as Bodhisattva.

12. **Sakyamuni Buddha: Tib. Shakya-Tubpa** or Tubpa "The enlightened one". Historically known as Gotama Buddha.

13. **Sixteen Arhats: Tib. gnas brtan bcu drug:** It is believed that they had been entrusted by Sakyamuni Buddha to protect the doctrine of Buddhism. The name of sixteen Arhats are Rahula, Cudapanthaka. Pindolabharadvaja, Panthaka, Nagasena, Gopaka, Abheda, Angaja, Ajita, Vanavasin, Kalika, Vajriputra, Bhadra, Kanakavastsa, Kankabharadvaja, and Bahula.

14. **Doljang: Tib. sgrol ljang.** The Green Tara is probably the form of Dolma incarnate in Wencheng, the Chinese wife of King Songtsen Gampo. She is usually seen seated with the right leg hanging down, in green colour, in peaceable manifestation, and with a dark blue lotus bud as a symbol. Cf. Finegan, Jack; *op. cit.*, 136.

15. **Sangyas Smamla:** In Sanskrit language equivalent to Baisajyaguru. The Medicine Buddha is the Buddha of healing, who is invoked to care for the sick. He wears the monastic robes of a Buddha and sits on a lotus blossom upon a lion throne. His body is dark blue and he holds an iron bowl in his left hand containing the medicinal plant. Here follows the name of eight kinds of Medicine Buddhas:
    1. Bhaisajyaguru
    2. Simhanada
    3. Saparikirtitanamsri
    4. Svaraghosaraja
    5. Savarnabhadravi malarat naprabhasa
    6. Acokottamasri
    7. Dharmakirtisagaraghosa
    8. Abhijnaraja

    Cf. Bune, Fredric W. *An Encyclopaedia of Buddhist Deities, Demigods, Godlings, Saints and Demons,* Vol. 1, D.K. Printworlds Ltd. New Delhi, 1944: 338.
16. **Mithug pa (Tib. mi athrugva pa):** He would be Buddha's form.
17. **Nasten cu dug (Tib. gnas brten beu drug) :** 16 Arhads
18. **Gyan drug chog nyis (Tib. rgyan drug mchog gnyis);** or Indian Pandits, here follows their names:
    1. kru sgrub
    2. thog med
    3. 'aphags pa lha
    4. dbyig gnyen
    5. phyogs glang
    6. chos grags
    7. yon tan 'od
    8. shakya 'od

9
Stongde Monastery of Zanskar

Introduction

Stongde monastery is situated in Zanskar region of Kargil district in Ladakh. It is 18 kms far away from the Padum on the road leading to Zangla. It is now the second largest monastic establishment of Geluk-pa order in Zanskar.

Approach

Perched on a rocky outcrop overlooking the oasis like village below the picturesque monastery of Stongde can be reached by foot in about 4 hours along the recently laid rough road from Padum. The climb upto the monastery is rather strenuous, but it is worth the trouble for the breathtaking scenery of the valley available from here.

Historical Background

It is said that the whole area of Stongde was under sea. Duve vang cuk[1], a Buddhist saint popularly known Lama Mar-pa navigated his boat there. However, while navigating his boat towards Stongde site, the boat all of a sudden collided with the underneath rock. As a result of strong jerked, Lama Marpa thought deeply: "There is water everywhere, I don't know how my boat collided with a rock? The heavy jerk as been recorded indicates that certainly there must be something unique here."

Lama Marpa meditated for a while, then performed rituals and offered prayers:

"May! a group of one thousand houses build here, the whole area turn to a village."

Thereafter, according to the prayer of Lama Marpa, Sea water from Stongde flushed out, people started to migrate here, many of them gradually settled down. Later in the following years one thousand houses were being constructed. Thus, named Stongde derived by the following two Bodhi words:-

'Stong'	:	One thousand
'sde'	:	A group of inhabitants Stong-sde
'Stong de'	:	Settlement of one thousand inhabitants or houses of one thousand.

Foundation of the Stongde monastery: This is a renowned monastery and was founded by Lama Lotas Mar-pa, later popularly known as stong-de-mar-pa-ling[2]. After sometime Lama Saskya zangpo[3] of Stong-de built new structure. Lama-Gyalsen-pa-Lundup-Pal-zang-po introduced Geluk-pa tradition of Mahayana Buddhism. Subsequently Lopon lozang[4], Lopon shesrab jugnas and Lana Paldan zangpo[5] of Stong-de village had made there valuable contribution for the development of monastic order.

Dukhang

The sprawling white-washed complex has a number of temples. Each a repository of the region's rich monastic legacy. However, has two Dukhangs one at the ground floor, the other is just above it. Inside the ground floor of Dukhang we can see the following wall paintings:

1. 35 Buddhas (Tib. ltung-bshag)
2. 16 Arhats (Tib. 'aphags p 'aignas brtan beu drug)
3. Sangyas smansla[6]
4. Gyalsen zhee[7].

Paintings on the Inside Walls of Upper Dukhang

1. Choskyong cu[8]
2. Gonpo[9]
3. Lhamo[10]
4. Chosgyal[11]
5. Bamsras[12]
6. Camsring[13]
7. Zhalzipa
8. Dub-pa

Besides, we can acknowledge the following clay statues of different Buddhist deities.

1. Yidam-jig jed[14]
2. Lha-cug-sum-pa
3. Avalokitesvara[15]
4. Standin[16]

The Gon-ekhang temple of the monastery has a particular interest, a well guarded room containing several fierce-faced deities which are mostly veiled; these are the guardian deities of the Buddhist pantheon.

Buddhist Text Books

1. Ka' gyur[17] : Brought from Tibet
2. Ka' gyur : Blocked (Traditional) Printed
3. Stangyar[18]
4. Tibetan religious pothis written by Buddhist scholars.

Festivals

In the monastery, the following rituals prayers are performed by the Lamas, according to the Tibetan calendar.

1. **Monlam:** Date 01 to 10 of the first month.
2. **Jig-jed prayer:** 13 to 15 of the first month.

3. **Chog-chod prayer:** 25 of the second month.
4. **Nyun-nas prayer:** On 15th of the Fourth month.
5. **Yarnas:** From 15th of sixth month to 30th of the seventh month.
6. **Monlam:** 18th of the ninth month.
7. **Lhabab Chorten:** On 22nd of the ninth month.
8. **Tsong-Kha-pa parinirvana ceremony:** On 25th of the 10th month of the year.
9. **Gu-tor:** About 60 lamas are resided in the monastery. Among them some lamas are chosen every year for sacred dances called Gu-tor which takes place on the 28th and 29th days of the 11th month of the year.

Economy: Stong-de monastery grow wheat and barley. Annually each monk of the monastery gets one *khal* wheat/ barley. Thus land is the main source of income, however, by virtue of rituals and prayers for the public lamas and *Gonpa* receives cash and kind as donation.

Head Lama: Nari Rinpoche is the Head of the monastery.

Notes and References

1. **Duve Vang Cuk:** Tib. gru p'ai dbang phyug. A famous Lama who visited Zanskar.
2. **Stong-de-Mar-pa-ling:** Tib. stong sde mar pa gling. The name of the stong-de by virtue of its foundation by Lama Mar-pa, called stong-sde-mar-pa gling.
3. **Lama Saskya Zangpo :** Tib. Lama shkya-bzang-po.
4. **Lopon lozang :** Tib. slo-dpon blo bzang.
5. **Lama Paldan Zangpo :** Tib. lama dpal-ldan bzang-po.
6. **Sangyas smanla :** Tib sngs-rgyas-sman gtso-'akhor. Medicine Buddha, normally in the Buddhist monastery one can see eight in number.
7. **Gyaltsen zhee:** Tib. rgyal-chen-bzhee. They are four in number as listed below :

(1) Virupaksha
(2) Dhritarashtra
(3) Virudhaka
(4) Vaisravana

8. **Choskyong cu:** They the Dharmpala, various forms of Mahakala.
9. **Gonpo:** Tib. mgon-po; the Dharmpala, has various forms viz.
   (1) mgon po phyag drug pa
   (2) mgon po ta ksad
   (3) mgon po stag zhon
   (4) mgon po legs ldan
   (5) mgon po beng
   (6) mgón po gur
   (7) mgon po phyag bzhi pa
10. **Lhamo:** Tib. lha-mo. As the monastery belongs to Geluk-pa, and Palden lhamo is the protector deity of Geluk pa.
11. **Chosgyal:** He is the Dharmpala. He is also known as " king of religion", in Sanskrit language equivalent to Dharmaraja, the chief protector of Tsong-kha-pa. Cf. Ladrang Kalsang; 'The Guardian Deities of Tibet; Little Lhasa Pub., Dharamsala ; 2000 : 43.
12. **Namisras:** Pali. Vassavana, Tib. 'Nam. thos-sras ; Phon. English Namtose. A guardian king or *devaraja lokpalas* whose dominion in the northern quarter of the world and autumn. He is the king and master of the yaksas. Cf. Bunce, Fredrick W. : An Encyclopaedia of Buddhist Deities, Demigods, Godlings, Saints and Demons, Vol. I ; D.K. Printworld Pvt. Ltd. New Delhi ; 1994 : 574.
13. **Camsring:** Tib. lcam-sring, equivalent to Beg-tse. A Dharmapala and a *jig-rten-las-'das-pa'i-sung-ma* of small importance in Tibet and called a maha-yaksa, lord commander of all ma-mo, head of the gshin-rje, god of war and protector of horses. His

father is the Dharmapala *gnod-shyin-zangs-kyi-ral-pa-can* "The yaksa who has looks of copper" and his mother is *srin-mo-khrag-gi-ral-pa-can* "The raksa with looks of blood" *la cam-sring* as synonymous with Mahakala. Cf. Bunce, Fredrick W. ; *op. cit.* : 290.

14. **Yidam-jig-jed:** In Sanskrit language is equivalent to Vajrabhairava. He is the most wrathful form of Manjusri. His anger is so terrific that it may consume even himself. He is the nature of emptiness which is express in the form the extreme rage. He has bull's head which symbolises the ignorance which is transmuted into discriminating wisdom. Cf Lobzang Tsewang 'Sakyamuni' ; Central Institute of Buddhist Studies, Leh-Ladakh; 2001 : 34.
15. **Avalokitesvara:** A Bodhisattva of compassion.
16. **Standin: (Tib. rta-mgrin-tho-brgyad pa) or rta-mgrin-rta-mgrin-rgyal-pa;** Phon. Engh. Tamdin, in Sanskrit language equivalent to Arya-Hayagriva, Krodha yamari "The horse-necked one". A Krodhadevatas and Dharmapala, and a protective who keeps away demons. Cf. Bunce, Frederic W.; *op. cit.* : 202.
17. **Ka'gyur:** It means 'translations of the word (bka', word or speech, i.e., of Buddha)."
18. **Stangyur:** (Tengyur), it means translations of treatises i.e, bstan-treatise commentarial works). In its complete form the Tanjur contains not only earlier translated commentaries but also newer works by Indian masters such as Atisa and Tibetan scholars such as Drokmi and Buston, and also books on grammar, logic, poetry, art, mathematics, chronology, astrology, medicine, and other sciences, these latter subjects being regarded as proper objects of study on the way to Buddhist doctrines. Although a very important part of the entire collection, The Tanjur is sometimes considered as only semi-canonical in comparison with fully canonical Kanjur. Cf Finegan, Jack: 'Tibet : A Dreamt of Image', Tibet House, New Delhi ; 1986 : 15.

10

Taru (Tib. ta-ru-dgon) Gonpa

Taru Gonpa is a branch of Spituk monastery belongs to Geluk-pa tradition. It is about 26 km from Leh on the right side of Leh-Srinagar highway.

Approach

This Gonpa can be easily approached by taxis and by bus from Leh.

Condition of the Building

The temple's main building is very old, therefore, acknowledged some cracks through the ceiling. However, new building is under construction.

Historical Background

This Gonpa was constructed during 17th Century A.D. In 1870 Chagzot Gendun Gyatso gave it to the temple shape. Therefore, historians believe that it was built by the Chagzot Gendun Gyatso and put it under the control of Spituk monastery.

Statues

There are four beams and a glass room in this Gonpa. Besides it is decorated by various Buddhist statues. Fig. 10.1 shows the details.

(c) **Avalokitesvara**[1]: (Tib. 'aphags pthugs rje chen po bcu gcig zal); has thousand hands and eyes, 6 feet in height and 4 feet width and made of brass.

(1) **Padmasambhava[2]:** Ferocious form, 4 feet in height and 3 feet width. It is made of clay.

(2) **Avalokitesvara[3]:** (Tib. 'aphags pa spyan ras gzigs), 4 feet in height and 3 feet width.

(3) **Dolma[4]:** (Tib. sgro-lma); white Tara.

(4) **Maitreya[5]:** (Tib. sangs rgyas tsed pag dmed); Red in colour.

(5) **Budha Chepakmed[6]:** (Tib. sangs rygs tsed pag dmed); Red in colour.

(6) **Dolma[7]:** 21 Dolmas.

Religious Books: In this Gonpa, there are many Tibetan pothis brought from Tibet. Some of them cited below:

1. Printed and Hand written Bum Pothis
2. Kangyur (Tib. K'a-'agyur) Pothis[8]
3. Bum Pothis written/printed during king Deldan Namgyal[9] and King Delegs Namgyal[10] period.

Paintings

We can see many old and beautiful paintings on the walls inside the temple. Fig. 10.2 shows the details:

(1) Four Lok-palas (Tib. Gyaltsen Zhee)[11]

(2) 16 Arhats (Tib. gnas brtan bcu drug)[12]

(3) 35 Buddhas (ltung shags rgyas slngs)[13]

(4) Three Padmasambhavas (Tib. gu rugtso 'akhor sum)

(5) Rigsum gonpo (Tib. rigs gsum mgon po)[14]

(6) Sangde jigsum (Tib. gsang bde 'ajig gsum)[15]

(7) Choskyong (Tib. chos skyong)[16]

Thankas

Popularly known as scrol paintings. In simple term these are the paintings on white cloth. In this monastery we can see many old thankas around 14th and 15th century period. Some of them listed below:

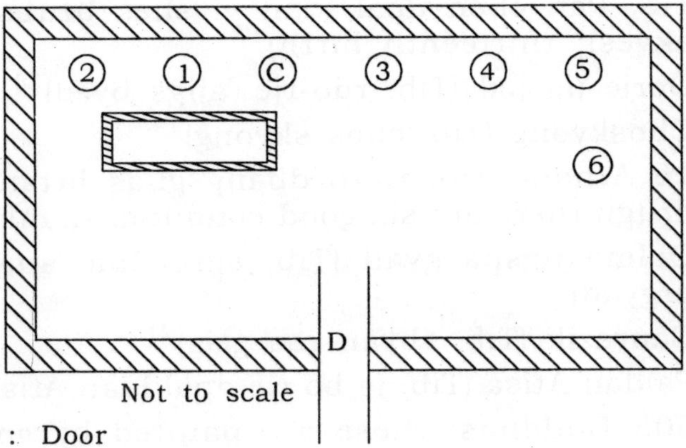

|D| : Door

O : Statue

▨ : Wall

Fig. 10.1 : Statues in Taru Gonpa

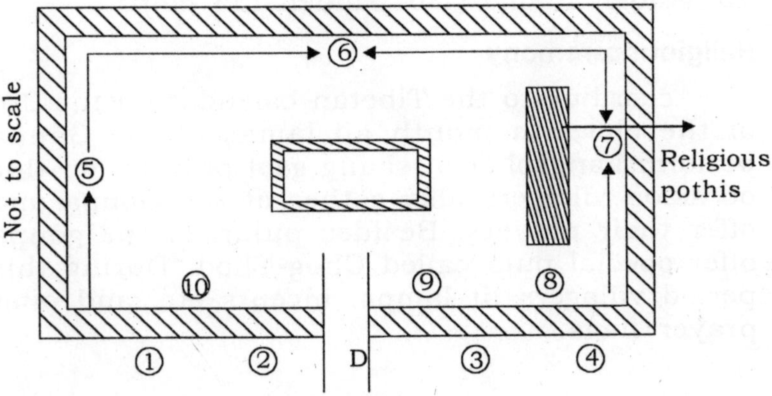

|D| : Door

O : Painting

▨ : Wall

Fig. 10.2 : Wall paintings on the wall of Taru Gonpa

Panchen rinpoche

1. Tib. Pan chen dpal ldan yi shes bzubs sku skyes); thirteenth birth)[17].
2. Dorje jig jed (Tib. rdo-rje 'ajigs byed)[18]
3. Choskyong (Tib. chos skyong)[19]
4. 16 Arhats (Tib. thub dbang gnas brtan bcu drug); there are six good condition thankas[20].
5. Dolma jigspa gyad (Tib. sgrol ma 'ajigs pa brgyad)
6. Canrazik (Tib. sbyan ras gzig)[21]
7. Paldan Atisa (Tib. jo bo rje dpal ldan Atisha)[22]
8. 505 Buddhas; these are painted by golden colour
9. Buddha: Past, Present and Future[23]
10. Thugje Chenpo (or Cuksikzal)[24]; this thanka was donated by king and queen of Ladakh
11. Chepakmed (Tib. tse dpag med)[25]
12. Thankas of various Buddhist deities
13. Palden lhamo (Tib. Palden lha mo)[26]

Religious ceremony

According to the Tibetan calendar on the 3rd of the eleventh month all lamas of the Gonpa perform kangsol (Tib. skang gso) prayers, on this occasion villagers also gather at the Gonpa and offer their prayers. Besides pujari of the gonpa offer special puja called Chog-Chod. During this period villagers lit lamps, incents etc. and offer prayer flags.

Notes and References

1. Avalokitesvara (Arya-Avalokitesvara): He has eleven heads and a thousand arms. The form with eleven heads is explained by the story that when Avalokitesvara looked down upon the many being in need of deliverance in the hell of yama, the god of death, his head broke into ten pieces out of his great compassion these were put together by his spiritual father Amitabha, thus in the figure there are nine gentle faces arranged in three tiers of three each, above that one wrathful face and at the top the head of Amitabha, and making eleven heads in all. With his thousand arms Arya-Avalokitesvara holds numerous attributes with which to communicate unlimited love to suffering being. Cf. Finegan, Jack : 'Tibet : A Dreamt of Image' Tibet House & Wiley Eastern Ltd, New Delhi, 1986 : 130-31.

2. Padmasambhava: Tib. Lopon Rinpoche or Guru Rinpoche. "Lotus Born One" an Indian Tantric invited by king Trisong Detsen in the eighth century A.D. He brought Buddhist Tantra in Tibet during 8th century and subdued the local deities and demons while constructing the first Samyas monastery in Tibet. He helped Santaraksita in his works on Buddhism in Tibet. During his period Buddhism was amazingly spread throughout in Tibet, therefore, he was recognised by Tibetans as the second Buddha. Cf. Batchelor, Stephan : *The Tibet Guide,* Wisdom Pub., London; 1987: 420.

3. Avalokitesvara: The lord who looks down with compassion is a manifestation of Amitabha, is shown in white colour, has 'Om Mani Padme Hum' as his mantra, is the special protector of Tibet, and is incarnate in King Songtsen Gampo and in the Dalai Lamas. Cf. Finegan, Jack ; *op. cit.* : 130.

4. Dolma: (The White Tara) or "White Savioress" is probably the form of Tara incarnate in Tshisun, the Nepalese wife of King Songtsen-Gampo. She is a companion of the Boddhisattva Avalokitesvara and also closely related to the Dalai Lamas as themselves incarnations of Avalokitesvara. She is usually seated, in white colour, in peaceable manifestation, and with seven eyes, the two normal eyes and the eye of wisdom in the forehead, together with one eye each in the palms of the hands and soles of the feet. In a form called Ushnisha Sitataptara. She has a thousand heads and arms, with an eye in the palm of each of the thousand hands as symbol of all-seeing compassion. Cf. Finegan, Jack ; *op. cit.* : 135-36.

5. Maitreya: Tib. byams-pa, Pron. Eng. Tampa. "The king one" and regarded as "Future Buddha". It is said that "Maitreya will come down in this world to liberate the sentient beings when Sakyamuni Buddha teachings will disappear from the earth". Cf. Lobzang Tsewang : Sakyamuni : An Exhibition of Rare Thankas, Central Institute of Buddhist Studies, Choglamsar, Leh-Ladakh 2001, p. 24.

6. Buddha Chepakmed: Tib. Ts'e dpag-med, Tsha-dpag-med, che-dpag-med, tshe-dpag-med-lha-dgu, Pron. Eng. Tsepame "Dispenser on long llife". The Bodhisattva of longevity who is invoked for long life, health and happiness. Cf. Bunce, Fredrick W. ; An Encyclopaedia of Buddhist Deities, Demigods, Godlings, Saints and Demons, Vol I. ; D.K. Printworld Ltd.; New Delhi; 1994 : 13.

7. Dolma: Tara, normally 21 statues of Dolma are placed in the Buddhist *gonpas*.

8. Kangyur (Tib. K'a-'agyur) pothis: It means "translations of the word (bka', or speech, i.e., of the Buddha)". The pothis contain the whole Theravada and Mahayana literature, as well as the Tantra which are the foundation of the Vajrayana, all of which is taken as the authoritative word of the Buddha. Cf. Finegan, Jack ; *op. cit.* : 14-15.

9. Deldan Namgyal: Tib. bde ldan rnam rgyal (Pron. lhachen Deldan Namgyal) received the most of Upper and Lower Ladakh, and reigned (1647-1694) as the twenty-fifth king in the succession from Pelgyigon and the seventh in the second

Dnasty of Ladakh. Cf. Finegan, Jack; *op. cit.* : 182.

10. Delegs Namgyal: Tib. bde legs rnam rgyal, he appears in the chronicles of the kings of Ladakh as the twenty sixth ruler in the succession from Pelgyigon and the eighth in the Second Dynasty of Ladakh. It is probable, that his actual position was only that of a prince associated with his father, and this for a relatively short time (1680-1691), and that he died before his father. Cf. Finegan, Jack; *op. cit.* 183.

11. Four Lokpalas: They are (1) Virupaksha (Mig mi bzan), Guardian of the West and king of the serpent deities (nagas, Tib. klu), is red in colour and holds a serpent in his right hand and a jewel in his left. (2) Vais'ravana (r Nam thos sras) or Kubera, Guardian of North and king of *Yakshas,* is yellow in colour and holds a banner of victory *(dhvaja)* and a mongoose *(nakula)* (3) Dhritarashtra (yul 'khor bsrang), Guardian of the East and king of the celestial musicians called *gandhavas,* is white colour and holds a stringed instrument. (4) Virudhaka (Phags skyes po), Guardian of the South and King of the malignant spirits called Kumbhanda, is dark blue in colour and holds a sword. Cf. Finegan, Jack; *op. cit.* : 134.

12. 16 Arhats (Tib. gnas brtan bcu drug): Here folllows a list of 16 Arhats:

1. Yan lag 'byung or Angaja
2. Ma pham pa or Ajita
3. Nags na gnas or Vanavasin
4. Dus ldan or Kalika
5. rdo rje mo'i bu or Vajriputra
6. bzang po or Bhadra
7. gser bi'u or Kanakavatsa
8. ba ra dhwa dza gser can or Kanakabharadvāja

9. Ba ku la or Bakula
10. sgra gcan 'dzin or Rāhula
11. Lam phran or Cūḍapanthaka
12. Ba ra dhwā dza bsdod snyoms les or Piṇḍolabharadvaja
13. Lam bstan or Panthaka
14. Klu'i sde or Bagasena
15. sbed byed pa or Gopaka
16. Mi phyed pa or Abheda

Besides the following Upāsaka are also sometimes comsidered as Arhats

1. dGe bsnyen dharma ta ha or Upasaka-Dharmatala
2. Hwa shang dge bsnyen or Upasaka-Hwa-shang.

13. 35 Buddhas (ltung shags rgyas slnga): Here follows a list of 35 Buddhas.

1. Shakya thub pa or Śakyamuni
2. rdo rje'i snying pos rab tu 'joms pa or Vajrag rbhapramardin
3. Rin chen 'od' phro or Ratnārcis,
4. Klu dbang gi rgyal po or Nāgesvararāja
5. dpa' bo'i sde or Virasena
6. dpal dgyes or Viranandin
7. Rin chen me or Ratnagni
8. Rin chen zla 'od or Ratnacandraprabha
9. mthong ba don yod or Amoghadarśin
10. rin chen zla ba or Ratnacandra
11. Drima med pa or Vimala
12. dpal byin or Suradatta
13. Tshangs pa or Brahma
14. Tshangs pa byin or Brahmadutta
15. Chu lha or Varuna
16. Chu lha'i lha or Varunadeva
17. dpal bzang or Bhadrasri

18. Tsan dandpal or Candanasri
19. gzi brjid mtha' yas or Anantauja
20. 'Od dpal or Prabhasaśri
21. Mya ngan med pa'i dpal or Aśokaśri
22. Sre med kyi bu or Narayana
23. Me tog dpal or Kusumasri
24. Tshangs pa'i 'od zer rnam par rol has mngon par mkhyen pa or Brahmajyotivikri-ditabhijña
25. Padma'i 'od zer rnam par rol bas mngon par mkhyen pa or Padmajyotirvikriditabhijna
26. Nor dpal or Dhanasri
27. Dran pa'i dpal or Smrtisri
28. mtshan_dpal shin tu yongs sbgrags or Suparikirtitanāmaśri
29. dbang po'i tog gi rgyal mtshan gyi rgyal po or Inderaketudhvajarāja
30. shin tu rnam par gnon pa'i dpal or Suvikrāntaśri
31. g 'yul las shin tu rnam par rgyal ba or Yuddhajaya
32. rNam par gnon pa'i gshegs pa'i dpal or Vikrantagamisri
33. Kun nas snang ba bkod pa'i dpal or Samantāvabhāsavyuhaśri
34. Rin chen padmas rnam par gnon pa or Ratnapadmavikramin
35. Sangs rgyas ri dbang gi rgyal po or Sailendrarāja.

14. Rigsum gonpo (Tib. rigs gsum mgo po):

1. spyan ras gzigs (or Avalokitesvara)
2. 'ajam p'ai dbyangs (or Manjusri)
3. bde mchog (or vajrapani)

15. Sangde jigsum (Tib. gsang bde 'ajig gsum)

1. gsang ba 'adus pa
2. 'ajags byed
3. bde mchog

16. **Choskyong (Tib. Chos skyong). Skt.** Dharmpalas, mgon-po, guardians of the doctrine. Here follows a list of Dharmpalas:

1. mgon po phyag drug pa or Sadhuja-Mahakala
2. 'brongzhal can
3. ta ksad seng ge zhon pa or Simhavahara Taksad
4. mgon po ta ksad? or Māhākāla-Taksad
5. mgon po stag zhon or Vyaghravahana-Mahākāla
6. mgon po legs ldan or Bhagavad-Mahākāla
7. mgon po beng or Daṇḍa (dhara)-Mahākāla
8. las mgon bya rog gdong can or Kakiasya-Karmanatha
9. mgon po gur or Mahākāla-pañjana?
10. mgon po phyag bzhi pa or Caturbhuja-Mahākāla.
11. Zhal bran gzugs or Brāhmanrūpa-Mahākāla
12. Ta ksad nag po or Kṛṣṇa-Takśad
13. lha mo dong skyong ma or Śankhapālī
14. lha mo dong sol ma or Dhāmavatī
15. dpal ldan lha mo phyag gnyis ma or Dvibhuja-Srimati Devi
16. Chos rgyal or Dharmaraja
17. Ta kki ra dza or Takkiraja
18. Dzi na mi tra or Jinamitra
19. Kse tra pa la or Ksetrapala
20. Tshe bdag mgon po or Āyuspati-Mahākāla

17. **Panchen Rinpoche:** In a related development there also came to be a second high spiritual head alongside the Dalai Lama. The Fifth Dalai Lama had been a pupil of an abbot of the Tashilhunpo monastery named blo-bzang chos kyi rgyal mtshan (1569-1662), and in his position of authority after 1642 the Fifth Dalai Lama, to show his gratitude to his teacher, confer upon Lopsang chokyi Gyentsen

the title of Pan-chen rin-po-che. This title means "precious great scholar" (Tibetan Pan Chen being derived from the Sanskrit ***mahapandita,*** great scholar), while in western accounts this dignitary is usually called the Pan-Chen Lama, or from the monastery which is his official residence, the Trashilhunpo Lama. The thirteen incarnation named dpal ldan yi shes bzubs sku skyes is mentioned here in Taru monastery. Cf. Finegan, Jack : Tibet. A Dreamt of Image; *op. cit.* : 116-17.

18. **Dorje jig jed (Tib. rdo-rje 'ajigs byed):** In Sanskrit language equivalent to Vajrabhairava. His wrathful form is the manifestation of Manjusri. He is the embodiment of total wrath. His anger is so terrific that it may consume even himself. He is the nature of emptiness which is expressed in the form of extreme rage. He has bull's head which symbolises the ignorance which is transmuted into discriminating wisdom. He has nine faces, sixteen hands and thirty four legs. His right legs are slightly folded and the left legs stretch. The central face is bull's face with two horns and its complexion is dark and in the angry form. The second face is of a demon and the top face is Manjusri's which is in peaceful form. Each and every face has three eyes. All hands hold different kinds of instruments to threaten the defilements. All hands and the body are decorated with many different kinds of ornaments. He crushes many evil spirits under this feet. His lowest arms holds his consort and the hands holds skull cups. His consort embraces him. Her complexion is also dark. She has two hands, one face and three eyes. He has many faces, so that he can look in all directions. It signifies the omnipresence of his anger. He has many arms

and legs, therefore nobody can escape from his fury. He has the wisdom of equanimity and thus treads equally on all aspects of ego. His consort feeds and reinforces his countless vengeance. He wears the following ornaments– Five-skull cron, writlets, anklets, necklace, garlands, and belts of skulls or heads, tiger or elephant skin a body covering. Cf. Lobzang Tsewang: Sakyamuni : An Exhibition of Rare Thankas; Central Institute of Buddhist Studies, Leh-Ladakh, 2001 : 34 and Bunce, Fredrick W. : An Encyclopaedia of Buddhist Deities, Demigods, Godlings, Saints and Demons, Vol. I. D.K. Printworld Ltd. New Delhi ; 1994 : 574.

19. **Choskyong (Tib. chos-skyong):** Skt. Dharmpalas, mgon-po, guardians of the doctrine.

20. 16 Arhats (Tib. thub dbang gnas brtan bcu drug): It is believed to have entrusted by Sakyamuni Buddha with the continuing task of protecting the Doctrine and of being present to reward virtue wherever good deeds are done. Only finally at the coming of Maitreya, their task will be completed, and all will then enter nirvana together. Cf. Finegan, Jack; *op. cit.* 132.

21. Canrazik (Tib. sbyan ras gzig); Skt. Avalokitesvara.

22. Paldan Atisa (Tib. jo bo rje dpal ldan Atisha): He is popularly known "The great lord" and his original name was Candragarbha and his monastic name was Dipankar (meaning "Maker of light" the name of the earthly Buddha prior to Sakyamuni), also Dipankarasvijnana (not be transcendent consciousness maker of light). He was born in 932, the son of a king in Eastern India. In his childhood he had a vision of the goddess Tara, who became his tutelary

deity. Later he went to Rajagriha, the capital of Magadha, and was initiate into the tantric cycle of Hevajra by Rahulaguhyavajra a practitioner of this system at the Black Mountain (probably one of the famous seven hills near Rajagriha), and he also spent three years in Uddiyana (Swat), where he participated in tantric ceremonies. At this point he was being established in the tantric methods of the Vajrayana or Tantrayana, but at the age of twenty-nine in obedience to instruction received from Sakyamuni Buddha in a dream he took up ordination and from then on studied the canonical scriptures and classical works of the Hinayana and Mahayana. At the age of thirty-one, after two years of study at the Buddhist University of Odantapuri, he had "mastered the problems of all schools". He then went abroad to study with the teacher Ser gling pa (Pron. Ser Lingpa), a teacher in Suvarnadvipa (the general name for Sumatra, Java, and the islands of the Eastern Archipelago), probably the famous teacher Dharmakirti at Śrivijaya (Palembang). After twelve years Atisa returned to India and became a famous teacher at the Buddhist University of Vikramasila. Cf. Finegan Jack; *op. cit.* : 61-62.

23. Buddha: Past, Present and Future: There are six Buddhas of the Past:

    1. Sangs rgyas man gzigs or Vipaśyin
    2. gtsug tor can or Sikhin
    3. Thams cad skyob or Viśvabhū
    4. 'khor ba 'jig or Krakucchanda
    5. gser thub or Kanakamuni
    6. 'Od bsrung or Kasyapa

However generally in Ladakh Past, Present and Future Buddha is known as 'dus gsum gyi sangs rgyas and listed below:

1. 'das p'ai sangs rgyas mar me mdzad
2. da lha b'ai snags rgyas sh'akya thub pa
3. ma' angs p'ai sangs rgyas byams pa.

24. **Thugje chenpo (or Cuksikzal):** In Sanskrit equivalent Avalokitesvara.
25. **Chepakmed (Tib. tse dpag med):** In sanskrit language equivalent to Amitayus. He is the Buddha of longevity. According to Buddhist custom is portrayed in red colour, in meditation posture holds pot which contains pills of longevity. Cf. Das, S.K. ; Tara : An Exhibition of Rare Buddhist Thanks; Central Institute of Buddhist Studies, Choglamsar, Leh-Ladakh; 2003 : 22.
26. **Palden lhamo (Tib. Palden lha mo):** "The Glorious Goddess" is one of the most important protectors of the Geluk-pa order of Buddhism and the guardian of Lhasa. Cf. : Batchelor, Stephen; *op. cit.* : 423-24.

11

Hanu Gonpa: A Geluk pa Order of Buddhism in Ladakh

Hanu Gonpa is propularly know Hanu og ma tasi thong zos gon[1] among Buddhist population of Ladakh. It was built by Lama tshultim zugnas[2] of Tashilhunpo monastery[3] of Tibet. He came in Ladakh during 18th century and practiced meditation in a cave at Hanu. In the passage of time Likir monastery had taken under its administrative control and renovated/decorated according to the Geluk-pa tradition.

Lama tshultim zugnas after completing meditation in a cave near Hanu came to Hanu gongma. He later built a ***gonpa***. The following are the main Buddhist statues in this monastery.

1. Camba Coskor[4]
2. Tsong-khapa[5]
3. Canrazik[6]
4. Do ba gug dol[7]

Thankas

In this ***gonpa,*** we can see many thankas of Bodhisattvas[8].

Religious Books

There are not many religious books as normally seen in the monasteries. Moreover 16 Bum pothis are very well preserved.

Chorten

Like other monasters, it has eight kinds of chortens.

Religious Things

The religious things which are used during rituals mostly made of stone and metals.

Pujari

To meet the villagers' requirements as to perform different religious festivals or other related events, Likir monastery depute a Pujari to Hanu ***gonpa*** who also lookafter the monastery.

Approach

We can go by taxi or bus to Hanu ***gonpa.*** It is about 150 km far away from Leh town in Ladakh.

Notes and References

1. **Hanu og ma tasi thong zos gon:** Tib. Ha nu 'og ma bkris thong mzos dgon (Pron. Hanu ogma tasi thong gon).
2. **Lama tsultim zugnas:** Tib. bla-ma tsul khrims 'abyung gnas.
3. **Tashilhunpo monastery:** Tib. bkra shis lhun po. In 1447, Genduntrup founded the Tashilhunpo monastery near Xigaze, where he was the abbot of the monastery and got parinirvana in 1475. This monastery was one of the important Geluk-pa order in Tibet. Cf. Finegan, Jack : *Tibet: A Dreamt of Image;* Tibet House and Willey Eastern Ltd. New Delhi, 1986 : 103.
4. **Camba Coskor:** Tib. gtso bo byams pa Maitreya. A Mahabodhisattva and the Bodhisttva who will be the Manushi Buddha of future age, the Buddha to be who will show the way to nirvana. Cf. Bunce, Fredrick W.: An Encyclopaedia of Buddhist Deities, Demigods, Godlings, Saints and Demons, Vol. I. D.K. Printworld Ltd. New Delhi ; 1994 : 323.

5. **Tsong-khapa:** He was the founder of Geluk-pa order of Mahayana Buddhism during the 14th century A.D. and considered to be a manifestation of Manjusri. Cf Batchelor, Stephen: The Tibet Guide, Wisdom Pub. London; 1987: 422.
6. **Canrazik:** Tib. Chen re ze. He has many forms such as:
   1. spyan ras gzigs phyag bzhipa (caturbhuja-Avalokitesvara)
   2. spyan ras gzigs padma dbang 'byed (Padmavikasana-Avalokitesvara).
   3. spyan ras gzigs kha sar pa ni (Khasarpani-Avalokitesvara)
   4. spyan ras gzigs seng ge'i sgra (Simhanāda-Avalokitesvara)
   5. spyan ras gzigs rdo rje chos (Vajradharma-Avalokitesvara)
   6. 'Jig rten dbang phyug halhala (Hālāhala-cokesvara)
   7. spyan ras gzigs padma gar dbang phyag gnyis pa (Dvibhuja-Padmanarteśvara-Avalokitesvara)
   8. Padma gar dbang phyag bco brgyad pa (Astadasabuja-Padmanarteśvara)
   9. 'Jig rten dbang phyug ha riha rila zhon pa (Hariharivahana-Lokeśvara)
   10. Khams gsum dbang 'dus spyan ras gzigs (Trailokyavaśamkara-Avalokiteśvara)
   11. 'Jig rten dbang phyug dmar po phyag bzhi pa (Caturbhuja-rakta-Lokeśvara)
   12. sgyu 'phrul dra ba'i rim pa'i spyan ras gzigs (Mayajalakrama-Avalokiteśvara)
   13. Don yod zhags pa (Amoghapāsa)
   14. spyan ras gzigs bhu kham dmar pa (Mahābhūmika?-rakta-Avalokitesvara)

15. bcu gcig zhal Edādaśamukha (Avalokitesśara)
16. Nam mkha' rgyal pa (Gaganarāja)
17. spyan ras gzigs sems nyid ngal gso (Cittavisramana-Avalokites'vara)
18. spyan ras gzigs yid bzhin nor bu (cintamani-Avalokiteśvara)
19. spyan ras gzigs rdo-rje snying pos rab tu'jomspa (Vajragarbhapramardin-Avalokiteśvara).

I have seen only two kinds of Avalokiteśvaras viz. Four Armed Avalokiteśvara and Thousand Armed Avalokiteśvara in most of the monasteries of Ladakh. Cf. Musashi Tachikawa, Masahide Mori and Shinobu Yamaguchi: There hundred and sixty Buddhist deities; Asian Iconography Series -II; Adroit Pub. New Delhi; 2003 : 13-14.

7. **Do ba gug dol (Tib. 'agro ba drug gol)**
8. **Bodhisattvas:**

The Bodhisattvas who are emanations of the five Tathagatas are the following:

1. Samantabhadra (Kun tu bzang po' pron. Küntu Sangpo)
2. Vajrapani (Phyag na rdo rje. Pron. Chhana Dorje)
3. Ratnapani (Phyag na rin chen, pron. Chhana Richhen)
4. Avalokitesvara (spyan ras gzigs' pron. chenresik)
5. Viśvapani (phyag na sna tshogs rdo rje. Pron. Chhak-na na-tshö Dorje).

Other important Boddhisattvas are:

1. Manjusri ('Jam dbyangs, Pron. Jamyang)
2. Kshitigarbha (Sahisnying po, pron. Sai nying-po). Cf. Finegan, Jack ; *op. cit*: 130-31.

12

Nyar-ma: An Ancient Gonpa of Ladakh

Location: Nyar-ma is situated in Leh district of Ladakh.

Approach: It is near Thiksey monastery[1] and about 1 km on the left side from Leh-Manali highway, can be approached by taxis.

Road: Link road, but not metalled.

How I approached Nyar-ma: It was 7th November 2004 morning, I was doing research work on Thiksey monastery. At 9 o' clock I arrived Thiksey monastery by bus, went to Geshes Tsultim Thercin's residence, nearby standing two chomos informed me that he had just left, however would return by evening. They offered me tea. In the mean time I asked:

"Kindly tell me, where is Nyarma Gonpa?"

"It is about 3 km. from here."

I decided to visit Nyar-ma. I followed Leh-Manali highway, travelling 2 km. turned left on link road and after one kilometer came to Nyarma Gonpa. Here six carpenters were busy in making design on woods. I asked: "Can you tell me the history of this craft art"?.

"In olden days Tibetan were making this wooden art on their doors, when Ladakh's religious and cultural relations were established with Tibet, some Ladakhis went there and learnt the same."

"Are you doing work for a new monastery here?"

"The foundation work for Chomo Gonpa has been finished, we are engaged for making doors and windows of the monastery."

"Where is Nyarma Gonpa?"

"These runis are of the Nyarma Gonpa. If you want to see old paintings, you should enter in a Rinchen Zangpo Chorten."

I went a few steps towards east and found a Rinchen Zangpo Chorten. After removing stones wall, entered inside the chorten. I saw beautiful old paintings of 11th century A.D. Among others there were various forms of Buddhas paintings. These paintings were in a very bad conditions, plaster had many cracks and holes in the middle.

Condition Assessment: Danger, the Gonpa complex is in a state of ruins.

Historical Significance

Lotsava Chenbo ban de yeshes popularly known Lotsava Rinchen Zanpo[2] at the age of 55 years in 1011 by his spiritual power built three monasteries, e.g., Nyarma in Leh, Khachar in Purang and Tholing in Guge. After the completion of these monasteries he performed Rabnas prayers together.

Nyarma Gonpa had eight temples, Buddha Marmezad was the main statue besides many other tantric deities. The main temple was 25 steps long, three feet broad and 13 feet in height. The boundary wall was built in the shape of yoga mandala. Extreme outside boundary wall at one side was 250 steps long, one and half feet broad and about eight feet in height. There were around one hundred chortens. They were decorated by five Buddhas, eight Buddhas chaza. Besides many Buddhist mantras were engraved nearby stone plates.

Local Belief: In oldan days there was a lake near Gonpa complex. When Nyarma Gonpa was destroyed, lake was started shrinking.Dorje chenmo statue of the Gonpa then shifted to shey Gonpa. The said lake dried soon and near Shey valley flood from the Indus river came, later this valley became more fertile.

What my field work speaks: In Nyarma I met Tsering Mutup kesar pa, he had key of a New Dorje chenmo temple, the old Nyarma Gonpa is completly ruined. Here also I saw some ruins of old Nyarma Gonpa (Fig. 12.1).

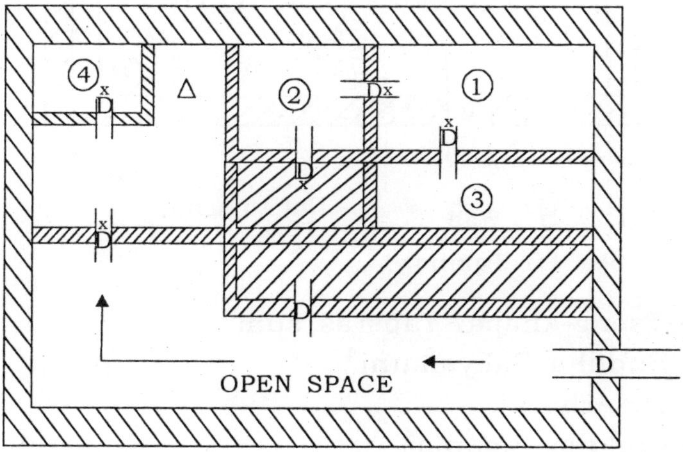

: New wall — △ : Chorten (possible) now ruined

(D) : Door

|D^x| : At present no door (now ruined)

▧ : Gallery

1\. : Possibility of temple
2\. : Possibility of temple
3\. : Possibility of temple
4\. : Possibility of temple
now ruined

(Fig. 12.1). Ground Floor of New Dorje chenmo temple at nyarma and nyarma Gonpa ruins.

Paintings in the New Dorje Chenmo, Nyarma

At the first floor I saw Dorje chenmo temple. The temple was small but had the following some beautiful wall painting (Fig.12.2).

Fig.12.2: The following

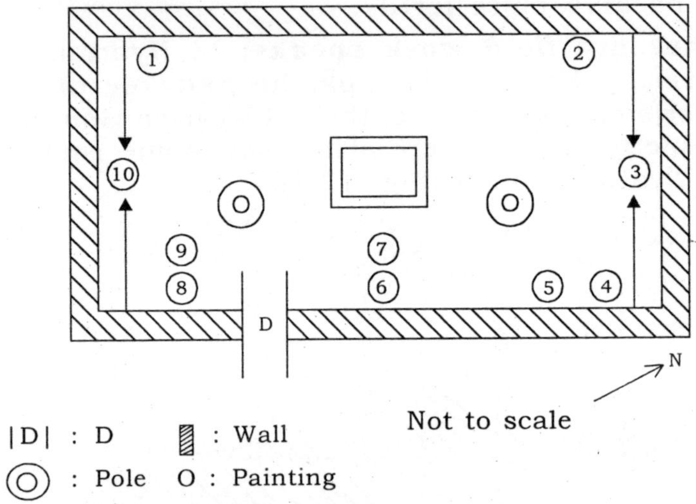

1. Tsong-khapa. Yabsras sum[3]
2. Buddha Sakyamuni[4]
3. 16 Arhats[5]
4. Buddha Smanla[6]
5. Green Tara[7]
6. Lokpal
7. Lokpal
8. Lokpal
9. Lokpal
10. 34 Buddhas in the mandala and at the centre Sakyamuni. Buddha, total 35 Buddhas.

    Here follows the details of New Dorje Chenmo temple (Fig.12.3).

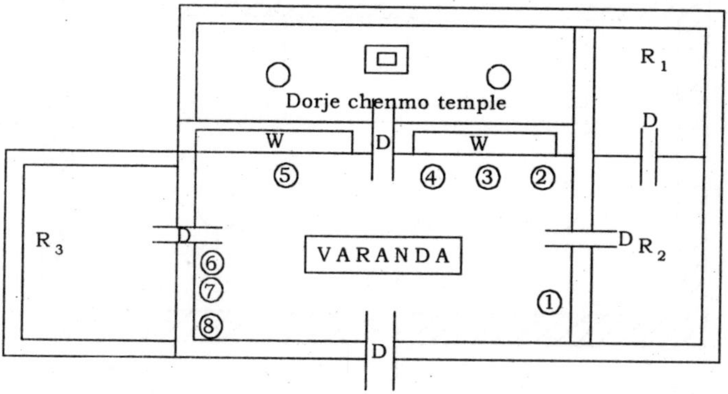

○ : D

Not to scale

|D| : Door

[W] : Window

N

▤ :

R_1 : Empty Room

R_2 : Kitchen

R_3 : Pujari Room

1. 2. 3. 5. 7. 8.

Tasi Targyat

4. : Lepoard

6. : Dregon

Fig. 12.3 Dorje Chenmo Temple at the first floor

Paintings inside the wals of Almirah in New Dorje Chenmo Temple

Inside walls of Almirah in New Dorje Chenmo temple we can see following black and white paintings (Fig. 12.4).

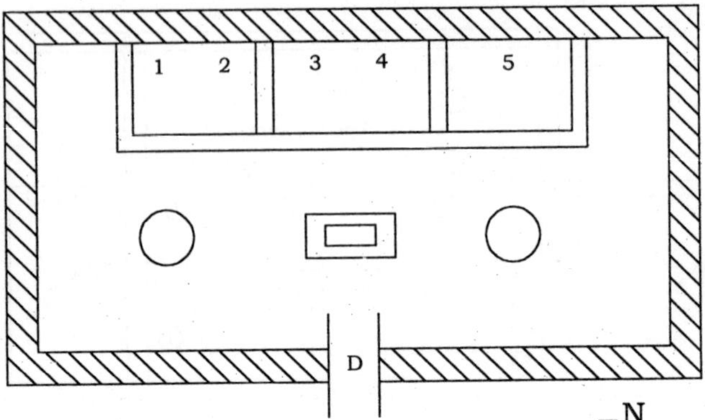

|D|: Door
○ : Pole
▤ : Almirah
| | : Walls

Not to scale

Fig. 12.4 Paintings inside the walls of Almariah of New Dorje Chenmo Temple

1. Gonpo[9]
2. Gonpo[10]
3. Kalcakra
4. Yamantaka[11]
5. Palden Lhamo[12].

Statues in the New Dorje Chemo temple

There are four statues of about 2-3 feet in height in this temple and placed inside the glass Almariah.

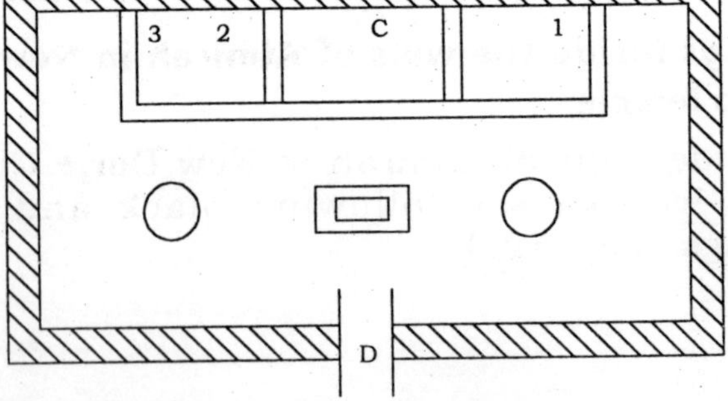

Fig. 12.5 shows the details:

|D| : Door

| | : Walls

▭ : Almirah

○ : Pole

→N

Fig. 12.5 Statues in the New Dorje Chenmo temple

(c): Padmasambhava, Sitting posture; 2½ feet in height

(1): seated, holds Nyola in his left hand and Norboo in right hand, 2½ in feet height

(2): Dorje Chenmo seated on horse; 2 feet in height

(3): Palden Lhamo; 3 feet in height

Thankas in the New Dorje Chenmo Temple

There are some small thankas exhibited through the celing and poles in the New Dorje Chenmo temple. Here follows the details:

1. Cakrasamvara
2. Buddha Sakyamuni
3. Jamyang with poth
4. Mandala

Dorje Chenmo was the Rinchen Zangpo family deity, When it was shifted to Shey monastery, under the tradition started appearing during Shey Subla festival and rest of the time stays inside the lake near the monastery.

Lotsava Rinchen Zangpo Meditation Centre:

The Lotsava Rinchen Zangpo Meditation Centre is about 1 km from the runied Nyarma Gonpa. In olden days there was source of spring water, Which was known as skyid kyinakha. Rinchen zangpo built 5 temples near source, Once while meditation Rinchen zangpo saw Thiksey Palace and forcasted:

"In future at the Thiksey Palace a monastery would be established."

What I saw here during field study:

On Novermber 2004 during study tour when I visited Nyarma, a local person informed me that the oldest nyarma Gonpa was on a hillock, 1 km towards north of the ruined Nyarma Gonnpa. According I climbed towards that hillock at first I climed directly from the front side, it was very difficult, I went back side of the hillock, later easily reached at the meditation centre.

The meditation centre was having various layers of romms or temples. It was built like a cave darker to darker with respect the capacity of yogi's power. I saw Lotsava Rinchen zangpo meditation centre at last. It has 12' in height 4' radius, circular structure. Fig. 12.6.

Shows the details:

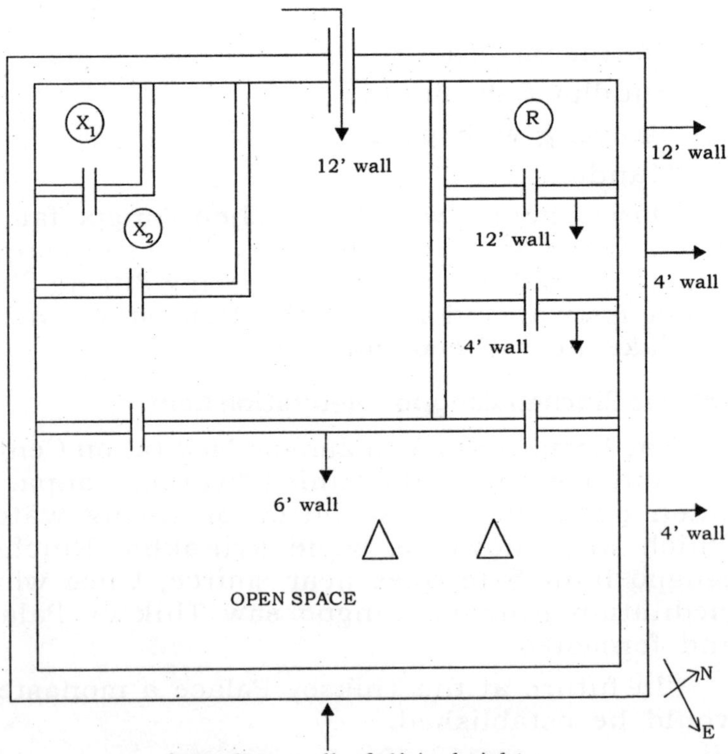

Not to scale

| | : Open space for entrance

X_1 : Meditation centre for Lamas

X_2 : Meditation centre for Lamas

(Possibly they assisted Rinchen zangpo)

: Pole

R : Here Lotseva Rinchen zangpo practiced Meditation

Δ : Chorten

The present condition of Lotsava Rinchen Zangpo is completly in ruined shape. It is said that the statues of this centre where shifted to new Dorje chenmo temple. The Dorje chenmo deity was the protector of Lotsava Rinchen Zangpo. Therefore, Nyarma Gonpa sometimes also known by Dorje chenmo Gonpa. Here follows the location of Lotsava Rinchen zangpo meditation centre (Fig. 12.7).

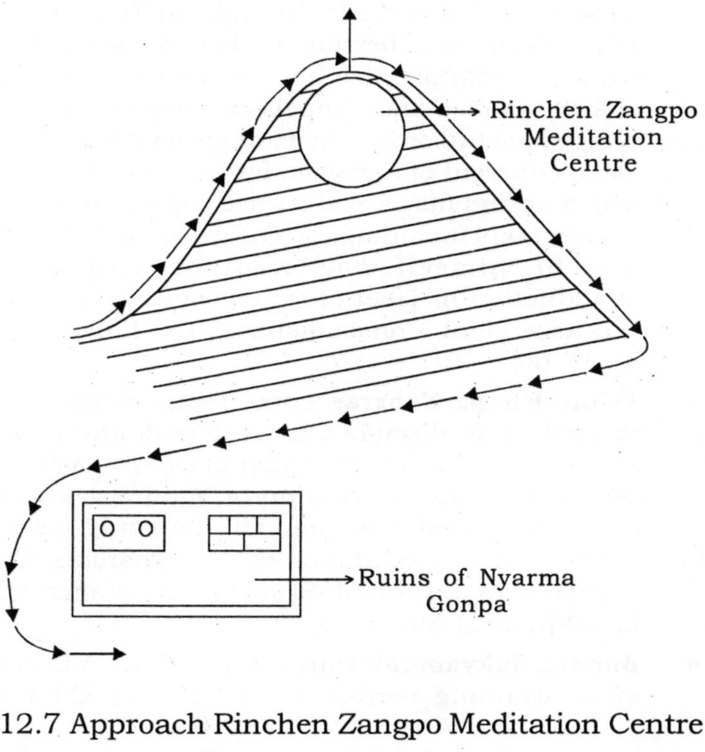

Fig. 12.7 Approach Rinchen Zangpo Meditation Centre

Notes and References

1. **Thiksey monastery:** It is about 15 km from Leh town and at a distance of 5 km beyond Shey on a prominent hill on the right bank of the Indus, with a sweeping view from Spituk in the northwest to the ravine that leads to Hemis in the southeast, is the monastery of Khri-rtse, Pron. Tiksey, belonging to the Geluk-pa. Cf. Finegan, Jack, *Tibet: A Dreamt of Image*: Tibet House, New Delhi; 1986:201.
2. **Lotsava Rinchen Zanpo:** He was born in 958 A.D., was ordiained at the age of thirteen, i.e. in 970 and died in his ninety-eighth year, i.e. in 1055. During his life time he made three trips to India, the first to Kashmir, while young and probably soon after his ordination when sent by Yeshe, O, a second to visit the Buddhist holy places in Magadha, and a third to Kashmir again. In all he spent seventeen years in India and studied with seventy five Indian masters. From India he brought to Tibet a number of panditas, and he himself became known as the Great Translator. Also he was famed as the builder of 108 temples and chapels in western Tibet. From his Indian studies Rinchen Zangpo evidently returned as an adherent of tantrism, for among the translation which he and his associates accomplished were many tantric texts including the Guhyasamaja and others, and he himself was credited with the first introduction in Tibet of tantric system named after "Transcendent Consciousness" Cf. Finegan, Jack; *op.cit.* 60.
3. **Tsong-Khapa Yabsras sum:** Tsong-Khapa and his two principal disciple viz. Gyal Tsab and Khasdup. Tsong-Khapa was the founder of Geluk-pa order and regarded as an incarnation of Manjusri who is the embodiment of wisdom. Cf. Lobzang Tsewang: Sakyamuni: An exhibition of Rare Thankas; Central Institute of Buddhist Studies, Choglamsar, Leh-Ladakh; 2001:50.
4. **Buddha Sakyamuni:** During 6th century A.D. Buddha after attaining perfect enlightenment showed the

right path to all fortunate beings, so that they could attain freedom from the cycle of existence.

5. **16 Arhats:** They had been entrusted by Sakyamuni Buddha with the continuing task of protecting the Doctrine till Maitreya will come down to earth.
6. **Buddha Smanla:** Medicine Buddha.
7. **Green Tara:** She was the wife of King Songtsen Ganpo of Tibet and had mother country China.
8. **Tasi Targyat:** Eight emblems of good fortune, they are:
   (1) Umbrella (Tib. gdugs)
   (2) Two golden fishes (Tib. gser na)
   (3) Vase (Tib. dung)
   (4) Lotus blossom (Tib. Pad ma)
   (5) Conch (Tib. dung)
   (6) Diamond-shaped mark (Tib. dpal beu)
   (7) Standard (Tib. rgyul mchan)
   (8) Golden Wheel (Tib. gser gyi' khor lo)
9. **Gonpo:** In Sanskrit language Mahakala. There are many kinds to Gonpo, however popular among them are :
   (1) Gonpo beng (Tib. mGon po beng)
   (2) Four Faced Gonpo
   (3) Gonpo chagzee (Tib. mgon po phyag bzhi)
   (4) Gonpo chag Drug (Tib. mgon pophyag drug)
10. **Kalacakra:** Tib. dpal-dus-kyi-hkhor-lo, the wheel of time.

A yidam and as terrifying god-form emanation of Dhyani Buddha Aksobhya. A complex supreme Tantric yogic deity Cf. Batchelor, Stephen: "The Tibet Guide", Wisdom Pub., London, 1987:416.

11. **Yamantaka:** Tib. Dorje Jigjed, in Sanskrit language to Vajrabhairava. His wrathful form is the manifestation of Manjusri.
12. **Paden Lhamo:** Tib. dpal ldan lha mo "The Glorious Godless" is one of the most important protectors of the Geluk pa order of Buddhism.

13
Korzok Gonpa of Ladakh

It is situated in Chang-Thang sub-division of Leh district, Ladakh; and about 208 km. far away from Leh, the main town of Leh district. In Tibetan language it is called as 'Karzok thupstan lingpo dubgyut tandar chos ling'. This monastery was built in between 1851-1861 by lama kunga Lotos and was sponsored by Spon Tsering Tashi Namgyal of Rikshot village. This monastery took four years in completion. Though the monastery was built, but didn't increase lama population. As a result they felt pitty and went to Gewang Dukpa Rinpoche, later requested:[1]

"Guruji paranam ! we did very hard work in the construction of a monastery but are sad as this monastery is not flourishing well, the lama population is very low, how monastic establishment will develop in Chang-Thang?"

"To follow Drukpa (Tib Drug pa) tradition, all will later go in smooth."[2]

Later 14th Karmapa gane a new name to Cumoor gonpa and called 'Thupstan Ningqo Dupgyud stardar chosling, and according to Korzok monastery Cumoor gonpa was built (Fig. 13.1)

Later they did the same and placed the following statues in the Cang Khang:

1. Buddha Sakyamuni[3]
2. Buddha
3. Padmasambhava[4]

4. Lama Tagtsang Raspa[5]
5. Opakmed[6]

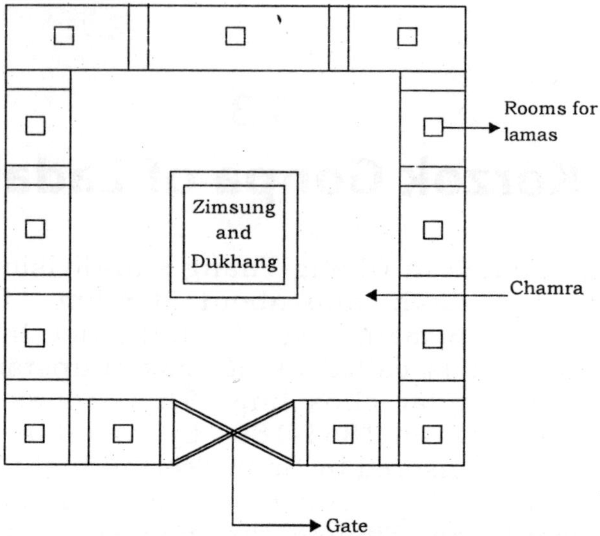

Fig. 13.1 A side map of Cumoor Gonpa.

In Dukhang the following Buddhist statues can be seen:

1. Jecum Mela, made of clay[7].
2. Phagzat-three statues.
3. Padmasambhava-three statues made of sandal wood.
4. Manjusri, made of wood[8].
5. Chepakmed.
6. Namgyalma-two statues[9].
7. Ikzin khor lo-three statues.
8. Mikyotpa-made of sandal wood.
9. Je-lama-made of sandal wood, three statues.
10. Ishe Duva.
11. Vasyakthul gyurmet Vangvo.
12. Rakduk thuvang, made of brass.
13. Gyalonancan.
14. Buddha, made of sandal wood.

15. Jamyang, naturally made.
16. White Tara, made of gold[10].
17. Dorje Sempa, made of sandal wood.
18. Padmasambhava, made of brass[11].
19. Guru Padmasambhava, made of sandal wood.
20. Five statues of Guru Padmasambhava made of sandal wood.
21. Maitreya, made of brass.
22. Guru Padmakari.
23. Mila Repa, made of brass.
24. Buddha, made of sandal wood.
25. Chepakmed, made of brass.
26. Thuvang Dardan ma.
27. Buddha, made of wood.
28. Avalokitesvara, made of wood.
29. Chepakmed, made of clay.
30. 21 Dolmas, made of brass.
31. Guru Rinpoche.
32. Buddha, made of clay.
33. Buddha, made of brass.
34. Thuvang Dordan ma, made of wood.
35. Nawang Namgyal, made of clay.
36. Buddha, made of sandal wood.

Thankas

This monastery has the following thankas:

1. Stanba Cokorsum[1] (i.e. three Buddhas)
2. Devacan gyi zinkhot[2] (About heaven)
3. Green Tara[3]
4. 16 Arhats[4]
5. Three thankas of Avalokitevara.
6. Thuthop kukuri[5]
7. Tesi zingkhot[6]

8. Lamcot 1000[7]
9. Tho Vo de nga[8]
10. Canrazik and Mahakala
11. Buddha
12. Kargyut se thing[10]
13. Sapchen Dorje Junu[11]
14. Buddha (Small Thanka)
15. Smanla
16. Sapchen Dorje Junu
17. Choslung tul sum lama chela
18. Zang dok spal ri
19. Cari tai zik got
20. Khotcaru cobo zing khot
21. Rigsum Gonpo, three thankas[12]
22. Guru Padma[13]
23. Canrazik
24. Ishes Gonbo Chag zee[14]
25. Guru Padmasambhava, two thankas
26. Palden Lhamo[15]
27. Chedak[16]
28. Canrazik lhazak[17]
29. Maitreya
30. Chagdo lhacak Gonsum[18]
31. Chorten Calu Khacor[19], naturally made
32. Je cun Dolma, white[20]
33. Padma zugnas lhacok[21]
34. Stonba Chagdor and Maitreya[22]
35. Thugze chenpozag zee[23]
36. Ca-sum[24]
37. Sangyas Smanla[25]
38. Thovo de dan[26]
39. White Tara[27]

40. Sirgdong ma[28]
41. Dolkar[29]
42. Khayunga[30]
43. Zangdong spal ri[31]
44. Dukar[32]
45. Lhachot[33]
46. Patkar casum[34]
47. Ge sung dolma[35]
48. Chagdor[36]
49. Guru Sangyat[37]
50. Dagpo Rinpoche[38]
51. Stonba[39]
52. Thuva lhacot[40]
53. Guru cokorsum[41]

Religious Books

In this monastery, the following religious books pothis written in Tibetan language are preserved:

1. Nar thang ka gyur phor
2. Kum khen palkargi
3. Ka bum cha can
4. Mi lu bum kar nak tha sum
5. Lu bum karn tha sum
6. Mani ka bum stot cha
7. Duspa tok zung
8. Seemyas kar chak
9. Pat kar zag lung ka nas na par pot cik
10. Padma ka kathang chal ma guru
11. Changyat
12. Ge cum Milai namthar tang gur bug
13. Da zang lum
14. Je yum Milai namthar disma

15. Ka thang pe nga bar ding pu lek
16. Mani ka bum barma nis la ligu chan, 136
17. Kun chog ci dus nis ton ning po
18. Je cun Mila namthar dispa
19. Be ngon
20. Do mang dis ma kanas evar cha cang
21. Dorje chotpa tima
22. Je Milai namthar marpa tang thamcat khen po namston

Notes and References

1. **Jamyang Gyaltsan (ed.) :** The History of Ladakh Monasteries. All Ladakh Gonpa Society, Leh-Ladakh; 1995 : 866-872.
2. *Ibid.*
3. **Buddha (Buddha Sakyamuni):** He was born in a royal family in 6th century B.C., married Yasodhara, later gave birth to a boy named Rahul. Subsequently practised all conducts and activities of Bodhisattvas, he attained the perfect enlightenment at Bodhgaya.
4. **Padmasambhava:** He was the great mystic saint from India who has tremendous miraculous powers. He brought Buddhist Tantra in Tibet in the 8th century A.D., later subdued the local deities and demons who were obstructing the construction of Samyas monastery.
5. **Lama Tagtsang Raspa:** He was a famous lama and siddha visited ladakh during King Singhe Namgyal and established Drugpa Kargyud pa monasteries in Ladakh, popular among is Hemis. Besides he was the ***Dharma Guru*** of King Singhe Namgyal.
6. **Opakmed:** Buddha Amitabha; he is the Buddha of infinite light, and popularly known as the fourth of the Dhayani Buddha.
7. **Jecun Mela:** Tib. Mi -la - ras - pa. He was one of the eighty four mahasiddhas and miracle workers. He was a great tantric of Mahayanism, the Mahaguru

and "Root lama ; and was one of the Tibetan guru who reintroduced the second era of Buddhism. Cf. Bunce, Fredrick W.: An encyclopaedia of Buddhist Deities, Demigods, Godlings, Saints and Demigods; Vol.I; D.K. Printworld Ltd., New Delhi; 1994 : 347.

8. **Manjusri:** He was one of the eight chief disciples of Sakyamuni Buddha, and a Bodhisattva, embodiment of wisdom. Buddhists believe that he is the role deity of wisdom won blesses the devotees to sharpen their memory and intellect. As a result, a devotee can penetrate the vast and profound meanings of the Buddha's teachings. Cf. Lobzang Tsewang: Sakyamuni: An exhibition of Rare Thankas, Central Institute of Buddhist Studies, Choglamsar, Leh - Ladakh; 2001: 22.
9. **Namgyalma:** Skt. Vijaya, deity of longevity.
10. **White Tara:** Tara, she is the female tutelary deity regarded as the manifestation of Avalokitesvara.
11. **Maitreya:** He is the future Buddha.

Glossary

1. Stanba Cokorsum : Tib. ston pa gto, 'a khor gsum.
2. Devacan gyi zinkhot : Tib. bde can gyi zhing bkot
3. Green Tara: Tib. sgrol lzang
4. 16 Arhats Tib. gnas brtan bcu drug
5. Thuthop Kukuri Tib. grub thop kukuri
6. Tesi zingkhot Tib. tise 'aizhig bkot
7. Lamcot Tib. bla mchot
8. Tho vo de nga Tib. Khro bo sde lng' ai
9. Canrazik Tib. sbyan ras gzig
10. Kargyat se thing Tib. bka'abrgyud gser phyeng.
11. Sapchen Dorje Junu Tib. dpal chen rdo rje gjhu nu.
12. Rigsum Gonpo: Tib. rig gsum mgon po'ai
13. Guru Padma: Tib. guru pdm'ai
14. Ishes Gonbo chag zee: Tib. ye shes mgon po phyag bzhi

15. Paden Lhamo : Tib. dpal ldan lha mo
16. Chedak: Tib.Tshe bdag
17. Canrazik lhazak: Tib. spyan ras gzigs lha zag
18. Chagdo lhacak Gonsum: Tib.Chag rdo lha zag mgon gsum.
19. Chorten calu khacor: Tib. mchod rten bya rung kha shor
20. Je cun Dolma: Tib. rje btsum sgrolma
21. Padma Zugnas lhacok: Tib bdma 'abyung gnas la lha tshogs
22. Stonba, Chagdor and Maitreya: Tib. Ston pa, phyag rdor and byams pa
23. Thugze Chenpozag zee: Tib. thugs rje chen po phyag bzhee
24. Ca-sum: Tib. rtsa gsum
25. Sangyas Smanla: Tib. sangs rgyas sman bla
26. Thovo de dan: Tib. khro bo sde ldang
27. White Tara: Tib sgro dkar
28. Singdong ma: Tib. seng gdong ma
29. Dolkar: Tib. sgro dkar
30. Khayu nga: Tib. khyung lnga
31. Zangdong spal ri : Tib. zangs mdog dpal ri
32. Dukar: Tib. gdugs dkar
33. Lhachot: Tib. bla mchot
34. Patkar Casum: Tib. pad dkar tsa gsum
35. Ge sung dolma: Tib. rje btsun sgrol ma
36. Chagdor: Tib. phyag rdor
37. Guru Sangyat: Tib. guru mtsan brgyad
38. Dagpo Rinpoche : Tib. dvags po rin po che
39. Stonba: Tib. ston pa
40. Thuva lhacot: Tib. Thub dbang lha mchog
41. Guru cokorsum : Tib. gu ru gtso 'akhor.

14

Coktsal Gonpa: A Branch of Spituk Monastery of Ladakh

Location: Coktsal Gonpa is about 5 kms. away from the Leh town in Choglamsar village.

Approach: We can aproach by taxis or by bus. Coktsal Gonpa has metalled road.

Old Gonpa Structure[1]: This structure was destroyed.

Tradition of the Gonpa : This Gonpa is a branch of Spituk monastery and belongs to Geluk-pa tradition of Mahayana Buddhism[2].

Historical Background: The Gonpa was built by Lopon Tsering Stopgyal in 1876 A.D. It was popularly known **'Lakchung'**. It is said that once Lopon or Minister of Ladakh was resided in Choglamsar village. After his death all the statues from his **Chotkhang** were shifted to **Lakcung.** Later it was turned into **Gonpa.** The Gonpa had four beams and main room was fitted by glass windows. There were following Buddhist statues in the Gonpa:

1. Avalokitesvara[3]
2. Jamyang or Manjusri[2]
3. Green Tara[3]
4. Chanrazik (Four hands)[4]
5. Buddha
6. Tsong - khapa[5]

7. Co-Rinpoche (made by sandal wood)[6]
8. 16 Arhats (small statues)[7]

Printing material

(i) Tarcok block
(ii) Block Printer

Religious Book

(i) Bum Pothi
(ii) Sar Ot Pothi
(iii) Dorje Chotpa
(iv) Domang Pothi: Printing of this pothi was started during king Nima Namgyal and later his son and king of Ladakh Deskyong Namgyal completed it. This pothi consists about 500 pages.

Important statue: In this **Gonpa** 4 hands Avalokitesvara statue of 10 inches in height was made by marble, treated to be the most important statue.

Thankas

(i) Skukes Cusumpa
(ii) Mithugpa Thousand made by gold colour
(iii) Chepakmed with 785 images
(iv) Tsong-Khapa Lamrim
(v) Chepakmed Largu
(vi) Dolma made of by gold colour
(vii) Smanla Desegyat[8]

Field Research: On 12th November 2004, I alongwith lama Lobzang Tander visited Choglamsar village monastery. At Choglamsar we met Dolkar, she was my student, requested for a cup of tea. We followed her upto the house. Her younger sister, who was also my student warmly welcomed us. We were seated in her glass room. After sometime Tsering Dolkar entered with tea and biscuits.

"Guruji ! Please have tea and biscuits."

"O.K. But tell me,where is Choglamsar *Gonpa*?"

"It is very near to my house."

"Can we see the ***Gonpa***?"

"At present ***Pujari*** is not here, if you want to see the ***Gonpa***, I may arrange key for you."

Tsering Dolkar sent her younger sister Tsewang Dolma to the nearby village to bring key of the ***gonpa***. After sometimes she brought key, we accompanied her upto the ***Gonpa***. She opened the door of the Gonpa, it was having beautiful paintings and Buddhist statues. Here follows the details.

Statues: The present Coktsal ***Gonpa*** is recently built. Therefore, has a very good condition with six beems. Fig.14.1 shows the details:

C : Central Statue Maitreya[9]

Height – 6 feet

Width – 3 feet

Pasture – seated

On its left and right are Avalokotesvara and Manjusri in standing, each of 1.5 feet in height.

Left side of the centre statue

1. **Tsong-Khapa[10]:** Height: 4 feet; below to this one framed photograph of 14th Dalai Lama is placed.
2. Behind the centre statues there are 17 small statues, most probably of 16 Arhats and one Avalokitesvara. 16 Arhats are 6 inches-7 inches in height and Avalokitesvara made by marble is 10 inches in height.
3. Two Namgyal chortens, 3 feet in height (each).
4. Here we saw two statues of Manjusri and Padmasambhava, each one of 3 feet in height.
5. Padmasambhava: 6 feet in height.

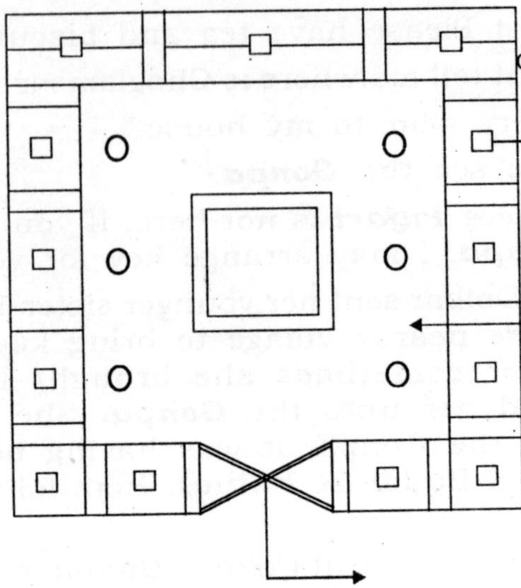

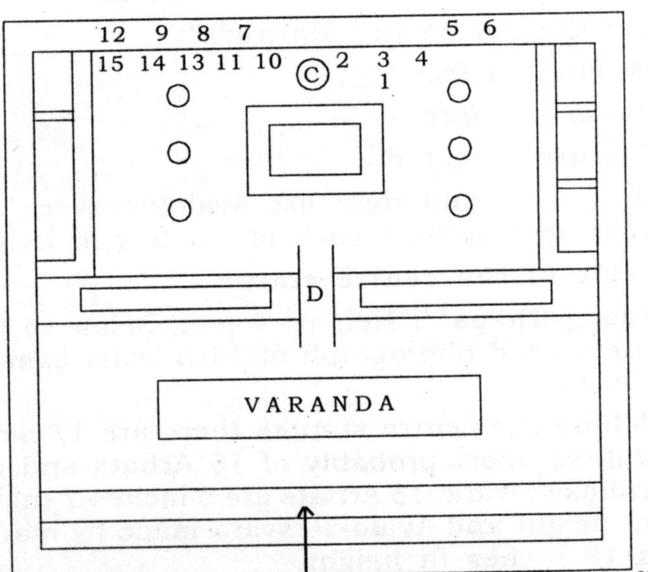

Not to Scale

© : Centre statue O : Beam

▣ : Window |D| : Door

Fig. 14.1 : Statues in Coksal Gonpa

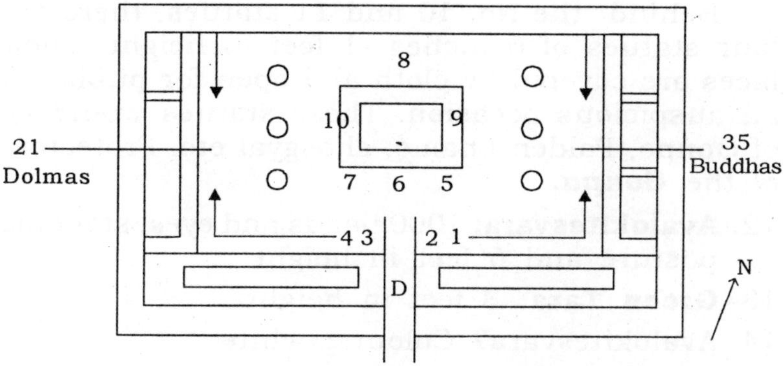

O : Beam |D| : Door ▭ : Window

Not to Scale

Fig. 14.2 : Paintings on the walls of Coktsal Gonpa

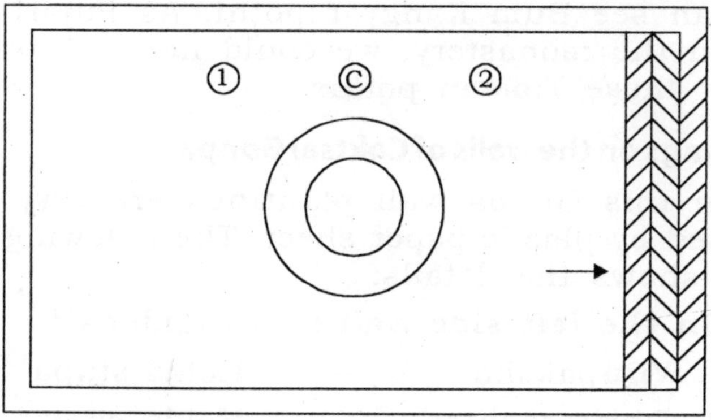

◎ : Mani Tungtur

Not to Scale

Fig. 14.3 : Paintings on Mani Tungtur

6. Buddha : 6 inches -7 inches in height

Right side of the centre statue

7. Tsong-khapa : 2 feet in height, on seated posture.
8. Tsong-khapa: 1 feet in height seated
9. Buddha: 2 feet in height, seated
10. Yabyum: ? , 1 feet in height, seated
11. Co-Rinpoche : 1 feet in height, seated

Behind the No. 10 and 11 statues, there are four statues of 6 inches -1 feet in height. Their faces are covered by cloth and open for public on an auspicious occasion. These statues would be of Gonpo, Palden Lhamo, chosgyal etc. Protectors of the ***Gonpa.***

12. **Avalokitesvara:** 1000 hands and eyes, standing posture and 6 feet in height
13. **Green Tara:** 3 feet in height
14. Avalokitesvara? Colour : white

    Head : Four

    Height: 3 feet
15. Green Tara: 3 feet height

Religious Books: Behind the Green Tara we can see Bum Kangyar pothi. As Pujari was not in the monastery, we could not say exactly about these Tibetan pothis.

Paintings on the walls of Coktsal Gonpa

In this Gonpa wall paintings are very well covered by plastic paper sheet. The following Fig. 14.2 shows the details:

On the left side wall : 35 Buddhas[11]

1. Virupaksha — Holds stupa[12]
2. Dhritarashtra — Holds sitar[13]
3. Virudhaka — Holds sword[14]
4. Vaisravana — Holds nyola[15]
5. Manjusri — Seated
6. Avalokitesvara — Posture-Seated Hands-Four
7. Chagdor[16] — Posture-Seated

On the Right side wall: 21 Dolmas

Normally Dharmpals are painted outside the door. Here I saw them on the walls inside the temple but on the left and right side walls of the door.

Paintings on Namkhang

8. Buddha with his two main disciples Sariputra and Mandgalyayana
9. Tsongkhapa
10. Padmasambhava[17].

All the above three main images are in sitting posture.

Coming out from the Coksal Gonpa I saw newly built Mani Tungtur. On one side wall was beautifully painted. (Fig. 14.3).

Paintings on the wall of Mani Tungcur

(c) : Avalokitesvara = Colour - White
= Hands - Four

1 : Manjusri[18]

2 : Chagdor

Notes and References

1. **Old Gonpa Structure:** This structure has been destroyed, as heavy cracks have been reported on walls, the wall paintings as well being destroyed by humidity or rain water.
2. **Geluk-pa tradition:** It was founded by Tsongkhapa after name of his own monastery 'Ganden'. Here follows the details that how the 'Gelukpa' name derived from Ganden.

   Ri bo dGa' ldonpa ≥ Ribo Gadenpa

   Ribo Gadenpa ≥ Galdenpa

   Galdenpa ≥ Gedenpa

   Galdenpa ≥ Geldokpa

   Geldok pa ≥ Glukpa

   Therefore, Tsongkhapa's monastery was first known as the Ribo Gadenpa, and from its strictness in monastic discipline it was called the Geluk-pa.
3. **Avalokitesvara:** He is the Bodhisattva who is one of the Five Tathagatas, is a manifestation of

Amitabha, is shown in white colour, and who looks all living beings with compassion.

4. **Jamyang or Manjusri:** Bodhisattva of wisdom and literature, and is shown in yellow, white, red, and black forms, with two lotus blossoms as his attributes, or with the sword of knowledge in his right hand and the book of transcedent wisdom (Prajnaparamita) in his left. During Sakyamuni Buddha's time he was one of his eight chief disciples. The wrathful appearance of Manjusri is Bhairava. There are various forms of Manjusri. Here follows the details:

(1) 'Jam dbyangs dkar po (Sita-Manjughosa)

(2) 'Jam dbyangs dpal gzhon nur gyur pa (Kumarabhuta-Manjusri)

(3) 'Jam dbyangs brtan pa'i khor lo (Sthiracakra-Manjughosa)

(4) 'Jam dbyangs gsang sgrub (Guhya-sādhana-Mañjughosa)

(5) 'Jam dbyangs seng ge'i sgra (Simhanāda-Mañjughosa)

(6) 'Jam dbyangs ngag gi rgyal po (Vadirad-Mañjughosa)

(7) 'Jam dbyangs chos dbyings gsung gi dbang.phyug brgyad pa (Astabhuja-Dharmadhatuvagisvara-Mañjughosa)

(8) 'Jam dbyangs sgra bzang dbang phyug rgyal po (Bhadravaresvararaja-Manjughosa)

(9) 'Jam dpal rgyal po rol ba (Rajalila-Manjusri)

(10) 'Jag gsum lhag par dbang du byed pa'i 'jam dbyangs (Trailokyavasyadhikara-Manjughosa)

(11) Mtshan brojod kyi 'jam dbyangs phyag bzhi pa (Caturbhuja-Nāmasamgīti-Mañjughosa)

12. 'Jam dbyangs shes rab' khor lo dang po (Prajnacakra - Manjughosa)

13 'Jam dpal rnon po (Tisna - Manjusri) Cf. Musashi Tachikawa, Masahide. Mori and Shinobu Yamaguchi. Three hundred and sixty Buddhist

Deities-Asian Iconography series - 11, Adroit Pub, Delhi, 2001: 13 and Finegan, Jack: Tibet: A Dreamt of Image, Tibet House, New Delhi, 1986: 131.

3. **Green Tara:** Tib. sGrol ma ljang gu, or "green savioress" is probably the form of Tara/Dolma incarnate in Wencheng, the Chinese wife of King Songtsen Ganpo. She is usually seen seated with the right leg hanging down, in green colour, in peaceable manifestation, and with a dark blue lotus bud as a symbol. There are many forms of Tara.

1. Seng ldeng nag 'bye sgrol ma (Khadivani - Tara)
2. Myur shing dpa'i sgrol ma (Pravīra ?-Tāra)
3. Sgrol ma zla mdang ma (Candrakānti? - Tāra)
4. Sgrol ma gser mdog ma (Kanakavarna -Tāra)
5. Gtsug tor sgrol ma (U s nīsa - Tārā)
6. Sgrol ma hum sgra sgrogs ma (Hūmsvaranādini - Tārā)
7. rNam par rgyal ba'i sgrol ma (Vijaya - Tārā)
8. Sgrol ma gzhan gyis mi thuba pa (Aparājita - Tārā)
9. Sgrol ma bdud 'joms ma (Mārasūdana - Tārā)
10. Mya ngan sel ba'i sgrol ma (s'okavinodana - Tārā)
11. 'Gra ba 'gugs pa'i sgrol ma (Jagadvasi ? - Tārā)
12. bka shis skye ba'i sgrol ma (Mangolotpadana - Tārā)
13. Sgrol ma smin byed ma (Pācaka -Tārā)
14. Sgrol ma khros ma nag mo (Kruddha Kālī-Tārā)
15. Zhi ba chen mo'i sgrol ma (Mahāsānti - Tārā)
16. Chags pa 'joms pa'i sgrol ma (Rāganisūdana - Tārā)
17. bde ba sbyin pa'i sgrol mo (Sukhada-Tārā)
18. Sgrol ma rnam par rgyel ma dkar mo (Sita-Vijaya - Tārā)

19. Sdug bsngal bsresgs pa'i sgrol ma (Duḥkhadahana - Tārā)
20. dNgos grub stsol ba'i sgrol ma (Siddhīda - Tārā)
21. Yongs su rdzongs pa'i sgrol ma (Paripūrna -Tārā)?
22. Dug nag sel ba'i sgrol ma (Janguli - Tārā).

4. **Chanrazik:** Tib. spyan ras gzigs phyag bzhi pa (Caturbhuja - Avalokitesvara); lord who looks all living being with compassion.
5. **Tsong -Khapa:** He was the founder of Gelukpa order of Mahayana Buddhism.
6. **Co - Rinpoche:** Buddha
7. **16 Arhats**: Tib. gnas brtan, Pron. nepten.
8. **Smanlla Desogyat :** Tib. sman bla bde gshegs brgyad. Here follows the name of these:
   (1) Sh'akye thub pa
   (2) Sman gyi bla
   (3) mngon mkhyen rgya po
   (4) Shos sgrags rgya mtsho
   (5) Mya ngan med mchog dpal
   (6) Gser bzang dri med
   (7) Sgra dhyangs rgyal po
   (8) Mtshan legs yongs bsgrags dpal
9. **Maitreya:** Future Buddha who will come down in the world to liberate the sentient beings when Sakyamuni's teachings will disappear from the earth. It is believed that at present, he lives in the Tusita Loka in the form of a Budhisattva. On the humble request of Asanga, he composed five books in order to disclose the implicit contents of the Wisdom Sutra of Sakyamuni Buddha. The different stages of the path., viz, the five spiritual paths and the ten grounds of Bodhisattva are the step that are to be traversed from the ordinary level i.e., Prthakjana stage up to the Buddhahood. Moreover, he is reported to have held that the sentient beings are innately endowed with Buddha nature (Tāthāgata - Garbha) and

therefore, it is proved that the sentient beings can attain Budddahood by eliminating the mental defilements, Cf. Lobzang Tsewang: 'Śākyamuni: An exhibition of Rare Thankas, Central Institute of Buddhist Studies, Choglamsar, Leh-Ladakh; 2001: 24.

10. **Tsong -Khapa:** The founder of Geluk-pa order of Mahayana Buddhism.

11. 35 Buddhas: Here follows the list of 35 Buddhas.

    1. Sakyamuni.
    2. Vajragarbhapramardin
    3. Ratnārais
    4. Nāgeśvararaja
    5. Vīrasena
    6. Viranandin
    7. Ratnāgni
    8. Ratnacandraprabha
    9. Amoghadarśin
    10. Ratnacandra
    11. Vimala
    12. Śruadatta
    13. Brahmā
    14. Brahmadatta
    15. Varuṇa
    16. Varuṇadeva
    17. Bhadraśri
    18. Candanaśri
    19. Anantaujas
    20. Prabhāsaśri
    21. Aśokaśri
    22. Nārāyana
    23. Kusumaśri
    24. Brahmajyotivikrīditābhijña
    25. Padmajyotivikriditābhijña

26. Dhanaśri
27. Smrtiśri
28. Suparikirtitanāmaśri
29. Indraketudhvajarāja
30. Suvikrāntāsri
31. Yuddhajaya
32 Vikrāntagamiśri
33. Samantāvabhāsavyūhaśri
34. Ratnapadmavikrāmin
35. Śailendrarāja

12. **Virupaksha:** Tib. Mig mibzan, Pron. Mig Midang; Guardian of the west and king of the serpent. He is the guardian king of west, red in colour and holds a small stupa in high right hand and a snake in his left.

13. **Dhritarashtra:** Tib. Yul 'Khor bsrung, Pron. Yul Khorsung, Guardian of the east and king of the celestial musicians called gandharvas, in white colour and holds a stringed instrument.

14. **Virudhaka:** Tib.'Phags skyes Po; Pron Phak kyepo, Guardian of the south and king of the malignant spirits called ***Kumbhanda,*** is dark blue in colour and holds a sword or ***Khadga***.

15. **Vaiśranavna:** Tib. rNam thos sras, Pron. Nam Those or Kubera, Guardian of the North and king of the **Yakshas** is yellow in colour and holds a banner of victory or ***dhvaja*** and a mongoose or ***Nakula.***

    Cf. Finegan, Jank; *op. cit* : 134.

16. **Chagdor:** Tib. phyay-na rdo-rje ; in Sanskrit language Vajrapani. He is the Bodhisattva of energy and power.

17. **Padmasambhava:** Tib. Lopon Rinpoche or Guru Rinpoche "Lotus Born One" an Indian Tantric invited by king Trisong Detsen in the eighth century A.D. He visited Tibet and subdued the local deities and demons while constructing the first monastery 'Samyas' in Tibet Cf. Batchelor Stephen: 'The Tibet Guide; Wisdom Pub., London. 1987: 420.

18. **Manjusri:** Tib. Jan dhyangs, Pron. Jamgyang "Charming Splendor" and is shown in yellow, white, red, blue and black forms, beautifully handsome young mahabodhisattva and bodhisattva and god of wisdom, science and agriculture. He is considered by the Northern Buddhists as one of the eight Dhyani Bodhisattvas. With his sword he destroys ignorance and darkness. He is frequently shown with Dhyani Bodhisattva Avalokitesvara and Dhyani Bodhisattva Vajrapani. These three together figures are known in Ladakh as 'Rig Sum Gonpo'. According to one tradition he attained perfect enlightenment countless aeons backs. He descended in this world as a Bodhisattva in order to remove the sufferings of all sentient beings. He is considered one of the chief eight disciples of Sakyamuni Buddha, thus one who wants to know the realization of emptiness, has to pray and recite bija mantra of Manjusri Cf. Bunce, Fredrick W.: 'An Encyclopaedia of Buddhist Deities, Demigods, Godlings, Saints and Demons; Vol. I; D.K.Printworld Ltd., New Delhi; 1994 : 331.

15
Bardan Monastery of Zanskar in Ladakh

Bardan monastery is situated about 12 km south of Padum, the capital town of Zanskar valley in Kargil district of Ladakh.

Old Establishment

The old Bardan Gonpa was constructed in 13th century on the top of a mountain called Thar-lha. It is said that a raven carried off from there a burning butter lamp and took it to the hill shaped like a white conch shell with its coil turning to the right the place where the present monastery is situated. To know the above fact that it is an auspicious sign, Siddha Lama Barapa scattered consecreted grain and blessed the site by performing rituals. Later he founded a monastery there. Since then it is the seat of Lama Barapa[1]. The name of the monastery also being derived from his name as Bardan in the following way:

Barapa Daphug ≥ Barapa Phug

Barapa Phug ≥ Bara Dug

Bara Dug ≥ Bardun

Bardun ≥ Bardan

The ruins of the old establishment of Bardan monastery and a stupa can still be seen at Thar-lha, about 2 km. away from the present monastery.

Present Establishment

The present monastery was founded by the Devang gyatso[2]. In the middle of 16th century A.D. Devang gyatso met Ladakh king Jamyang Namgyal[3] and requested him to give support in the construction of new Bardan monastery in Zanskar. King Namgyal accepted the request. Later with his kind support Devang gyatso constructed **Chot-Khang** and **Tashak** for lamas in the monastery. He later gave new name to the monastery as **Bar-dan sangyas chos ling.** Then with the hard work of Devang gyatso and his follow disciples, the number of lamas in the monastery had been increased considerably within a short of time[4].

Role of Tagtsan Raspa

While constructing Bardan monastery in Zanskar, evil spirits of the site disturbed Devang gyatso. This was the time when Mahasiddha. Tagtsang Raspa on his journey to Urgyan (Pron. Urgyan) came in Zanskar. When Devang gyatso came to know about his journey, he didn't want to miss the chance and decided to meet him.

Accordingly he met him and requested to visit the construction site of the monastery. At the site of the monastery he said :

"Guruje, I have no interest in the construction. I know, monastery will not harm anybody, however, will help to strengthen Buddhism. But unfortunately evil spirits don't happy with this auspicious work. They all the time disturb me some or the other way. Therefore, kindly stay here for at least one month ; look their activities, and if possible to control them. Your presence will definitely help to make peace and harmony at this region."

Lama Tagtsang Raspa delightfully accepted the request of Devang gyatso, later stayed at

Bardan for one month and purified monastery's place. He spent most of his time in meditation. In this way evil spirits stopped their nonsense activities. Thereafter, Devang gyatso successfully able to construct Bardan monastery.

Principal Image of Maitreya

There are many important Buddhist images in the Bardan monastery. But Buddha Maitreya has got its especial significance as:

(1) It is made according to Gandhara art.

(2) It is a small statue of two feet in height, but can speak with devotees.

(3) It is *savayambhu* statue and brought here from Kashmir.

(4) It is made of precious metals of gold and brass.

Today Bardan monastery is a well developed monastic structure in Zanskar, situated at an isolated place with three big Dukhangs in the middle surrounded by Tashaks and has about 50 monks resided[5].

It is one of the big *Drug pa kargyud* monastery in Zanskar. It controls several small establishments including Sani monastery in this region. The large assembly hall around which all other structures are organized, contains beautiful statues of Buddhist divinities and small stupas of clay, bronze, wood and copper. Perched a top rocky crag, rising vertically from the Lungnak river bed. The monastery is right on the trekking trail to Manali[6].

The temples of Bardan monastery are beautifully decorated by statues, wall painting and Buddhist texts. Here follows the details:

Gonkhang (Tib.mgon khang)

Gonkhang temple does not have windows. Here protector deities are placed in a dark room.

Statues in Gonkhang

(1) Four hands Gonpo (*Tib. mgon po phyag bjhee*)[7]

(2) Gon carag docan (*Tib. mgon bya rog gdong can*)[8].

(3) lha mo dud rol ma (*Tib. lha mo dud grol ma*)

(4) Dechog khor lo dom pa skyu nyan (*Tib. bde mchog 'akhor lo sdom p'ai sku brnyan*)[9]

(5) Gonpo kagyud (*Tib. mgon po bk'abrgyud*)

Dukhang (Tib.'adu khang)

It is a assembly hall where lamas of the monastery set at their respective alloted seats and offer prayer.

Statues in Dukhang

In Dukhang Stonba (*Tib. stonba*) or Sakyamuni Buddha[10] is placed in the middle of 108 kangyur (*Tib. K'a*[11] *'agyur*) texts. The other main statues are:

(1) Padmasambhava[12]

(2) King Nawang Namgyal of Ladakh.

Wall Paintings in Dukhang

The inside walls of the Dukhang are decorated by frescoes e.g. khor lo dom pa (*Tib. 'akhor lo sdam pa*)[9] and the paintings of lamas representing to various Buddhist orders.

Statues in Chot-Khang (*Tib. mchod-khang*)

This temple has one principal statue of Avalokitesvara ***(Tib. sbyan ras bzias)***[13] of sandal wood. In addition there are many Buddhist texts of worth value such as:

(1) Dugkpa kagyud Namthar (*Tib. bk'a brgyud gong ma rnams kyi rnam thar*)

(2) Sumbum (*Tib. sung 'bum*)

Zimsung (Tib. gzim shung)

The monastery has two Zimsungs (or V.I.P. rooms) for Rin-po-che and other respected persons.

Mane khang

In this room devotees offer Mane prayer for peace and harmony.

Famous Lamas and their Contribution in Bardan Monastery

After Devang gyatso, Lama Dorje zin pa[14] took initiative to renovate old temples and to contruct new temples in the monastery. Thereafter Dagnas Chorje Nawang Gyaltsen[15]. Chorje Jamyang Patkar[16] and Dorje Zinpa offered their valuable services for the manastic activities in Zanskar. Subsequently, Tashi Stanphel of Stagna[17] monastery, Leh arrived in Zanskar with the motive to strengthen the Drugpa ka' gyud school of Buddhism. He stayed in the Bardan monastery and made all needed improvements in the monastic discipline, vinaya rules and regulations.

Dus chod (Tib. dus mchod)

In the Bardan monastery the following ritual prayers are offered by the lamas in the Dukhang.

1. From 22nd of 12th month of the year to about one month, lamas of the monastery perform daily rituals or prayers in the honour of the following deities:
   (1) Gonpo chag jhee (*Tib. mgon po phyag bjhee*)[18]
   (2) Yidam (*Tib. yi-dam*)[19]
   (3) Dechok (*Tib. mde mchog*)[20]
   (4) lha cu sum (*Tib. lha bcu gsum*)
   (5) jee tho dam pa rigs gya (*Tib. jee khro dam pa rigs brgya*)[21]
   (6) Tordag (*Tib. tor zlog*)
   (7) lha nga (*lha lnga*)

(8) lha cu (*Tib. lha cu*)

(9) la ma chod pa (*Tib. bla ma mchod pa*)

2. On 10th of the 1st month of the year according to Tibetan/Ladakhi Bodhi calendar, lamas of the monastery gather in Dukhang, read padmasambhava pothis, offer prayers and intermíttently play monastic musical instruments according to rituals. Devotees on this occasion offer prayer and lit lamps.
3. On 15th of the 1st month of the year devotees offer prayer to Gyalva Chmba in Chot khang and lit lamps.
4. From 14-15 of 4th month of the year lamas of the monastery practice cham for Gonpo ka-gyat.
5. On 15th of the 4th month of the year, lamas offer Ge-ca prayer for all living beings.
6. From 15th of the 7th month of the year lamas gather in the main Dukhang and participate in the Sozong prayer for 5 days.

Notes and References

1. Thupstan Paldan : Guide for Ladakhi Gonpas; 1976 : 22 and Barapa: *Tib. 'bar-ra-pa*, was the established Buddhist yogi.
2. Devang gyatso : *Tib. bde-ba-rgya-mtho:* He was the geat Buddhist Saint of Zanskar Valley during 16th century A.D. He was born in a royal family in Padam (Padum), the Tashil headquarter of Kargil district, Ladakh.
3. King Jamyang Namgyal (*Tib. 'ajam dbyangs rnam rgyal*) helped Devang gyatso for the construction of Bardan monastery in Zanskar. He became king of Ladakh after the death of king Tshewang Namgyal.
4. Jina, Prem Singh : '*Ladakh : The Land and People*' Indus Pub. Co. New Delhi ; 1996 and Tashak: Rooms for Lamas of the monastery.

5. Ladakh : Kargil and Zanskar, a booklet published by Jammu and Kashmir Tourism Department : 29.
6. *Ibid.*
7. **Four hands Gonpo** (*Tib. mgon po phyag bjhee*): One face, fierce with three eyes and flame-like hair; four hands. He is one of the Dharmapala.
8. **Gon carag docan** (*Tib. mgon bya rog gdong can*) **:** He would be *rdo rje kyung kha* vajragaruda (Sabala)?
9. **Dechog khor lo dom pa skyu nyan (***Tib. bde mchog'akhor lo sdom p'ai sku brnyan***) :** It would be Sricakrasamvara.
10. **Sakyamuni Buddha :** In 6th century B.C. Skyamuni Buddha descended to the world to show the right path to the fortunate beings, so that they may attain freedom from the cycle of existence.
11. **Kangyur** (*Tib. k'a 'agyur*): It means "translations of the word (bka' word or speech, i.e., of the Buddha)". The Kanjur contains the whole Theravada and Mahayana literature, Cf. Finegan Jack : Tibet : A Dreamt of Image; Tibet House, New Delhi, 1986 : 14-15.
12. **Padmasambhava :** He was the great mystic saint from India who had tremendous miraculous powers. He brought Buddhist Tantra in Tibet in the 8th century A.D. and introduced its learning and practice. Cf. Lobzang Tsewang: 'Sakyamuni' C.I.B.S., Leh-Ladakh, 2001 : 26.
13. **Avalokitesvara** (*Tib. sbyan ras bzias*) : The lord who looks down with compassion ; is a manifestation of Amitabha, is shown in white colour and has various forms such as :
    1. Caturbhuja—Avalokiteśvara
    2. Padmavikāsana—Avalokiteśvara

3. Khasarpana—Avalokiteśvara
4. Simhanāda—Avalokiteśvara
5. Hālāhala—Lokesvara
6. Vajradahra—Avalokiteśvara
7. Dvibhuja-Padmanartèvara Avalokiteśvara
8. Astadasabhuja-Padmanarteśvara
9. Harihariivāhana-Lokeśvara
10. Trailokyavaśamkara Avalokiteśvara
11. Caturbhuja-rakta-Lokeśvara
12. Nilakantha-Lokeśvara
13. Mayajālākrama-Avalokiteśvara
14. Amoghapāśa
15. Mahābhumika? - rakta Avalokiteśvara
16. Ekadasamukha Avalokiteśvara
17. Gaganarāja
18. Cittaviśrāmana Avalokiteśvara
19. Cintāmani Avalokiteśvara
20. Vajragarbhapramardin Avalokiteśvara

14. **Lama Dorje Zin pa : *Tib. bla ma rdo rje adzin pa*.** He was the famous lama of Bardan monastery after Barpa and Devang gyatso.
15. **Dagnas Chorje Nawang Gyaltsen :** Tib. ***'abrug nas chos rje ngag dbang rgyal mtsan.*** He was the head lama of Bardan monastery.
16. **Chorje Jamyang Patkar : *Tib. chos rje 'ajam dbyangs bad dkar.*** He was also a head of the Bardan monastery.
17. **Dorje Jinpa: *Tib. rdo rje dzin pa.*** He was an active lama of the monastery, who helped in the improvement of monastic discipline.
18. **Tashi Stanphel : Tib. Bkris bstan aphel.** He visited Zanskar from Leh for the propagation of Drugpa K'agyud order of Buddhism there.
19. **Gonpa chag jhee (*Tib. mgon po phyag bjhee*) :** He is one of the Dharmapala.

20. **Yidam (Tib. Yi-dam) :** The Yidams (Sanskrit Ishtadevata, ***Tibetan yidam lha***). The yidam is usually represented together with his ***Prajna.*** It is considered that a tutelary got more efficacious if worshipped in company with his consort. Cf. Finegan, Jack; *op. cit.* : 132-33.
21. **Dechok (*Tib. mde mchog*) :** In Sanskrit language equivalent to chakrasamvara. He belongs to vajrayana and usually represented in twelve-armed form embracing his consort Vajravarahi.
22. **Tordag (*Tib. tor zlog*) :** Possibly it would be ***Tib. Dur khrod bdag po,*** equivalent in Sanskrit as Citipati.

16
Kar-sha Monastery of Zanskar in Ladakh

Introduction

Kar-sha[1] is the largest monastery in Zanskar valley of Kargil district in Ladakh. It has many carved images of Maitreya, .therefore named after as ***Kar sha chams pa ling***[2].

Establishment

Kar-sha monastery was established by Phags pa Shesrab[3] in 1080 A.D. as evident by the following Tibetan Inscription.

Text

Om Savasti

Tog mar gon devs zang kar lo tsava

Cag chal lo

Translation

Om Savasti

Salute to Zangskar lotsava

(Who) built the (monastery)

Explanation

Zangskar lotsava (Zanskar lotsava)[4]

built the monastery

Shesrab Zangpo arrived Zanskar and developed three villages

Rin chen zabs came at last

I salute to all these three great personalities[5].

Canvings on Rocks and Other Important Statues.

(1) 21 Feet High Avalokitesvara Carving

At the north of the Kar-sha monastery there is a huge carving of Avalokitesvara of 1000 hands and eyes[6] of about 21 feet on a Rock. Today supporting to this a temple is built and named 'Ciling'.

(2) Phakspa Lhundup

It is said that once Pujari Phur-bus went to Phur-das for meditation, he offered prayer to his Ishtadeva, thereafter walking a few distance found half feet high Phakspa Lhundup[7] image at the north direction.

(3) Avalokitesvara Image

Phur-bus, when visited to Lang-me village, saw a huge image of Avalokitesvara of about two storyed in height.

(4) Savayambhu Buddha and Avalokitesvara

When Phur-bus visited beyong the Dorje Jong monastery, saw thousand ***Savayambhu***[8] Buddha images and one Avalokitesvara image.

(5) Savayambhu Maitreya images

In Kar-sha village one ***Savayambhu*** Maitreya image[9] is carved on a rock. The chapel is built with the support of rock. ***Savayambhu*** Maitreya image is at the centre of Chapel. Later one clay statue is made. Below this on the left side of rock one more ***Savayambhu*** Maitreya image was found, later painted according to Buddhist tradition. After sometimes, another Chapel was constructed with the support of the same above said rock. Further down near water fall one more **Savayambhu** Maitreya image was found.

Introduction of Geluk pa Order

During 1443 Cang Shes rab zang po[10] visited Kar-sha monastery. He stayed there for some time and put the monastery under Geluk pa tradition[11]. Thereafter, propagated this tradition in the other parts of Zanskar valley. After the **Parinirvana** of Cang Shes rab zang po, Lama Dung-do-de-rinchen took the responsibility to strengthen the Geluk monastic tradition and Vinaya rules in the monastery. He followed the path of Cang-shes-rab-zang-po and later made his statue and placed it in Tus-Chod-Lhakhang.

Galdan Tsewang Invasion

In 1681 Sokpo Galdan Tsewang invaded Ladakh and plundered many important monuments. It is said that when his forces were entering into Zanskar valley, the pious statue of Cang-Sems Shesrab-Zang-po started weeping. Thereafter, it is considered a powerful statue in Zanskar and among Buddhist community. At the consequence, every year on 18th of the 11th month of Tibetan/ Ladakhi Bodhi calendar, lamas of the Kar-sha monastery gather in the main Du-khang and offer **'Skang so'** prayer.

Dogra Invasion

In1835 Dogra force under the command of Zorawar Singh[12] destroyed many important Buddhist monuments. The Kar-sha was among them. Later they carried away precious statues to Jammu.

The Role of Do-de-shes-rab

When the old structure of Kar-sha monastery was dis-used, Do-de shes-rab[13] visited Zanskar and re-built the present structure. Thereafter Zhadpa Dorje[14] devoted his life for painting works, he decorated the inside walls of the temples of kar-sha monastery by Buddhist Gurus, Bodhisattvas, Taras, protected deities etc. In addition he made Do-de-rinchen-shes-rab statue and inserted his bone relices.

Rin-chen-zang-po temples

The two ***Rin-chen-zang-po***[15] temples named : ***Thugs-je-chen-po-lha-khang*** and ***Lha-khang-khar-po*** are located near kar-sha monastery. These temples lookafter by Kar-sha monastery and are very well preserved. However, it is very unfortunate to say that some of the old paintings of 11th century A.D. are being damaged by moisture penetration[16].

Other Old Temples at the Vicinity of Kar-sha Monastery

There are some old temples near the Kar-sha monastery viz. Pu-rang[17], Kha-sar[18] and Nang-va-phal[19]. These temples have very old statues of Avalokitesvara and Maitreya of about 10-11th century A.D.

Dorje Dzong[20]

It is an old Nunnery, occupying a hilltop to the west of about 8 km of the main monastery. The ruins around the Nunnery is believed to be the origional monastic foundation of Kar-sha. The present complex was founded during the 14th century. An old stupa surviving among the ruins is still adorned with the original murals reflecting Indian artistic influence.

Tradition to Visit Sacred Sites

As said above, there are many sacred sites at the surrounding of the main monastery. During 1972 many renowned Buddhist lamas visited there. Popular among them are:

1. Lama Phunchok of Nubra, Leh district.
2. Nawang Norbu of Korzok village, Leh district.

3. Lama Rigzin of Rug Rug.
4. Lama Chetan-thu-khyongs of Phey village, Leh district.
5. Lama Nawang.
6. Lama Ishey Sangroop.

Today it becomes a tradition to visit nearby temples while visiting the main monastery Kar-sha.

One year calendar of monastic activities in the Kar-sha monastery according to Tibetan/ Ladakhi Bodhi calendar

1. **Ist month of the year :** From 14 to 15/, in two days lamas of the monastery celebsrate nyen nas and myung nas.[21] On this occasion six old Thankas of Padmasambhava[22] and one Tsong-kha-pa[23] exhibited.
2. **IInd month of the year :** Lamas of the monastery offer Panchen Lozang-chos-gyan prayer, and make Chodpa. On this occasion devotees visit the monastery, offer prayer and lit lamps.
3. **IVth month of the year :** From 19 to 25 lamas of the monastery offer Ge-ca[24] prayer.
4. **Vth month of the year :** On 25th lamas of the monastery offer Gansol prayer[25] at the Gon-khang.
5. **VIth month of the year :** From 15th onwards lamas perform **Yarnas.**
6. **VIIth month of the year :** From 1 to 7, lamas make Kalacakara mandala and perform rituals.
7. **Xth month of the year :** On 21st and 27th day lamas perform Gaden Namchod.
8. **XIth month of the year :** On 21st and 25th day lamas practice **'Cham'** without masks. On 27th, they practice **'Cham'** with complete tantric costumes and masks of Buddhist deities. Finally from 28 to 29 i.e. in two days lamas of the monastery perform 'cham' at chamra

called **'Gu-tor'**.[26] On this occasion devotees and visitors are gathered in large number.

9. **XIIth month of the year :** From 4 to 26, lamas gather at the main Dukhang of the monastery, practice Buddhist Philosophical debate and enrich their knowledge of Buddhism.

Lama population : There are 160 registered lamas in the monastery, 75 per cent of them reside in the rooms of monastery, the rest reside outside. Here follows the details :

Table 16.1
Number of Lamas Resided in and Outside the Kar-sha Monastery

S.No.	*No. of Lamas*	*Particulars*
1.	120	Reside in monastery
2.	003	Maysoor, for higher studies
3.	020	Tashilhunpo monastery in Maysoor, Karnataka; for higher studies.
4.	004	Tibetan Institute of Higher Studies, Sarnath, Varanasi; for Higher Studies.
5.	002	Gantok, Sikkim ; for Higher Studies.
6.	011	Working in Govt. jobs.

Source : Survey conducted by Dr. Prem Singh Jina, during 2004-05.

Thus, in the monastery about 70 per cent lamas are engaged in monastic activities and dedicated their life in rituals or religious works.

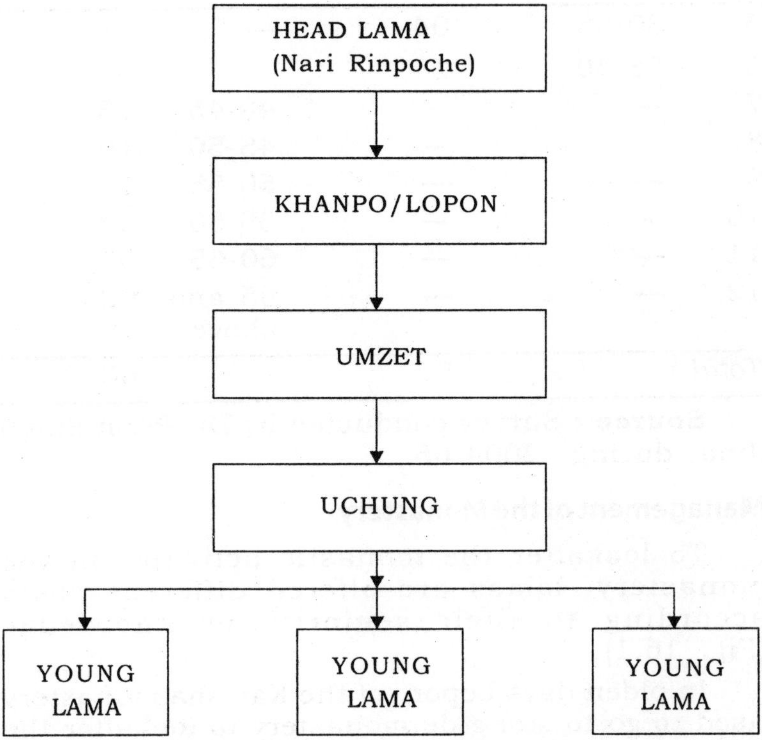

Fig. 16.1: Administrative posts in the Kar-sha monastery.

The rest 30 per cent are young and partially engaged in monastic religious works. Table 16.2 shows the details.

Table : 16.2

Agewise Lama Population in Kar-sha Monastery

S.No.	*Age Group*	*Lama population*	*Age Group*	*Lama Population*
1.	0-15	10	—	—
2.	15-20	19	—	—
3.	20-25	25	—	—
4.	25-30	10	—	—

(Contd.)

5.	30-35	04	—	—
6.	35-40	24	—	—
7.	—	—	40-45	18
8.	—	—	45-50	10
9.	—	—	50-55	15
10.	—	—	55-60	20
11.	—	—	60-65	03
12.	—	—	65-and above	02
Total		92		68

Source : Survey conducted by Dr. Prem Singh Jina, during 2004-05.

Management of the Monastery

To lookafter the monastic activities in the monastery, lamas are offered different posts according to their seniority or knowledge (Fig. 16.1).

In olden days Lopon of the Kar-sha monastery used to go to stong-de monastery to lookafter the monastic activities and discipline. Now-a-days this tradition is almost stopped.

Villages Attached with Kar-sha Monastery

Today maximum villages of Zanskar valley are attached with Kar-sha monastery. However, popular among them are:

Abrang, Hamiling, Skagum, Remala, Manda, Phey, Rentak Sa, Tung Re, Takskeng, Khasar and Techa.

Kar-sha' the main monastery depute lamas to the above villages to meet villagers religious demands. In response they donate their children to monastery to become lamas.

Conclusion

To sum up I would say Kar-sha is the largest monastic establishment of Geluk-pa order in zanskar valley of Kargil district in Ladakh. It is neatly white washed comprising several chapels, beside residential rooms for its 160 lamas.

The said monastery is built along the steep gradient of the mountain side above the steep River, can be seen from far and wide.

This monastery has a long assembly hall called 'Dukhang'. The temples of the monastery are decorated by Buddhist statues and paintings. Among popular images are : Maitreya, Avalokitesvara, Gurus or Acharyas of Geluk tradition.Inside walls are painted by Buddhist traditional lamas and Indian Acharyas. Besides it has throne for incarnated lama which is used for all elaborate prayer sessions.

There are three adjoining chapels. Besides statues, they have various art objects viz. Silver and copper objects, chortens are worth value.

A set old thankas of Buddha, Bodhisattvas and Indian Acharyas adorning the wall of the chapel is worth beholding.

The Lhabrang, a large chamber accessible through a vent in the roof, has some damaged frescos of 15th century A.D.

At the end Kar-sha Gu-tor is a famous festival in Zanskar. The two days festival normally held in every July month of the year. On this occasion thousand devotees and tourists witness the ***cham*** ritual dances performed by mask-wearing lamas of the monastery.

Notes and References

1. **Kar-sha :** ***Kar*** means clean mind and **Sha** to involve in welfare works. Therefore, the name of monastery is derived from the clean hearted villages who had been devoted their life for Dharma and during the construction of monastery, helped wholeheartedly through cash and kind.

2. **Kar-sha Chamas Pa Ling : *Tib dkar-sha-byams-pa-ling dkar-sha*** means clean mind and heart person who works for the welfare of all animal being ***'byams-pa-ling'*** here laying maitreya or ***'Fulure Buddha'*** statues, purify the minds of all people who come and offer prayers.
3. **Phags pa Shesrab :** Tib phags pa Shes rab. He was a famous lama in Zanskar and was known as **'Lotsava'** like Richen Zangpo.
4. **Zangskar lotsava (Zanskar Lotsava):** He was phags pa shesrab zangpo, a great scholar and translator during 11th century A.D. He alongwith Lotsava Rinchen Zangpo ***(Tib. Rin - Chen - Bzang - Po)*** constructed many temples in Western Tibet and decorated them by wall paintings.
5. **Three Great Personalities:** (i) Phags - pa - Shesrab zungpo (ii) Rin chen zabs and (iii) Cang shes rab zang po (probably).
6. **Avalokiteśvara of 1000 hands and eyes:** He is called Arya Avalokiteśvara. It is said that when Avalokiteśvara looked down upon the many beings in need of deliverance in the hell of Yama, the god of death, his head broke into ten pieces out of his great compassion; these were put by his spiritual teacher father Amitabha, thus is the figure three are nine gentle faces arranged in three in three tiers of three each, above that one wrathful; face and, at the top, the head of Amitabha, thus making eleven heads in all. Cf. Finegan, Jack: 'Tibet': A Dreamt of Image; Tibet House; New Delhi; 1986: 130-31.
7. **Phakspa Lhundup:** Tib. phags pa lhun grup. He would be phags pa shesrab, a great scholar and translator.
8. **Savayambhu:** Natural statue or not made by human being.
9. **Maitreya:** Tib. byams-pa, Pron. Champa or Maitreya, is a manifestation of Amoghasiddhi and Viśvapani, is a Bodhisttva or known Future Buddha.
10. **Cang Shes Rab Zang Po: Tib. byang sems shes rab bzang po.** He was a great scholar and lama of

Geluk pa order, came in Ladakh from Tibet during 15th century A.D. Later he propagated Geluk-pa order in Ladakh including Zanskar valley of Kargil district.

11. **Geluk Pa Tradition:** Model of virtue, derivation from the tradition of Atisa and Drom it was called the New Kadam-pa and from its strictness in monastic discipline was called Guluk-pa order and was founded by Tsong-khapa. Cf. Finegan, Jack, op.cit: 101.

12. **Zorawar Singh:** He was born in a Rajput family of Kahlur (Bilapur) in 1786 Zorawar Singh Kahlura when sixteen, he killed his cousin over a property feud and immediately left Kahlur for Hari Dwar. Here, he came in contact with Rana Jaswant Singh, a ***Jagirdar*** of Marmat Galihan who took him in his service and brought him back. Even as a child Zorawar had possessed remarkable physical prowess, under Jaswant Singh's patronage, he became dexterous in handling the weapons of offence and defence. After some time Zorawar Singh entered the service of the Dogra Chief Gulab Singh. In 1815, the latter put him in charge of the defence of Riasi fort a job which he did admirably when it was attacked by Mian Dewan Singh, another contender for the possession of Riasi Jagir. Soon after, Gulab Singh accepted Zorawar's proposal for the better utilisation of supplies to troops and appointed him Inspector. He did remarkable work as a result of practical achievement Gulab Singh was very much impressed and appointed him Governor of Kishtwar and Kussal in 1823, soon after gave him the title of ***Wazir***. In 1834, he started an adventurous career and attacked Ladakh, after conquering put it under the Jammu and Kashmir high Government i.e. Maharaja Gulab Singh Sikh's empire. Cf. Datta, C.L. Ladakh and Western Himalayan Politics : 1819-1848, Munshiram Monoharlal Publisher Pvt. Ltd. New Delhi, 1973:105-07.

13. **Do-de-shes-rab: Tib drung-mdo-sde-shes-rab.** He was a scholar lama and, was responsible to impliment strict monastic discipline in Kar-sha monastery.

14. **Zhadpa Dorje: Tib. bzhad-pa-rdo-rje.** He prompted Buddhist painting works and decorated the temples of Kar-sha by painting of Buddhist Gurus, Bodhisattvas and other deities according to Buddhist tradition. Besides, he followed the ***Do-de-rinchen-shes-rab*** tradition and implimented the same in the said monastery.
15. **Rin-chen-bzang-po: Tib. Rin-chen-bzang-po.** Pron. Rinchen Sangpo. He was born in the year 958, was ordained at the age of thirteen, and died in his ninety-eighth year, i.e. in 1055. During his life time he made three trips to India, the first to Kashmir while young and probably soon after his ordination when sent by Yeshe O, a second to visit the Buddhist holy places in Magadha, and a third to Kashmir again. In all he spent seventeen years in India and studied with seventy-five Indian masters. From India he brought to Tibet a number of panditas, and he himself became known as the Great Translator. Besides he built 108 temples and Chapels in Western Tibet. He was responsible to introduce Tantric system in Tibet. Cf. Finegan, Jack, *op.cit*, 60.
16. **Thupstan Paldan:** Guide for Ladakhi gonpas: 1976:21.
17. **Pu-rang:** This monastery is located in Lang-me Zanskar valley.
18. **Kha-sar: Tib. Kha-gsar.** This monastery is also located in Lang-me village.
19. **Nang-va-Phal: Tib. snang-ba-phal.** About tbis monastery it is said that when a Zanskari villager of Kha-sar started digging the foundation of his house, suddenly stranged to see a ***savambhu*** Avalokitesvara statue. He felt happy and decided to donate the land to monastery. Later on this land Nang-va-phal monastery was built and derived its name Nangva-phal means ***'I am happy'***.
20. **Dorje Dzong: *Tib. rdo-rje-rdzong*.** It is a nunnery and located at the top of the valley at the west of Kar-sha monastery. The ruins around the nunnery is believed that once Kar-sha monastery was founded here.

21. **Nyen nas and myung nas:** Tib. ***bsnyan gnas*** and smyung gnas.
22. **Padmasambhava: *Tib. Pad ma byun'g gnas*** *Pron.* Pema Jungno called the Pad ma thang yi (Pron. pema Thangyig) or Padma thang scroll, pictures him as the spiritual son of the Buddha Amitabha who, in many previous existences, learned and taught the nine vehiles of the Vajrayana. In his earthly existence at Padmasambhava he was born from a lotus flower in Lake Dhanakosa in the country of Urgyan (Pron. Urgyen), which was the Sanskrit Uddiyana, ancient Swat, then under the rule of the blind king Indrabhuti. Eventually, after study and travel in many places and attainment of fame as a powerful exorcist, Padmasambhava accepted the invitation of King Trhisong Detsen to come to Tibet. There he was able to wield spell and charms by which many evil spirits hostile to Buddhism were subdued and even turned into formidable protectors of faith Cf. Finegan, Jack, op. cit: 50.
23. **Tsong-Kha-Pa: *Tib. Tsong Kha-pa-blo gros grags pa*** (pron. Tsongkhapa Lotro Trakpa), also known as rJe Rin Foche. He was born in the district of Tsong Kha, in the vicinity of Lake Kokonor in Amdo, where in 1578 the Kumbum monastery was founded at his birth place. At a very early age he received a consecration from ***Rol Pa'i rdo rje***, who was he Fourth Gyelwa Karmapa, and as a boy of eight the received a further consecration and an introduction to the disciplinary rules of the Vinaya, and to the Tantra, from a great spiritual friend named Don grub rin chen, who also gave him the monastic name of blo-bzang grags pa. At the age of sixteen Tsongkhapa went to Central Tibet and for many years studied with famous teacher of the Nyingma-pa Sakyapa, Jonang-pa, Kagyu-pa, Tshal-pa, Phakmotru-pa, Shalu-pa, and Kadam-pa. He was the incarnation of Manjusri and the founder of Geluk-pa order. Cf. Finegan, Jack, op. cit. 100-01.
24. **Ge-Ca: Tib.qe-rtsa.**
25. **Gansol Prayer: Tib. gnang slol prayer.**
26. **Gu-tor :** It is the annual festival of Kar-sha monastery in which lamas of the monastery perform cham.

17
Zanak : A Famous Long Mani Wall

Nima Namgyal was the eldest son of king Delegs Namgyal, after the death of his father he came on throne of Ladakh kingdom. He was a good administrator and administered royal law not simply on the basis of whatever came to his mind but rather in compliance with the advice of leaders of good counsel. He had two younger brothers: Nawang Namgyal[1] and Tsewang Namgyal. When Nima Namgyal became king of Ladakh in 1694, Nawang Namgyal became lama and went to Thiksey monastery[2] and Tsewang Namgyal also became Lama in Hemis monastery[3].

King Nima Namgyal married Nima Saskyong Vangmo. He had two children from her: Deskyong Namgyal and Norgin Vangmo. After sometimes queen Nima Saskyong Vangmo died[4].

To know the sad news of queen's death, Ladakhis had doubt that king would marry with some one, Deskyong Namgyal who was a handsome Prince would loose his chance to come on Ladakh throne. Therefore, a girl from Shey village sung the following song[5] in the praise of prince Deskyong Namgyal and warned king Nima Namgyal that after marriage he should be remembered the ability of prince Deskyong Namgyal and should not be forgotten that after his death or after him Deskyong Namgyal would become future king of Ladakh.

On the hill in the back there is the chorten of white crystal:

In the front there is the lake, blue like a turquoise.

On the shore flowers are in bloom.

They grow in my fatherland together with its future.

On the shore large yellow flowers are in bloom.

In the castle of Sheh (or Shey) the milk (of abundance) flows.

On the high summit there lives.

The eloquent god of the summit.

Whenever our gracious prince goes.

Oh God, protect his life!

To Deskyong Namgyal, the (future) lord of men.

Give blessing during his lifetime.

The lama who is loved by the girl.

Is beautiful like a picture of the gods in the temple.

With pure and holy words.

Bring offerings to God !

With pure and holy words ?

Give alms to the poor !

The above song reveals that people of Ladakh took a particular interest in Prince Deskyong Namgyal, and committed him to care to his guardian deity, so that he would became the next king of Ladakh.

Marriage with zi-zi Khatun: After the death of queen Nima Saskyong Vangmo, king Nima Namgyal decided to marry. In this connection he got offer from Purig, later married Zi-Zi Khatun of Purig. He had two issues from her: Trashi Namgyal and Trashi Wangmo[6].

Contribution of Nima Namgyal: King Nima Namgyal was a kind hearted person. He respected simple and honest people. In his kingdom scholars and old people were given full respect. He had established political, economic and cultural relations with his neighbouring countries. He encouraged printing works in Ladakh, many printing wooden blocks were made, later under his direction many volumes of Kangyur and Tangyur pothis were printed.[7]

King Nima Namgyal had strong faith on Buddhism. He donated silver, gold and precious things for the statues in Tibet as well as in Ladakh monasteries. He constructed many Mani walls: Chivang, Usla, Yungdung, Tingmogang, Le-do, Zanak. The Zanak is the longest Mani wall of about 3.6 feet wide, 5 feet in height and 1950 feet long. For the construction of this Mani wall King Nima Namgyal employed 500 people. This Mani wall is towards north-south direction and runs parallel to the Leh-Choglamsar main road. On its north end is I.T.B.P. Camp, east side has residential building, south side has a small bridge and Choglamsar market, and on west side Leh-Manali highway. It is a long horizontal wall structure with a wide surface that consisted of thousands stone slates engraved with Om Mani Padme Hum—Avalokitesvara Mani Mantra in Tibetian language. It also consists of long prayer flags fluttering on the top base[8].

At present the structure is deterioration due to lack of maintenance. Last year i.e. 2005 and this year in the last week of July 2006 flood came at the south side ***nallu*** of the Mani and washed away a portion, however later renovated. But due to the increase in population and migration from the remote villages of Lakakh to Choglamsar, the land adjoining to the above structure being converted into residential buildings, thus pollute the sacred site of Mani wall as well its beauty.[9]

Besides King Nima Namgyal constructed Cagras (Tib. lcag-ra-sa) Khar which is 15 km. from Sumoor, Nubra in 1718 and planted many Ayum plants in Sabhu village on the request of his second wife Zi-Zi Khatun. At last this great king died on 1738 at Mulbek[10].

Deskyong Namgyal : The New King of Ladakh

King Nima Namgyal was very well aware the capability of his son Deskyong Namgyal. Therefore, when he became old, he understand the feeling of his public and appointed his elder son Deskyong Namgyal as the King of Ladakh. But queen Zi-Zi Khatun was not happy with the decision. She wanted her son Trashi Namgyal should be given a part of Ladakh and would be appointed as the king of that region. King Nima Namgyal discussed queen Zi-Zi Khatun's proposal with his ministers and other high ranked officials. But no one was agree with the proposal, as every one was in the favour of undivided Ladakh. Therefore, advised king that he should request his son Trashi Namgyal either to become lama or to live quietly at Tingmogang palace. King did accordingly. But queen Zi-Zi Khatun objected. When differences between king and queen Zi-Zi Khatun became acute, old king Nima Namgyal withdrew all powers from Deskyong Namgyal and he was dethroned. Therefore, Nima Namgyal once again became the King of Ladakh Kingdom and ruled Ladakh for several years.[11]

Division of Ladakh Kingdom: After the death of King Nima Namgyal, under rule Deskyong Namgyal came on throne of Ladakh. But his step mother Zi-Zi Khatun didn't happy and according to her earlier proposal she asked a portion of Ladakh Kingdom to her son Trashi Namgyal, finally she succeeded to occupy a portion of Ladakh kingdom was divided Trashi Namgyal became vassal king of Bodrik and lived in Mulbek palace. He married with Stanin Wangmo, unfortunately she died childless in 1758[12].

Marriage of Trashi Wangmo: While queen Zi-Zi Khatun succeeded to occupy a portion of Ladakh kingdom, she now thought to marry her daughter. Later she married her with the king of Kishtwar. After sometimes, queen Zi-Zi Khatun invited her son-in-law and daughter in Ladakh. Both came in Ladakh. During her stay Trashi Wangmo told her mother that she had been tortured by her in-laws and she wouldn't want to go back again until some proper solution would be taken by her in-laws. Zi-Zi Khatun listened carefully all the problems of her daughter, later said she should need not to worry. After sometimes when king of Kishtawar decided to return to Kishtawar along with his wife queen Trashi Wangmo, queen Zi-Zi Khatun made a tricky plan, she brief her army officer, who would be sent alongwith the couple to kill Kishtawar king on the way. Later on the way to Kishtawar Ladakh army officer Sangyas Gyatso pushed king Kishtawar from the bridge at Paldar. King drawn into the river, queen Wangmo returned Leh along with army officer. Thereafter she married with the Cho of Khapulu.[13]

In conclusion Nima Namgyal though ruled his kingdom skillfully, but queen Zi-Zi Khatun's wilful attitude, he could not able to give throne of Ladakh kingdom to his son Deskyong Namgyal. After his death Deskyong Namgyal became the king of Ladakh but he had to give a portion of Ladakh kingdom to Trashi Namgyal. Thus, caused the division of Ladakh kingdom.

Notes and References

1. **Thupstan Paldan:** 'Buddhist monasteries and Royal castles in Ladakh' 1976 : 5 and Sonam Phuntsog: 'Ladakh', 2000 : 140.
2. **Thiksey Monastery:** It is about 19 km. from Leh, located on a prominent hill on the right bank of the Indus with a sweeping view from Spitak in

the northwest to the ravine that leads to Hemis in the southeast, is the monastery of Thiksey (Tib. Khri-rtse); belonging to the Geluk-pa order of Mahayana Buddhism. Cf. Finegan, Jack: Tibet: A Dreamt of Image, Tibet House, New Delhi; 1986, 202.

3. **Hemis Monastery:** It is about 45 km. from Leh and is situated on the left bank of Indus River in the Shang valley. It is the most famous monastic institution of the Druk-pa Kagyu-pa order in Ladakh. Cf. Finegan, Jack, *op. cit.'* 204.
4. Sonam Phuntog, *op. cit.*
5. The song was translated by A.H. Franke? : 'History of Western Tibet' New Delhi; 1907: 125.
6. Franke, A.H.,*op. cit.,*125.
7. *Ibid.*
8. Sharma, Janhwij: 'Architectural Heritage: Ladakh' The Indian National Trust for Art and Cultural Heritage in association with Har-Anand Pub. Pvt. Ltd., New Delhi; 2003: 88-89.
9. *Ibid.*
10. Sonam Phuntog, *op. cit.*
11. Francke, A.H. *op. cit.*
12. Sonam Phuntog, *op.cit.*
13. *Ibid.*

18

Architectural Description of Namgyal Tsemo Temples

Location

Namgyal Tsemo[1] is situated behind the Leh palace[2] on the rock above Leh town.

Approach

It can be approached by road and by trek.

(1) By Road

Visitors can visit Namgyal Tsemo from old Leh Bus stand, now-a-days is alloted to Taxi Union, following Leh-Nubra road.

(2) By Trek

Following the steep winding pathway from polo ground visitors can reach Namgyal Tsemo.

Age

Approximately 600 years old.

Historical Background and Architectural Description

Ladakh king Drags pa Bum de[3] erected 'Red chapel' on the Namgyal Tsemo hill behind Leh town. This chapel has two portions both of which are built over rocks. A portion of this rock provide base for the construction of the present structure.

The 'Red Chapel' or 'Tsemo Gonpa' is the outcome of two structures, one of which is single storey and the other is two storeys high. Inside the temple has a three storey wood and clay made statue of Maitreya[4]. The other two statues Avalokitesvara[5] and Manjusri[6] are flanked on its right and left.

The walls of this temple are made of mud bricks and plastered over by the mud. The roof is flat and also made of mud, small sticks and popular beams. The topmost edge of the roof has black band runs along the periphery[7].

Both the above structures are entered through a small doorway. The single storey has white colour building where as the other structure is Red or Maroon colour surface[8].

During king Tashi Namgyal[9] period this temple was repaired and later taken under the administrative control of Shankar Gonpa, a branch of Spituk monastery of Geluk-pa order.

Gon-Khang (m Gon-Khang)[10]

It is a dark and dingy room temple of two storey structure and exterior walls are painted red.

Historical background

This temple was built in 1520 during King Tashi Namgyal regime. According to Ladakh chronicle it was built on the corpses of Hors[11]. died during war. Here follows the details :

"During King Tashi Namgyal Hors invaded Ladakh from Nubra side, battle took place in Nubra Valley between Ladakh army and Hors. Ladakh army won the war, later king Tashi Namgyal ordered to bring dead bodies of Hors to Leh. These bodies were placed under an image of Mahakala over which a temple devoted to the guardian deities was built. The idea behind was to crush evil spirits who instigated Hors to attack Ladakh. By doing so evil spirits would not have further courage to attack from the Nubra border[12]".

Material used

Mud bricks for walls and flat roof is made by wood sticks and mud.

Wall paintings

Inside the temple walls are beautifully decorated by the paintings of Sakyamuni Buddha with attendants[12], Tashi Namgyal, Tsong-Khapa[14], Nas cu (Tib. gna bcu) or Sixteen Arhats, Dolma[15] and Rigsumgonpo[16].

Architectural Description

Rectangular structure, does not have windows has only small wooden doorway on the west side.

Statues

Inside the temple the following Buddhist statues are placed:

1. Nasten **(Tib. nang rten)**[17]
2. Yidam **(Tib. Yidam rdo rje)**[18]
3. Jigjed **(Tib. 'ajigs byed)**[19]
4. Gonpo Chag-tug **(Tib. mgon po phyag drug)**[20]
5. Tamcan chosgyal yab yum **(Tib. dam-can-chos-rgyal yab-yum)**[21]
6. Palden Lhamo **(Tib. dpal lden lha mo)**[22]
7. Namsras **(Tib. rnam sras)**[23]
8. Camsing **(Tib. lcan sring)**[24]

Notes and References

1. **Namgyal Tsemo :** (or Namgyal peak), on the summit of this peak high above the city are the ruins of the fortified palace built by Tashi Numgyal, still of impressive magnitude and the anchor point for long strings of colourful prayer flags. Immediately below the fort are the temples of Tsemo Khang and Gonkhang.
2. **Leh Palace :** Much lower down on the slope of the Namgyal Tsemo and above the Leh city

is the Leh palace, which was built by Senge Numgyal. It has nine stories and contains about one hundred rooms. The palace entrance is the Lion portrayal, so called from the lion heads in the wood carving around the door. At the fifth floor level there is court open to the south and provided with small wooden balconies. Cf. Finegan, Jack : Tibet : A dreamt of image; Tibet House; New Delhi, 1986: 197.

3. **Drags pa Bum de :** He was the son of king Thri-sung-de **(Tib. Khri-btsung-lde)** and ruled Ladakh kingdom during 15th century A.D.

4. **Maitreye :** Tib. byams pa, Pron. champa, is a manifestation of Amoghasiddhi and Visvapani is waiting now as a Bodhisattva in the Tushita, and will come as the future Buddha. Cf. Finegan, Jack; *op. cit.*, pp : 132.

5. **Avalokitesvara : (Tib. spyan ras gzigs, Pron. chenrsik)**, the "lord who looks down with compassion" is a manifestation of Amitabha, is shown in white colour, has "Om Mani Padme Hum" as his mantra and is incarnate in king Songtsen Gampo and in the Dalai Lamas. He is represented in various forms : as Padmapani, holds the lotus as Amoghapasha, he is a standing figure with six or eight arms, or a seated figure with twenty arms; as Ekadashamukha, he has eleven heads. There is a variant of this form called Sitatapatra in which he is seated and with two of twelve arms holds an umbrella as Arya-Avalokiteśvara he has eleven heads and a thousand arms. The form with eleven head is explained by the story that when Avalokiteśvara looked down upon the many beings in need of deliverance in the hall of Yama, the god of death, his head broke into ten pieces out of his great compassion; these were put by his spiritual teacher father Amitabha; thus is the figure there are nine gentle faces arranged in three

tiers of three each, above that one wrathful face and at the top, the head of Amitabha, thus making eleven heads in all. Cf. Finegan, Jack; *op. cit.* : 130-31.

6. **Manjusri:** It has many forms some of them as follows:
   1. Sita-Manjughosa
   2. Kumarabhuta-Manjughosa
   3. Sthiracakra-Manjughosa
   4. Guhyasādhama-Mañjughosa
   5. Simhanāda-Mañjughosa
   6. Vādirad-Mañjughosa
   7. Astabuja-Dharmadhātu
   8. Vāgìsvara-Mañjughosa
   9. Bhadravarśvararaja Mañjughosa
   10. Rājalīla-Manjusri
   11. Trailokyavas'yādhikāra Manjughosa
   12. Caturbija-Namasamgiti Manjughosa
   13. Prajñacakra-Mañjughosa
   14. Tiksna-Mañjusri

   In brief Mañjuśri (Tib.'Jam dbyangs, Pron. Jamyang), "Charming splendor" is the Bodhisattva of wisdom and literature, and is shown in yellow, white, red and black forms with two lotus blossoms as his attributes, or with the sword of knowledge, in his right hand and the book of transcendent wisdom in his left, incarnate in king Trhrisong Detsen land in Tsongkhapa. Cf. Musashi Tachikawa, Masahide Mori and Shinobu Yamaguchi : Three Hundred and sixty Buddhist Deities; Adroit, Pub. Delhi; 2001: 13 and Finegan Jack : Tibet : A Dreamt of Image; Tibet House, New Delhi; 1986 : 131.

7. Sharma, Janhwij: Architectural Heritage Ladakh; The Indian National Trust for Art and Cultural Heritage and Har-Anand Pub. Ltd., 2003, : 62 = 72.
8. *Ibid.*
9. King Tashi Namgyal : He was the younger son of **lha-chen-Bha-gan** the founder of Namgyal dynasty and ruled Ladakh during 16th century A.D.
10. *Gon-Khang*: Tib. mgon khang belongs to Mahakala or the protector.
11. **Hors :** Turkish-Mongolian force, normally know Mongols.
12. **Thupstan Paldan**: Buddhist monasteries and royal castles in Ladakh; 1973 : 13.
13. **Sakyamuni Buddha**: The compassionate Lord Buddha, who was one of the thousand princes vowed to become Buddha countless Kalpas ago, appeared in this world in the form of the supreme emanation body and later become known in the name of the Fourth Spiritual Leader. It is said that having generated the bodhimind in the hell realm by seeing hellish being who was tortured by the envoys of the hell, he accumulated the dual merits throughout three countless aeons and finally attained the complete and perfect enlightenment in Akinstha Heaven. However, for the sake of benefiting sentient beings, he demonstrated the mode of taking birth in a royal family in Lumbini descending from Tusita Heaven. Later, when he grew up, he married Yasodhara who later gave birth to a boy named Rāhula. Inspite of being endowed with every kind of worldly pleasure he, having disgusted with them renounced them and chose the path of asceticism in search of truth. Practising all conducts and activities of Bodhisattvas, he attained the perfect

enlightenment at Bodhgaya. Thereafter, he turned the three wheel of Dharma in three different places namely: Vārānasi Grdrakūpa and Vaiśali where he delivered both the profound and extensive Dharma according to the interest, sense faculties and aspiration of the sentient beings and did great welfare to them whenever he is depicted in the meditation posture, he is seated in the cross-legged posture on a throne supported by for lions. The mat on which he is seated is decorated with lotus flower. He is flanked by two attendents; Sariputra on the right and Maudgyalayanaputra on the left. Das, Sanjib Das; Tārā; CIBS, Leh, Ladakh; 2003 : 18.

14. **Tsong-Khapa :** The founder of Geluk pa order of Mahayana Buddhism
15. **Dolma :** Tārā, is a female tutelary deity with various forms and is regarded as the manifestation of Avalokites'vara.
16. **Rigsumgonpo :** (Tib. rig gsum mgon po), consisted the paintings of Manjusri, Vajrapani and Avalokiteśvara
17. **Nasten (Tib. nang rten) :** The sixteen Arhats named : Añgaja, Ajita, Vanavāsin, Kalika, Vajriputra, Bhadra, Kanakavatsa, Kanaka Bharadvaja, Bakula, Rahula, Cudapanthaka, Pindola Bharadvaja, Mahapanthaka, Nagasena, Gopaka and Abheda.
18. **Yidam (Tib. Yidam rdo-rje) :** It is a deity of tantric system.
19. **Jig ced (Tib. 'ajigs byed)** Yamantaka or Vajrabhairava, he is the most wrathful form of Manjusri.
20. **Gonpo Chag-tug (Tib. mgon po phyag drug):** In sanskrit equivalent to sadbhuja-Mahakala, one of the Dharmapala.

21. **Tamcan Chosgyal yab-yum (Tib. dam-can-chos-rgyal :** He is the chief protector of Tsongkhapa, in Sanskrit equivalent to Dharmaraja.
22. **Palden Lhamo (Tib. dpal lden lha mo) :** "The Glorious Goddess", is one of the most important protectors of the Geluk pa order of Buddhism and the guardian of Lhasa. History tells us that Palden Lhamo was the jewel protector, extremely aggressive and was the custodian of religious properties. She was initiated by Chagna Dorje and was given the name Dorje Naljorma. Later Padmasambhava bound her to follow the exhaustive instruction and came to Tibet with him. Cf. Ladrang Kalsang : 'The Guardian Deities of Tibet, Little Lhasa Pub. Dharmasala Pub., 2000 : 17.
23. **Namsras (Tib. rnam sras) :** The namthos–sey or rnam thos sras, one of the Four Directional Protector.
24. **Camsring (Tib. lcam sring) :** He is equivalent to Beg-tse (*beg-rtse* or *Bhegtse*). A Dharmapala and **'jig-rten-las-'das-pa'i-sung-ma** of some importance in Tibet, and called a **maha-yaksa**, lord commander of all **ma-mo,** head of the **gshin-rje** god of war and protector of horses. His father is the Dharmapala **g nod-sbyin-zangs-kyi-ral-pa-can** "Yaksa who has locks of copper" and his mother is "**Srin-mo-khrug-gi-ral-pa-can"** the raksa with looks of blood, lcam-sring as synonymous with Mahakala. Cf. Bunce, Fredrick W. : *An Encyclopaedia of Buddhist Deities, Demigods, Godlings, Saints and Demons*, Vol. 1, D.K. Print World Pvt. Ltd., New Delhi, 1994 : 290.

19

Iconographical Guide for Buddhist Monasteries of Ladakh

Shakyamuni : Tib. Shakya Tubpa or Tubpa "The enlightened one" or "the awakened one". Historically Known as Gotama Buddha. In 6th century B.C. he descended the world to show the right path to the fortunate beings, so that they may attain freedom from the cycle of existence. He practiced Bodhisattva activities for countless acons to attain perfect enlightenment. He is identifed by his thirty-two major and weighty minor bodily signs. In Latitavistar I have studied 54 names of Buddha. Hindus worship him as ninth avatar of Vishnu, while painting on walls or thankas, he is shown sitting in the full lotus posture on the discs of sum and moon. Body: golden colour, legs: two; hands; two. In his left hand he holds the blue iron begging bowl of a monk, while his right hand touches the earth in the 'earth witness gesture' or ***Bhumi sparsha mudra,*** invoking the earth as a witness to his realisation. He wears the three robes of a monk, his hair is dark blue, and the golden emblem of enlightenment rises above the protuberance on his head[1].

Maitreya: ***Tib. Byams-pa***, Phon. Eng. Jampa "The Kind One" A Mahabodhisattva and the Bodhisattva who will be the Manushi Buddha of the future age, the Buddha to be who will show the way to nirvana. He is a Bodhisattva who is equally respected by the Theravadists and the Mahayanists. He will be the next Buddha to appear in this world, while painting on wall or cloth and as a statue form is shown as a Buddha Dharmachakra mudra, with his feet resting on a moon disc and a lotus. In painting he is depicted as a Bodhisattva with a yellow body, wearing the clothing and ornaments of a Bodhisattva and holding the stems of two lotus blossoms that bear his emblems—a vase and a Dharma—wheel. He can be shown seated either in the full lotus posture or with his legs extended down to the floor. Maitreya may also be recognised by a white or golden stupa in his hair[2]. Maitreya's various forms or emanations are[3]:

1. Anucara - Maitreya
2. Bhattaraka - Maitreya
3. Caturbhuja - Maitreya
4. Dasa - bhumi - pati -Maitreya
5. Dvibhuja - Maitreya
6. Nirrtipada - Kruma Bhattaraka - Maitreya
7. Trimukhacaturbhuja - Maitreya

Amitabha: ***Tib. 'Od-dpag-med,*** hod-dpag -med, Phon. Eng. Opagme, "Immeasurable light" or "Infinite light". He is one of the five Dhyani Buddhas, the personification of the five Buddha energies. He represents the lotus energy, which transmutes passion into spiritual purity. His family of emanations includes Avalokitesvara. He is the Buddha of the pure land of the west called Sukhavati or Dewa chen. He is red in colour, wears the monastic robes of a Buddha, and with his hands in the meditation gesture holds a begging bowl. He is sometimes shown seated on a peacock throne. His recognition symbol is the lotus, water and the night are his association[4].

Aksobhya: ***Tib. Mi-hkhrugs-pa,*** Mi-bskyod pa, phon. Eng Mikyopa "the Unshakable" or

"Unagitated". A Dhyani Buddha. His recognition symbol is the thunderbolt (Vajra). He is generally depicted as in calm with one face, two hands; right hand in Bhumisparsha mudra, left hand holds vajra (rdo-rje) in dhyani mudra; legs: two; dhyanasana; colour: blue, ornament: five leafed crown; vahana: pair of elephants, shakti: Mahakali or Locana[5].

Amoghasiddhi: *Tib. Don-hgrub, Don-yod-grub-pa.* Phon. English Tonyo Trup-pa, Donyo Dhupa "flawless perfection". A dhyani Buddha oriented in the North. His recognition symbol is the crossed thunderbolts. Depicted generally as: One calm face, two arms: right hand in abhaya and left in dhyana holding a crossed thunderbolts. Asana: dhyanasana, colour: green, vahana: lotus throne; Shakti Tara[6].

Ratnasambhava: *Tib. Rin-Chen-'byung-ldan* Rin-hbyun, Rin-byan, Rin-chen, hbyun - ldan, Phon. English. Richen Jungden "Precious birth". A Dhyani Buddha whose heavenly quarter is the south. His recognition symbol is the jewel. Spring is his season. Generally depicted is the form of one calm face, two arms carrying jewel in his left hand and right hand in varada mudra. Mudra: Varada and dhyana; legs: two; asana; dhyanasana; colour: yellow, Vahana: pair of lions or horses; Shakti: Vajradhativari or Mamaki[7].

Vairocana: *Tib. r Nam-par-snag-mdzed, rNam-par-snan-mded,* Phon. English: Nampar Nangdze, shortened form: rNam - snam, Phon. English. Namnang "sun scion". A Dhyani Buddha whose dominion is the centre of the world. His recognition symbol is the wheel. Winter is his season. His Dhyani Bodhisattva is Samantabhara. Tace: one, calm, arms: two, holds wheel at his hand in dharmachakra mudra, legs: two, asana: dhyanasana colour: white, vahana: pair of dragons, Shakti: Locana or Tara[8].

Medicine Buddha: *Tib. Sanggye smanla,* in Sanskrit language equivalent to Baishajyaguru. The Medicine Buddha is the Buddha of healing, who is invoked to care for the sick. He wears the monastic robes of a Buddha and sits on a lotus blossom upon a lion throne. His body is dark blue and he holds an iron bowl in his left hand containing the medicinal plant arura. He may also holds a stem of the arura plant in his right hand. Eight Medicine Buddhas are often depicted in the mandala of Sakyamuni Buddha. The name of these are follows:[9]

1. Bhaisajyaguru
2. Simhanada
3. Suparikirtitanamasri
4. Svaraghosaraja
5. Suvarnabhadravimalaratnaprabhasa
6. Acokottamasri
7. Dharmakirtisagaraghosa
8. Abhijnaraja

Sometimes Sikhin or Ratnashikhin is included in the Shakyamuni Buddha company.

Four-Armed Avalokitesvara: *Tib. Chenrezi-chak. zhi pa.* Bodhisattva of compassion, sets in the fall lotus posture on sun and moon discs supported by a lotus blossom. Body: white, cloths: five silk robes, ornaments: Bodhisattva ornaments. Hands: Four, holds a wish-fulfilling gem by his two arms rest before his heart. Two of his hands: holds a crystal rosary right up near shoulder, blue flower of compassion left up near shoulder, a green grey deep skin draped over his left shoulder[10].

Thousand-Armed Avalokitesvara: *Tib. Chenregi chak-tong chen -tong.* Bodhisattava who once took a vow to save all beings from suffering, when he realised the magnitude of his task his head exploded into countless pieces. His body was reassembled by Amitabha and the Bodhisattva Vajrapani into much more powerful form. Heads: eleven, Arms: Thousand, each of his hand has an eye in the centre of the palm, symbolising the union of wisdom (eye) and skilful means (hand). In this form he has a white body and stands on moon disc and a lotus flower. He has eight main hands, the first two of which hold a wish-fulfilling gem, the next five hold a lotus, bow and arrow, vase, rosary, wheel and the eighth is held in the open-palmed gesture of generosity. He has three rows of three faces coloured: Red, white and green, symbolising the three principal aspects of Buddhahood, while above these nine heads are the blue wrathful face of Vajrapani and the red face of Amitabha.[11]

Thus Avalokitesvara can look in every direction and one of the most popular Bodhisattva in the world of Buddhism. He is the embodiment of compassion[12].

Manjusri: ***Tib Jampeyang;*** a Bodhisattva of wisdom, is shown as a beautiful youth with a golden yellow complexion. In his right hand he holds aloft the flaming sword ignorance while in his left hand in the stem of a lotus blossom bearing a "perfection of wisdom" scripture. He is often depicted in a triad known Rig-sum-gon-po[13]:

1. Avalokitesvara: Compassion-White
2. Manjusri: Wisdom-Golden Yellow
3. Vajrapani: Power-Blue

Vajrapani: ***Tib. Chana Dorje.*** He is the Bodhisattva of energy and power. Hands: Two; standing on a sun disc. His body is dark blue in colour and he wears a tiger skin around his waist and snake around his neck. While in yab-yum form he holds vajra in his right hand and bell in left hand, ornaments: five skull crown, garlands of freshly severed human heads, shakti: two armed; during peaceful aspect he is represented as a blue Bodhisattva holding a lotus flower.[14]

Amitayus: *Tib. Tsepame.* Bodhisattva of longevity. His body is red and wears Bodhisattva ornaments and cloths. Hands: Two, in Dhyana mudra, and holds a golden vase containing the nector of immortality and a sprig of the myrobalan plant (bell fruit), and often depicted in trinity together with white Tara and Vijaya[15].

White Tara: *Tib. grolma Kar po.* She represents the fertile aspect of compassion. Her body is white and sits in the full lotus posture on moon and sun discs upon lotus flower. Hands: Two, holds a stem of blue lotus of compassion in her left hand and right hand is in varada mudra. She is recognised by her seven eyes: Three in her face, two in the palms of her hands, and two in the soles of her feet.[16]

Vijaya: *Tib Namgyalma.* She is a goddess of longevity: Arms: Eight. She holds a double vajra, a hook and a snare, a bow, an arrow, and image of Buddha, and a vase containing the nectar of immortaility. Her two other hands display the gestures of generosity and fearlessness. She has three faces; each face contains three eyes, her right face is blue, left face yellow. Her body is white and seated on lotus throne[17].

Green Tara : *Tib. Drolma Jang.* She represents the motherly aspect of compassion. Her body is green, sits in the royal posture on the moon disc and lotus flower, her right leg extended, with its foot resting on a small lotus blosoom. Hands: Two, both hold two blue lotus flower of compassion[18].

Vajrasattva: *Tib Dorje Sempa.* He is the Bodhisattva of purification and is known as the primordial Buddha; white in colour wears robes and ornaments of Bodhisattva. Face: One, Arms: two, holds a vajra to his heart and a bell to his left hand placed to his left hip[19].

Vajradhara: *Tib. Dorje Chang.* He is the tantric manifestation of Sakyamuni Buddha. Face: one, calm; arms: Two, Vajrahumkara mudra which are crossed at his heart holding a vajra and a bell, symbolising the enlightened union of bliss and emptiness, legs: two; asana: dhyanasana, colour: dark-blue or gold. When in the yab-yum pose with the Shakti, they represent that the distinction between "Duality and Oneness Absolute"[20].

Yamantaka: Tib. Dorje Jigjed, in Sanskrit language equivalent to Vajrabhairava. His wrathful form is the manifestation of Manjusri. He is the 'Destroyer of Death', belongs to the supreme yoga tantra division of the Vajrayana and is the protector of Geluk-pa order. Head: nine; arms: 34, legs: sixteen. His main head is that of a buffalo and his uppermost head is that of Manjusri. He has three eyes in each head except Manjusri. His body colour is blue; ornament; wears bone ornament, hangs a snake around his neck and a garland of fifty one freshly severed human heads. He holds a skull cup and a curved flaying knife in front of him. Underfoot he tramples upon eight Hindu deities, eight mammals and eight birds. Shakti: Ro langsma; a fearsome manifestation of Dhyani Bodhisattva Manjushri whose duty is to overcome Yama, the god of death.[21]

Samvara: Tib Demchok, in Sanskrit language equivalent to ***chakrasamvara.*** He belongs to vajrayana and usually represented in twelve-armed form embracing his consort ***vajravarahi. (Tib. Dorje Pagmo).*** Together they symbolise the union of emptiness and bliss. His body is dark blue, wears tiger skin around his waist and holds an elephant skin across his back. Ornaments: bone garland and a necklace of fifty one freshly severed head. Face: Four, coloured yellow, blue, green and red. In his hands he holds: a vajra and bell, a skull cup, a snare, the head of Brahma, a tantric staff, an elephant knife, a flying knife, a trident and a drum. He is enhaloed in flames, trampling the Hindu god Bhai rava and his consort. His consort, Vajravarahi is red and has two arms and one face. She carries skullcup and curved knife, Mudra: Vajrahumkara; asana: ardhaparyankasana.[22]

Vajrayogini: *Tib. Dorje Naljorna* or Naro Kachoma. A terrifying goddess-form emulation of Dhyani Buddha Ratnasambhava. A dakini, and goddess of initiation who personifies the female wisdom energy of emptiness. She is generally appears naked crushing underfoot the Hindu god Bhairava and is functionally equivalent to ***Vajravarahi.*** She is depicted in the form of 'Naropa's dakini'; red colour wears bone ornaments, and a necklace of fifty-one skulls; holds a curved knife in her right hand a skull cup from which she drinks blood in her left. A tantric staff rests on her left shoulder symbolising the essence of bliss[23].

Guhyasamaja: *Tib. Sangdu.* He belongs to yoga tantra. Face: Three, Arms: six, seated on lotus throne. His body and central face are dark blue. His right face is white and left face red. He embraces a light blue consort who has three and six arms. Both carry same emblems: a vajra, bell, sword, jewel, wheel and lotus. Thus Guhyasamja is a protection deity (Tib. Yi-dam), an Istandevata. In tantra a god of the initiation ceremonies.[24]

Hevajra: *Tib. Kye Dorje.* He is the yoga tantra deity dark blue in colour, Faces: Eight, Arms: Sixteen, Legs: Four, embraces consort Nairatma and they together dance of four lesser deities, who symbolise the four demonic forces. He wears bone ornaments, a tiara of five skulls and a necklace of fifty-one severed heads he holds a skullcup. The skullcups in the right hands contain eight Hindu gods. His consort is also dark blue. She has one face and two arms, and holds a skullcup and a curved knife. She wears bone ornaments, necklace of fifty one freshly severed heads. They are encircled by flames and dance, in the 'Bow and Arrow' posture. Thus he is a Yi-dam and terrifying emanation of ***Dhyani Buddha Aksobhya,*** and a popular tantric deity particularly for the Sakya Order. A form of Heruka when shown in the body in yab-yum position pose with Prajna.[25]

Hevajra's various forms are: Citta-Hevajra, Garbha-Hevajra?, Kapaladhara-Hevajra, Kapala-Hevajra, Kaya-Hevajra, Sahaja-Hevajra, Sastradhara-Hevajra (Buddha), Sri-Hevajra, veg-Hevajra[26].

Kalcakra: *Tib. dpal-dus-kyi- hkhor- lo, Dus-'k'or,* Phon. English. Palduchi Khorlo, Dus-kyi-hkhor-lo, Phon. English abbreviated Dukhor "The wheel of Time" A yi-dam and a terrifying god-form emanation of ***Dhyani Buddha Aksobhya,*** A complex supreme tantric yogi deity[27].

Face: Four-Dark blue, red, white and yellow Eye: Fierce, three eyes each.

Arm: Twenty four-eight lower are dark blue or dark; Middle eight are red and upper eight are white. Right hands hold: Vajra (rdo-rje), sword (khadga), trident (trishula), Knife (churi),' fire arrow (bana), thunderbolt, hook (ankusha), wheel (chakra), and axe (parasha). The left hand hold: bell (ghanta), plate, ritual wand (khantvanga), skullcup (kapala), bow (dhanus), noose (pasha), Jewel (ratna), chain and several head of Brahma.

Leg: two.

He wears a tiger skin around his waist golden ornaments, vajra ear-rings, bracelets belt and necklace. His right leg is red and left is white, trample two Hindu deities Ananga and Rudra and their repective consorts. He embraces his consort ***Vishavamati*** with his two principal arms, whose hands hold a vajra and bell. She is golden in colour with four faces, eight arms and two legs; right leg is red while the left is white; asana: yab-yum in alidhasana.[28]

Hayagriva: ***Tib rta-mgirn*** *or* ***rta-mgrin-royal-po,*** Phon. Eng Tamdin, in Sanskrit equivalent to ***aka Arya-Hayagriva, Krodha Yamari.*** "The horse-needed one". A krodhavatas and dharmapala, and a protective deity who keeps away demons. Some say an emnation of ***Dhyani Buddha Aksobhya or Dhyani Buddha Amitabha*** while others say an emanation of Dhayani Bodhisattva Avalokitesvara[29]. Thus Hayagriva is a wrathful emanation of Avalokitesvara and functions as both a powerful protector who destroys evil spirits and a deity (*yidam*) in tantric practice. One of the Hayagriva form has three faces, six arms and four legs. His body is red, right face is white and left face is green; wears a tiger skin around his waist, a tiara of five skulls, and a necklace of fifty one fleshly severed heads. Across his back are elephant skin a human skin and the unfurled wings of a garuda. He holds: a lotus, skullcup, snare, sward, an axe and a club; embraces a blue consort, who wears a leopard skin and holds a skullcup and lotus. Together they trample underfoot male and female corpses. He is identified by horse head that protrude from the top of his main head[30].

Palden Lhamo: In Sanskrit she is equivalent ***shri Devi,*** Hindu worship as ***Kali Devi.*** "Glorious Goddess", is one of the main protectors of Geluk-pa. order. Force: one, Arms: two, holds a club in her right hand and skull cup full of blood in her left. She has dark blue body wears a tiger skin around her waist and human skin over her shoulders. In her mouth she holds a corpse, hanging from her earrings are a snake and a lion: Her hair streams upwards. The moon rests in her hair and the sun in her navel. She sits astride a mule on a cannibal skin saddle and rides across a sea of menstrual blood. She is usually attending by her two companions the blue 'Lion-headed one' and the red 'Crocodile headed one'. Sometimes, she has four hands.[31]

Songtsen Gompo: He was the king of Tibet in the seventh century A.D.; responsible for the introduction of Buddhism in Tibet; and considered to be a manifestation of Avalokitesvara: He is depicted with a white or flesh-coloured complexion, seated on throne, wearing the royal attire of a king. Holds wheel in his left hand and lotus in his right, and on his head he wears a white turban, which is folded around an image of a red Amitabha Buddha.[32]

Trisong Detsen: He was the great religious king of Tibet during the eighth century A.D. He is a manifestation of Manjusri, the Boddhisattva of Wisdom, and holds lotus with sword in his right hand and lotus with scripture in his left.[33]

Padmasambhava: Tib. Lopon Rinpoche or Guru Rinpoche "Lotus Born One" an Indian tantric invited by king Trisong Detsen in the eighth century A.D.; seated on a lotus blossom that rises from a lake, his right foot resting on a smaller lotus blossom. Face: One, body: flesh colour, hands: two, holds vajra in her right hand and left holds skullcup containing a vase of the nectar of immortality; carries a tantric staff surmounted with a trident in the fold of his left arm. He wears the folded red hat of the Nyingma order of which he is the founder.[34]

Milarepa: He was a founding figure of the Kagyu order usually depicted sitting on a yogin's antelope' skin in a cave, wears a single white cotton robe. He has two hands and leg, holds an skullcup in his left hand and his right hand presses his ear forward in the attitude of singing his songs of realisation.[35]

Atisa: Tib. ***Jowo-je*** in Sanskrit language equivalent to Dipankara Shrijana Atisa. Indian Buddhist who helped revive Buddhism in Tibet during the eleventh century A.D. is depicted with a gold or flesh coloured body seated on a lotus throne, hands: two in Dharmachakra mudra, wears the robes of a monk, and a red hat, easily identified by the stupa at his right side, and basket of scriptures placed at his left side.[36]

Tsongkhapa: He was the founder of Geluk-pa order of Buddhism during the fourteenth century, and considered to be a manifestation of Manjusri; Body; golden or flesh colour, Hand : Two, holds a stem of lotus with a bear sword in his right hand and a stem of lotus with scripture in his left. His two hands in the middle before his heart is in Dharmachakra mudra.[37]

Dalai Lama: He is the manifestation of Avalokitesvara, has two hands, holds Dharma wheel in his left hand and right hand holds lotus flower. All the Dalai lamas are represented in a similar form but with various gesture.[38]

Dhritarashtra: He is the guardian king of the east, white in colour and plays a lute.[39]

Virupaksha: He is the guardian king of west, red in colour and holds a small stupa.[40]

Virudhaka: He is the guardian king of the South, is blue in colour and carries a sword and scabbard. He is lord and master over the kumbhandas giants, demons and gnomes. Face One, angry, helmeted; arms: two, body: richly dressed; legs: two, vahana: elephant.[41]

Vaishravana: ***Tib. Namtose,*** also known as Kubera and Jambhala. He is the guardian king of the north and Buddhist god of wealth. Vahana:

white lion, golden yellow in colour, he has a large rounded body. Hands: two, holds silk banner of victory in his right hand, holds—a mongoose that vomits jewels in his left hand.[42]

Notes and References

I. Batchelor, Stephen: *The Tibet Guide,* Wisdom Pub., London; 1987: 378 and Bunce, Fredrick W.: *An Encyclopaedia of Buddhist Deities Demigods, Godlings, Saints and Demons,* Vol. I, D.K. Printworld Ltd., New Delhi; 1994 : p. 73.

2. Batchelor, Stephen; *op. cit.* and Bunce, Fredrick W.; *op.cit.* p. 323.

3. Bunce, Fredrick W., *op. cit.*

4. Batchelor, Stephen; *op. cit.* pp. 323-24, Bunce, Fredrick W.; *op. cit.*, pp. 11-12.

5. Bunce, Fredrick W., *op. cit.*, p. 9.

6. *Ibid.,* p. 16.

7. *Ibid.,* pp. 427-28.

8. *Ibid.,* p. 527.

9. *Ibid.,* p. 338.

10. Butchelor, Stephen, *op. cit.*, p. 399.

11. *Ibid.,* p. 400-401.

12. Bunce, Fredrick W., *op., cit.* p. 35.

13. Batchelor, Stephen; *op. cit.*, pp. 402-403.

14. *Ibid.,* pp. 403-404, Bunce, Fredrick W., *op. cit.*, p. 588.

15. Batchelor, Stephen, *op.cit.*, p. 405.

16. *Ibid.,* p. 406-407.

17. *Ibid.,* p. 407.

18. *Ibid.,* p. 404.

19. *Ibid.,* p. 408.

20. *Ibid.,* p. 409 and Bunce, Fredrick W., *op.cit.*, p. 577.

21. Batchelor, Stephen, *op. cit.*, pp. 409-410 and Bunce, Fredrik W., *op.cit.*, p. 544.

22. Batchelor, Stephen *op.cit.*, pp. 410-12 and Bunce, Fredrick, W., *op. cit.*, p. 90.

23. Batchelor, Stephen, *op.cit.*, pp. 412-13 and Bunce, Fredrick, W., *op.cit.*, p. 579.
24. *Ibid.*, p. 415 and Bunce, Fredrick, W., *op.cit.*, p. 190.
25. *Ibid.* pp. 415-16 and Bunce, Fredrick, W, *op.cit.*, p. 207.
26. Bunce, Fredrick, W., *op. cit.*, p. 207.
27. Batchelor, Stephen; *op. cit.*, pp. 4416-17.
28. Bunce, Fredrick, W.; *op. cit.*, p. 241.
29. *Ibid.*, p. 202.
30. Batchelor, Stephen; *op.cit.*, p. 417-18.
31. *Ibid.*, pp. 423-24.
32. *Ibid.*, pp. 417-18.
33. *Ibid.*, p. 419.
34. *Ibid.*, p. 420.
35. *Ibid.*, pp. 420-21.
36. *Ibid.*, p. 422.
37. *Ibid.*, p. 422.
38. *Ibid.*, p. 423.
39. *Ibid.*, p. 426.
40. *Ibid.*
41. *Ibid.*
42. *Ibid.*, p. 425.

20

Ladakh: The World's Highest Tourist Spot

The world's highest inhabited plateau, Ladakh, has created history by attracting in last five decades, after suffering a tourist drought in the aftermath of the Kargil conflict.

Ladakh has beated all the records in the past as the highest number of more than 30,000 tourists have been visited the frontier region. There is a flood of tourists particularly foreigners and we expect that if the present trend will continue it will cross the 50 thousand mark. The following are some facts which attract foreigners in large numbers.

(1) The main reason is its setting among of the greatest mountain ranges in the world. Running through this mountainous desert are the Great Himalayan Range, the Zanskar Range and Ladakh Range. These huge mountain ranges make Ladakh into a high altitude desert. Both the geographical and geological formations of the mountains make the scenery spectacular and these arid, barren mountains have especial beauty of their own. The sharp jagged mountains of Zanskar makes an interesting contrast with the rolling rounded mountains situated along the Indus valley. The most beautiful features of these mountains are their colour. Every shade of brown, grey, blue and pink can be seen during the different time of the day in respect of amount of cloud or sun in

the sky. One can sit for days at a time watching the colours change and one never sees the same shade twice. As the seasons advance from spring to summer to autumn the level of snow, like icing sugar sprinkle on the mountain peaks can be seen falling and rising. Above all the most striking feature of Ladakh is the clear weather and clean blue sky.

(2) Each village which has grown up by a river side, the river water formed by snow melting has a charm and beauty of its own. The colour in all season various from green in spring and summer and the gold in autumn contrasts vividly with the bare mountains and every colour appear brighter. Ladakh, as called moonland, has always attracted foreign tourists, who have outnumbered the domestic tourists since 1974 when the frontier region of Jammu and Kashmir was opened to them.

The tourist inflow in Leh and other parts of Ladakh registered an increase of 400 to 500 per cent in the present season and projects are underway to make this northern region the hub of foreign tourist activity in the country.

The development of Leh-Manali and Leh-Shimla roads at the cost of Rs 8.5 crore would help in bringing in new people to hilly region, where tourism and agriculture remains the major sources of livelihood.

The rich cultural potential Ladakh is wrapped in the golden silence of rocky terrain, it is repository of myriad cultures, traditions, heritage spots, scenic sites and religious influences. Besides, it has 30 to 40 old ancient Mahayana Buddhist monasteries, two high altitude lakes, two dozen-mountain peaks, nine mountaineering virgin peaks, multiple bewitching and picturesques places and rich flora and fauna attract every tourist of the world.

Tourist traffic to Ladakh has grown significantly. During 1998,22,030 tourists including 15,238 from foreign countries visited Ladakh. But after Kargil war in 1999, tourist arrivals fell to 11574 in 2000 and 8079 in 2002, but now it again increased at the rate of 22 per cent per year. Today Leh district gets about 24.75 crore rupees per year from tourism and hence more than 2000 unemployed youths are getting jobs.

Today Leh district has all kinds of facilities for tourists (Table 20.1).

Table: 20.1
Facilities for Tourist in Leh District

S. No.	*Facilities*	*Number*
1.	Hotels	65
2.	Guest Houses	111
3.	Restaurants	92
4.	Taxis	483
5.	Guides	180
6.	Antique shops	150
7.	Horses	180
8.	Travel Agencies	30

Source: Tourist Reception Centre, Leh.

Wayside Facilities: In order to increase tourism State and Central Governments sponsored various schemes (Table: 20.2).

Table 20.2
Various Schemes for the Development of Tourism in Leh District

S.No.	*Schemes*	*Total cost (Rs.)*
1.	**Central Schemes:**	
	(a) Wayside Facilities : 7 schemes	205.40 lac.

(*Contd.*)

(*Contd.*)

S.No.	Schemes	Total cost (Rs.)
	(b) Refurbishment of monuments There schemes	76.04 lac.
2.	**State Sector Schemes**	
	(a) Wayside facilities : 12 schemes	174.30 lac
	(b) Refurbishment of monuments. Seven secheme	105.22 lac
	(c) Holding of annual Ladakh Festival since 1993	65.75 lac
3.	**Beautification of Leh town under State Plan:**	
	(a) Street lighting	45.00 lac
	(b) Two incinerators operating through N.A.C. Leh	48.00 lac
	(c) One loader and one tipper operating through N.A.C. Leh	21.12 lac
4.	**Wayside Facilities under District Plan**	
	(a) Tourist Bungalow Saspol	—
	(b) Tourist Bungalow Sakti	—
	(c) Tourist Bungalow Rumtse	—
	(d) Registration Office Upshi	—
	(e) Registration Office Khaltse	—
5.	**Identification of Monuments**	
	(1) Sculpture at Dras	—
	(2) Rock Sculpture at Mulbekh	—
	(3) Lamayuru monastery	—
	(4) Likir monastery	—
	(5) Alchi Chos-Khor	—
	(6) Phyang monastery	—
	(7) Hemis monastery	—
	(8) Leh Palace	—

(*Contd.*)

(*Contd.*)

S.No.	*Schemes*	*Total cost (Rs.)*
	(9) Old Castle Tsemo	—
	(10) Stupa at Tisru	—
	(11) Shey Palace	—
	(12) Thiksey monastery	—
	(13) Tsemo Gonpa	—
6.	**Tourism Incentive Scheme:**	
	(a) Leh block	
	(1) Hotels 12 (9 Approved)	—
	(2) Resorts 02 (1 Approved)	—
	(3) Paying Guest Houses 27 (19 Approved)	—
	(b) Nubra block	
	(1) Hotels 01 (Approved)	—
	(2) Paying Guest Houses 20 (11 Approved)	—
	(c) Nyoma block	
	(1) Paying Guest Houses 1 (Approvd)	—
	(d) Khaltse block	
	(1) Paying Guest House 3	—
7.	**Proposal for Relaxation of Inner line:[2]**	
	(a) Hunder-Phyang trekking route for 5 days	—
	(b) Rongjuk-Sakti trekking route for 3 days	—
	(c) Rongjuk-Durbuk trekking route for 3 days	—
8.	**Circular road of Lakung on the bank of Pangong lake:[3]**	—
9.	**De-restristion of link road from Bodhkharbu in Khaltse area:[4]**	—

Source: Compiled from Tourist Reception Centre, Leh.

(1) The government of India has declared the said historical monuments as national importance under Archaeological Survey of India.

(2) All the places which fell along the trek routes as cited, i.e. upstream of Siachen river from Rongjuk to Sasoma including the famous monastery of Inja and villages along both the sides of the Siachen river. Few villages beyond Hunder upto Turtuk including the villages of Partapur, Skampuk, Terchey, Skuru, Largyap Pachathang, Changmar, Bogdang and Turtuk.

(3) The circular road of Lukung-Chushul on the bank of Pangong Lake and Lungparma including the famous Shachukul monastery to Tangtse and the area beyond Mahy bridge to Demcok and famous monastery of Henley included under the proposal for the relaxation of inner line.

(4) In Khaltse (or Khalsi) area a proposal is made for de-restriction of the link road from Bodhkharbu via the famous historical village of Chiktan to Sanjak including the Khaltse-Dha-Hanu-Batalik-Kargil road.

Training to local youths: To uplift the tourist facilities, Tourism Department at Leh district has started a training scheme and which through the Department 14 youths were trained in catering and hotel management from the Institute of Hotel Management and Catering Technology, Nehru Park, Srinagar for a period of 10 days in the year 1999. This is a welcome step.

Environment Protection Service: In order to protect the Environment of Leh and its vicinity Tourism Department at Leh has taken an encouraging step under which two incinerators, one loader and one tipper were sponsored under state plan for lifting litters and biodegradable garbages for combustion. Besides, the department through its various systems of dissemination of information educates the tourists and persons not to pollute the environment.

Suggestions and Recommendations

1. At the vicinity of historical monuments no new construction will be allowed.
2. Necessary arrangements should be taken to clean Leh city.
3. There should be made proper numbers of toilets in the Leh town.
4. District administration should check whether hotels and guest houses have followed the Environment Protection norms or not. If any other fails to do so, may be punished.
5. Restriction to be imposed to prevent pollution of water, air and sound including dumping of domestic commercial and other kind of wastes in the vicinity of Leh town or at the surroundings of historical and religious important monuments and places.
6. The Indian Airlines service is very poor, therefore, more and more private Airlines should be allowed to operate flights from Delhi, Chandigarh, Srinagar and Jammu to Leh and vice-versa. The Air fare is very high, it should be reduced upto economic level.

21
Cultural Tourism in Ladakh

The cultural heritage of Ladakh is protected by the high snow clad mountains. Buddhist monasteries here have strange architecture character which are not only the main life of Buddhist culture, have together many Buddhist temples and rooms for Monks. These temples represent Kaya: Buddhist deities in the form of images and on the walls as paintings; Vaka: ka'gyur and stangyur pothis in which Buddha teachings have been written in Tibetan (Bodhi language; and Chitta: Chortens (or stupas).

The Buddhist images and paintings may be seen in peaceable manifestation and in wrathful manifestation as may be appropriate to guardians against evil or as may signify the destruction of hindrances to emancipation.

Besides, we can often see the male and female deities in the union is called yab yum. Philosophically the male deity stands for ***upaya*** which expresses ***karuna*** (compassion), and the female deity stands for ***prajna*** which recognizes ***sunyata,*** so correlates of compassion and emptiness as is being seen in Hindu tantrism in which male is conceived as passive and female Sakti as active, here the male is seen as active and female as passive.

Sculpture is usually made of metals viz. gold, silver, copper, zink and iron, sometimes combination of metals called bronze. But maximum sculptures are made by clay. Besides, there are many statues made by butter and barley flour, called ***torma.***

These images visualize as to help in the process of meditation on the Vajrayana path. The posture, dress, colour, symbols etc. are made according to the Buddhist texts, are included in the Stangyur.

In brief the paintings and sculptures in the monasteries are classified in the following categories.

(i) Enlightened beings: Buddha, Bodhisattvas, Arhats, Gurus etc.

(ii) Ishtadevas: Personal deities, deities of tantric systems.

(iii) Dharamapales: Mahakalas, guardians of the doctrine.

(iv) Lokapalas: Four great kings; guardians of four directions.

(v) Goddesses: Dolma viz. Green, white, yellow, etc.

(vi) Mandales: Tib. dkyil' khor.

(vii) Ilustrations of the teachings: The wheel of existence.

Ladakh has rich folk culture. Ladakhis are found of singing and dancing. In all fest and festivals they actively take part and attract tourists in large number. The state tourism department every year organises Ladakh and Kargil Festivals from the first week of September.

Monastic festivals that provide the average Ladakhi with the spice of life. No other festival can match them in religious and entertainment value. These are held to Commemorate the founding of a monastery; the birthday of its patron saint or major events in the evolution of Tibetan or Mahayana Buddhism. Table: 21.1 shows the details of Monastic festivals.

Table: 21.1

Time-table of Monastic Festivals in Ladakh

S.No	*Name of Monastery*	*Name of Festival*	*Month of Celebration*
1.	Spituk	Spituk Gustor	January
2.	-	Dosmoche	February
3.	Gur-phug	Stok Guru Tsechu	February
4.	Matho	Matho Nagrang	March
5.	Hemis	Hemis Tse-chu	June
6.	Lamayuru	Yuru Kabgyet	July
7.	Karsha	Karsha Gutor	July
8.	Phyang	Phyang Tsedup	July
9.	Dakthok	Dakthok Tse-chu	July
10.	Thiksey	Thiksey Gustor	October
11.	Chemday	Chemday Angchok	November

Source: Field study by Author during 2000-2005.

Table 21.1 reveals that 45.5% big monasteries celebrate annual festival during summer season; the rest (i.e. 54.5%) monasteries celebrate the same during winters. Before 1974, Ladakh was not opened for foreign tourists. Therefore, maximum monasteries were celebrating annual festivals during winter season, as Ladakhis have had no works in their fields and thus turned out to see these festivals. Today, situation has been changed, their living standard accordingly improved, many of them do not stay in Ladakh during winters, they go to Chandigarh, Jammu, Delhi and Dehradun and spend their winter holidays there. The rest who have not much money, remain in Ladakh and enjoy with colourful monastic festivals.

Dosmoche, in which Lamas of different monasteries after wearing masks perform the sacred dance. This tradition was started by the kings to Ladakh. In olden days it was celebrated at the courtyard of the chapel below the gates of the Leh Palace. Today this festival is better known as the festival of the scapegoat, celebrated, with fervous at Leh. As statecl in the above said Table 21.1 that it falls in the second half of February. At this festival, a great wooden mask decorated with streamers and religious emblems is get up outside Leh. At the appointed time; offerings of 'storma', ritual figures moulded out of dough, are' brought out ceremonially cast away into the desert, or burnt. These scapegoats carry away with them the evil spirits of the old years, and thus the town is cleansed and made ready to welcome the new year.

The Ladakhis believe implicitly in the influence of gods and spirits on the material world, and undertake no major enterprise without taking this influence into consideration. The lamas are the vital intermediaries between the human and the spirit worlds. Not only do they perform the rites necessary to propitiate the gods in private houses as well as in the monasteries; they also often take the role of astrologers and oracles who can predict the auspicious time for starting any enterprise, whether ploughing the fields, or taking in the harvest, arranging a marriage or going on a journey and advise as to the auspicious way of going about it.

The most famous monk oracles are of Matho monastery. It is a unique kind of fair also: This started with two priests who have to undergo strict meditation for two or three months. After sometimes when they purify themselves for their arduous role, they are possessed by the deity. This time their inner eye exposes to them everything. The whole process is somewhat supernatural. The deity then control of the monks and acquire supernatural powers. Thus Spirit enables them to perform feats that would be impossible to anyone in a normal state such as cutting themselves with knives, or sprinting along the gonpa's topmost parapet.

Both the monk-oracles before coming in the public, cover their eyes with dark cloth but through their tantric power they could see every thing. Hence, run here and there among the people. They run and jump over walls and roof but their steps never falter. They walk forward and backward on walls and roof, blind-folded, but they never fall. When the festival is over, they become normal and the cloth over their eyes is removed.

Hence, it can safely be said that the monks in Ladakh possess tantric powers. There are also oracles and healers in the villages who have special powers. Some men and women who have such powers are believed to be capricious, and not always entirely benevolent, and some people resist being possessed by them. Once they have accepted, however, they undergo a process of initiation and training by monks and senior oracles, and only after this is completed, later they may start practising.

There may be many Nunneries in Ladakh region, however, the Nunnery of Rizong monastery has its own importance. Rizong monastery is surrounded by apricot orchard and Nuns of the monastery are fully engaged' to look after the orchard. Thus, Nunnery is the centre of economic activities based on apricot and its byproduct production and are directed towards the Rizong monastic community. This group of celibate women from the most productive sector of the said monastic society because their celibacy minimises their material needs and the two central factors in production, time and labour power. However they remain central to the productive process of the primary of their human power rather than their ability to set some mechanized system into operation. They have nonetheless renounced any further generation of their key value by this very celibacy. And this celibacy is demanded by the religion and its economy. By the fact of their centrality in the economy, the nuns are drawn into the closest contact with the monastic community which while contact to permit controlled faminity in an ideal sense, it cannot permit the physical presence of woman to threat on the reproduction of the religious system as emanating from a male custodians.

In marked contrast to the situation prevailing in the nunnery where goods and services tend to be predominantly uni-directional, in the main village attached to the monastery times and produce are constantly being juggled between the different areas of economic activity in an effort to ensure the continuity of a productive system a religious structure and this fundamental component-human power. This continuity, further must be established and maintained in separate locations, the village and the monastery, and again as at the nunnery, women are the central features in this continuity. The processes of physiological reproduction from the essence of the whole system under consideration because they provide manpower for the religion and the economy. Women in the village are the process of the products and assume a primary value in their capacities for human reproduction rather than economic production, since inevitable dependencies and drains upon economic resources result from this role. Indeed it is interesting to note that in this context the village is under considerably more pressure to provide its own daily subsistence than is the nunnery which tehds to receive much of this sustenance through the process of redistribution. By and large I would say Nuns have important role in the primary Rector from where concern monastery get primary product. Therefore it is more important for each monastery to educate them so that they may read religious books and offer prayers at their respective temples.

In conclusion I have an opinion about cultural tourism that Ladakh has good cultural tourist potential as tourists can see Buddhist monuments in large number throughout in Ladakh. During study tour I have recorded that every year each big monastery in Ladakh earn Rs. 5 lac to Rs. 10 lac from cultural based tourists.

References

1. Jina, Prem Singh; *Tourism in Ladakh Himalaya*; Indus Pub. Co., New Delhi, 1994.
2. ___________; *Ladakh: The land and the People*; Indus Pub. Co., New Delhi, 1996.
3. ___________; *Ladakh: Past and Present*; Gyan Publishing House, New Delhi, 2000.
4. ___________; Development of Ladakh: Recent Researchers; Kalpaz Pub., New Delhi, 2002.
5. ___________; Monasteries in the Economy of Leh Ladakh, In: All India Conference, CIBS, Leh-Ladakh, 1998.

22

Prospects of Tourism in Ladakh and Spiti Valley of Himachal Pradesh

Ladakh and Spiti valley are situated in the high land crystalline mass of Trans-Himalayan zone, which are one of the highest altitude region with low density of population. The climate of these regions are cold and arid with frozen waste land, inhabited areas lie in between subzero temperature as low as –20°C. The nature of the enveloping mountain crest has exerted a strong impact on the natural attributes of these regions. Laying in the Trans-Himalayan terrain shadow zone, Ladakh and Spiti valley have almost devoid of natural vegetation. Therefore, basic constrains hindering the process of economic development at large scale in these regions are:

1. The mountainous terrain
2. The scarcity of water
3. Adverse climatic condition.

It has been found that more than fifty per cent area of these two regions is unfit for vegetative and human life. Only about 30 per cent land is under cultivation. This is mainly due to thinness of soil cover and sarcity of water. Therefore, on the basis of human response to inclement environment Ladakh and Spiti regions can be divided into two parts:

1. Pastoral area
2. Agricultural area.

The Pastoral areas in Ladakh region are in Chang-Thang sub-division of Leh district and Dras and Zanskar valleys in Kargil district. Besides, all the higher parts of Ladakh and Spiti valley are used for grazing purpose. Here climatic condition is excessively cold and arid.

The cultivated areas are confined to the lower parts along the Indus and its tributaries in Ladakh, whereas in Spiti the same correspond to the Spiti River. However, there has been cultivated lands along the streams of melted glaciers. Therefore, I would say both regions have subsistance agriculture farming.

Ladakh was opened for foreigners in summer 1974, since'then every year their percentage increased. Now-a-days about 25-30 thousand tourists are visiting Leh and its surroundings. As a result the living standard of Ladakhis has been increased tremendously.

Keeping in view to the above facts Himachal Government also declared to open Spiti valley for foreigners in 1992. Therefore, foreign tourist flow into the valley has been increased considerably. Later various developmental programmes all together have been brought here and changed the infrastructure.

In Ladakh Tourism has developed as a Tourist Industry. The Cultural, Social, Agricultural, Architectural, Landscapes, Adventures, Sports, Historical places, Monuments, Fairs and Festivals all being explored very well for the intertainment of tourists. Similary Spiti valley also have good tourism potential, so needful action should be taken to explore the following sectors:

1. Cultural Sector

[i] Cultural Tradition

[ii] Monastic Tradition
[iii] Costumes
(iv) Ornaments
(v) Folk dance
(vi) Folk song
(vii) Rituals and Festivals

2. Social Sector

(i) Customs
(ii) Social system
(iii) Social structure
(iv) Social means and behaviour

3. Agricultural Sector

(i) Traditional Agricultural techniques
(ii) Traditional Agricultural irrigation system
(iii) Ritual means and beliefs of Agriculture
(iv) Traditional system of village organisation

4. Handicraft Works

(i) Wooden craft works viz. Tsokse, Dragon and other decorative items
(ii) Thanka paintings
(iii) Statues

5. Architectural Structure

(i) Houses
(ii) Monasteries
(iii) Chortens / Stupa
(iv) Mani walls
(v) Forts
(vi) Palace
(vii) Cave

6. Bridge

(i) Rope bridge

(ii) Log bridge
(iii) Big Iron bridge

7. Landscapes

(i) Lakes
(ii) Rivers
(iii) Mountains
(iv) Glaciers

8. Adventures

(i) Trekking
(ii) Mountaineering
(iii) Driving

9. Sports

(i) Traditional games viz. Polo, Archery etc.
(ii) Ice hockey
(iii) Ice skating
(iv) Skating
(v) Rafting
(vi) Boating

10. Historical Monuments/Places

(i) Chortens
(ii) Rock carvings site
(iii) Inscriptions site on rocks and stones
(iv) Rock/Stone sculptures site.

The cultural sector in Spiti valley includes a primary sphere of activity which stemming or attracting tourism into the valley. The 10th century A.D. period monasteries in the valley are the main source of tourist attraction. Here follows a list of monasteries which are important for the development of tourism in the valley:

(i) Tabo Choskhor
(ii) Kaza monastery
(iii) Kee monastery

(iv) Hansa monastery

(v) Kungri monastery.

Spiti inhabitants are rich in their traditional folk dances, folk songs, fairs and festivals. These all together attract Indian and western tourists.

Social sector accelerates tourism. The simple, hospitable, friendly social behaviour attracts tourists most. Tourists do not like social and economic tension, money making, cheating etc. such social evils hinder tourism. Like Ladakhis, Spiti people are simple and cultured, therefore foreign tourists feel happy to visit Spiti.

In Spiti we find traditional agriculture based on rituals, village level co-operation and organisation. Therefore, Westerners would like to visit Spiti and enjoy their primitive agriculture.

Ladakh as well as Spiti valley have good potential of architectural structures such as old houses, monasteries, chortens, Mani walls, forts, palaces, caves etc. Hence, Spiti valley certainly attract good number of tourists from India and abroad.

Ladakh and Spiti have similar landscapes and topography. Lakes, mountains, rocks, glaciers, rivers etc. In the remote peaceful environment when tourists get the opportunity to see the above said geographical treasury become very happy and would like to visit here time and again.

Spiti valley has wide scope of mountaineering and trekking. These are very much popular among tourists. As adventurious tourism foreigners like adventure games. Ladakh and Spiti would definitely fulfil their requirements.

Normally Ladakh and Spiti valley have tourist traffic during summers. But, if concern governments make some efforts through advertisements in order to attract winter tourism

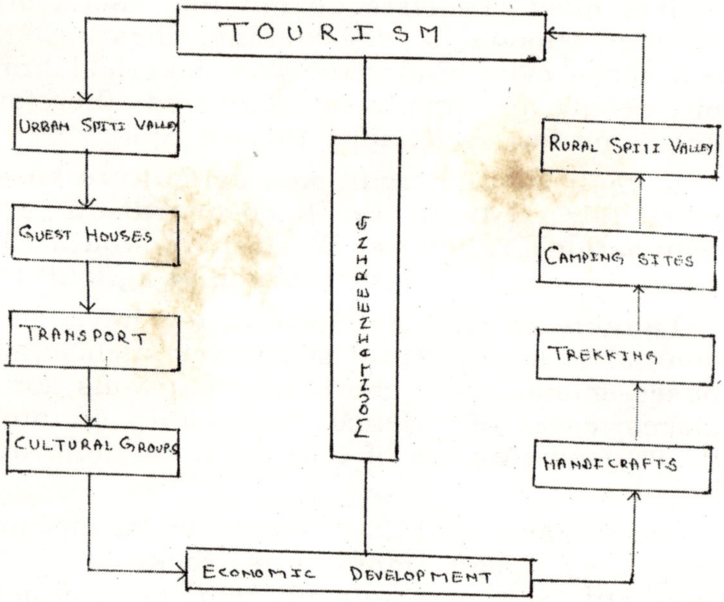

Model 22.1: Tourism and Economic Development of Spiti Valley (H.P.).

as both regions have good scope for winter games viz. Ice hockey, Ice skating etc.

To sum up I would suggest the following Model 22.1 for the economic development of Spiti valley through tourism.

Conclusion and Recommendation: In Leh district of Ladakh of Jammu and Kashmir state, tourism has been developing very well. Except winter sports, almost all sectors are being used for the development of tourism in Ladakh. Therefore, following recommendations can be made for the development of tourism in Spiti valley.

(i) Government should give subsidies for the construction of guest houses or hotels in a accountable manner.

(ii) Banks and other financial institutions in Spiti valley should be increased so that they can provide loans for the construction of guest houses / hotels after the clearance of environmental constrains.

(iii) Department of culture, Government of India may give grants to the Buddhist monasteries in Spiti valley in order to preserve the monastic culture. However, strict monitoring should be needed while distributing funds for the same.

(iv) Infra-structure should be developed in Spiti region and all monasteries are needed to link with the main road.

(v) World-wide advertisement through Indian Embassies and Indian Government Tourism Departments will help to accelerate tourism in Spiti valley.

(vi) To organise annual festivals in monasteries and in villages.

(vii) Fax / S.T.D. and internet facilities may be updated in Spiti valley.

(viii) To prepare documentary films on monasteries and village life of Spiti valley.

(ix) To organise sèminars and workshop about Buddhist culture and religion of Spiti valley.

(x) To arrange concessional tickets for those who are interested to visit Spiti valley.

(xi) Necessary steps should be taken to preserve historical sites and monuments.

(xii) In order to increase adventure tourism, river rafting and mountaineering facilities should be provided to interested tourists.

(xiii) Trekking has wide scope in Spiti, therefore, trekking routes should be opened for tourists.

(xiv) Handicraft works should preserved and encouraged according to the needs of tourists.

23
Folk Dance of Ladakh

Folk dance of Ladakh has close relations with its history. Jammu and Kashmir state is divided in three regions—Jammu, Kashmir and Ladakh. The Ladakh region is itself further divided into two districts—Leh and Kargil. Leh is Buddhist dominated whereas Kargil is dominated by Balti or Shia Muslims. The folk dance of Ladakh is very much popular among Buddhist community, however, Muslims also take equal part. In view of its strategic importance and geographical position, it has age old relations with its neighbouring countries is Central Asian countries, *i.e.*, Tibet, Himachal Pradesh, Baltistan etc.

In Ladakh we have broadly four races viz. Dard, Mon, Balti and Mongol. Dards and Mons were possibly migrated here well before 10th century A.D. Mongolian race came with Skilde Nimagon during 10th century A.D. Gradually they subdued Dards and Mons. During 14th century A.D. and later during King Jamyang Namgyal period Baltis migrated Ladakh and settled down in Kargil region and near Leh areas in upper Ladakh. Consequently, they brought their art, culture and religion here.

Therefore, Jabro dance from Tibet, Shondol dance from Himachal Pradesh and Dok dance by Dards later became the main dances of Ladakh. Besides, other types of dances were introduced from Central Asian countries, with the passage

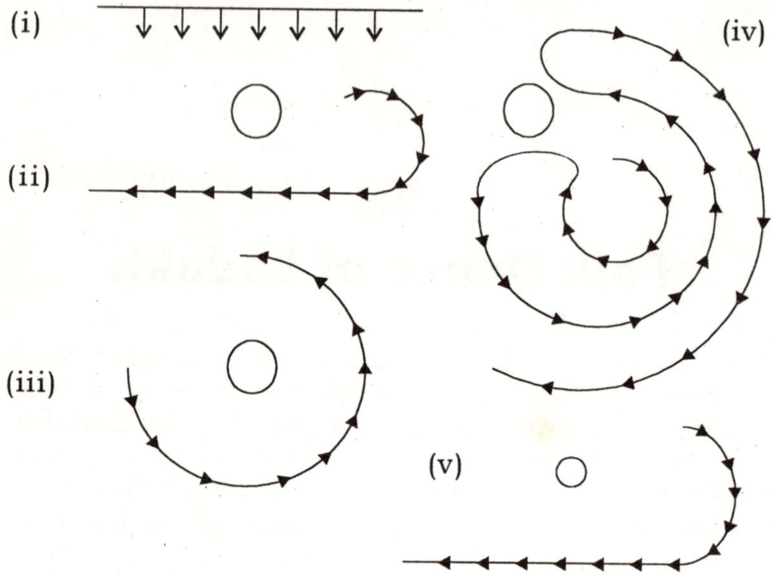

Fig. 23.1: Pucha-Sches (Male dance) at different stages.

of time the dances which were vogue in Nepal got popularity in Ladakh with slight change.

Dard Dance: The dances performed during olden days were at Male dance, Female dance and confined dance. These folk dance before 10th century A.D. were brought in Ladakh by Dards, therefore, sometimes known Dard dance. Through the ages these dance tradition being followed by Mongolian race who migrated from Tibet. Now-a-days called Tashichot folk dance. Here follows further details :

Male Dance (Ladakhi, Pucha-sches): In all cases it started with salutation i.e. by saying 'Juley' by the dancers. As this folk dance is performed by males, therefore, they after salutation put forward their first step from right foot. They use *skerak* while dancing. *Skerak* is the indication of glorification of the deity 'Lha-Gyallo'. They turn right and left hands with the movement of steps, accordingly they move *skerek* between right and left through back. (Fig. 23.1).

Female Dance (Ladakhi Pomo sches)

Female dancers start the dance with salution by putting forward their left step first with the tune of Ladakh musical instrument *'Daman'*. They present dance with movement of their fingers, like male-motion of their hands and steps. The movement of their fingers depict plucking of flower and their presentation to God. The dance has great significance and spiritual values. For a Ladakhi it gives him consolation in this world and a good reward in the life hereafter.

Combined Dance: It is a mixed dance. In this dance male and female in a single row come to the stage or on dancing ground. All the dancers carry *skerak* which they move with their steps and according to the tune of music. While dancing they in the middle say 'Yasha'...... 'Yasha' accordingly the dancing rhythm also increase. The leader of this dance should be expert dancer, the second has to follow accordingly, the rest dancers should also have a good knowledge of dance. The musicians play the tune meant for male power.

Kompa Sumsak: This is male and female mixed dance. Dancers male after female come into the stage or on dancing ground. They dance with three steps with the movement of hands and music tune.

Shondol Dance: This is a female dance who start dance after salutation. Dancers hold one another hands and dance with less movement and slow music.

Chabskyang Dance: Male and female dancers come one after another with Chabskyang pot[4], start dancing with the music and with the movement of hands along with Chabskyang. It is said that in olden days villagers from Wanla performed this dance on agricultural fields. In this dance usually eight dancers present folk dance.

Notes

1. Skerak: It is long bed sheet like cloth but less in width.

2. Daman: Ladakhi musical instrument similar to *Tabla*, but they are two in number. One for heavy tune other for fine. Musician plays daman by two sticks.

3. Shondol Dance: Dancers dance by singing glory song of Ladakh king.

4. Chabskyang Pot: It is a *chang* (local beer pot).

24

The Changpa of the Ladakh Himalayas :

Some Observations On Their Economy and Environment - A Case Study of Chang-Thang

This paper very briefly presents some observations on a few aspects of the interaction between pastoralists and their natural environment in the Chang-Thang subdivision of Leh district of the Ladakh Himalayas (Map 24.1) chang-Thang stretches from Chushul in the southeast into Tibet and is now cut across by the Ladakh - Tibet border. Its inhabitants are known as Chang Pa; a term also applied to the 'Tartar' shepherds of these northern plains. This vast high altitude plateau is criss-crossed by mountain ranges and is liberally scattered with salt lakes, such as those of Pakchak Kurutso, Tsokar and Tsomoriri. While a great deal of these 21,000 sq. km are desert, they do include vast arid grazing lands. The observations and analysis presented here focus on aspects of ecological adaptation as especially on pastoralism and ago-pastoralism as they are practised on this huge elevated plateau. This paper was published in 'Nomadic Peoples' Research journal NS (1999). Vol. 3, Issue 1, Germany, 94-105 and is reproduced below with minor alterations:

The Ethnographic Context: The Chang Pa are said to have originally migrated from 'Hor' in Tibet around 800 A.D. The term ***Hor*** was first

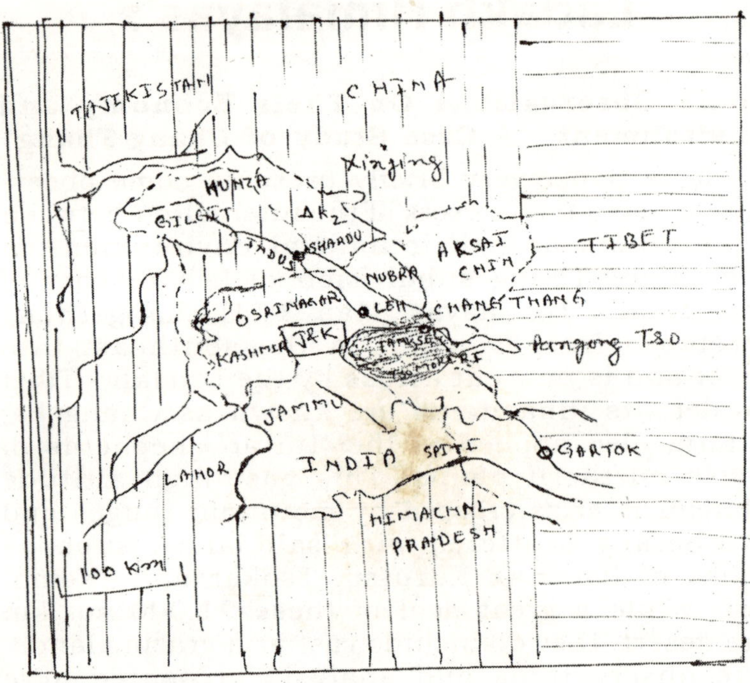

Map. 24.1: Map of the Chang-Thang Region : The shading indicates the area of study.

applied to the Vighurs, found in Kanchow, and the contemporary nomadic Horpa of the West (Nur Hor) in Tibet may still bear their name. Later the term was used for the Mongols of Genghiz Khan and it is from these that the five Hor principalities of Khan (around Kandze and Beri) claim descent. In the past, the Chang Pa and Ladakhis did not inter-marry. However, when the Ladakh King Singe-Namgyal[1] married 'Kal-zang, Dolma, a girl from the family of Rupshu Goba[2], the custom of inter-marriage with Ladakhis began.

Originally, most Chang Pa must have led a largely nomadic, pastoral life in the upland valleys. Today, they live and use one of two major ecological zones—the ***drok*** and the ***rong***—depending on the zone lived in there are differences in culture too. Almost every inhabited place extends downwards, along the narrow valleys and thus zones are formed corresponding to altitude. Pastures on the upper slopes are known as ***brog or drok,*** while ***rong*** designates the high altitude mountain village; where Tibetan Buddhism of ***ka-rgyutpa*** sect is practised. It would seem that Chang Pa living here gradually took to a somewhat more sedentary lifestyle, grazing their livestock near their respective villages. Thus groups of Chang Pa started leading a semipastoral, seminomadic life.

Drok culture	*Rong culture*
- non-caste society	- broadly speaking no caste system, but status groups[3]
- economy based on pastoralism	- economy based on trade, agriculture and trade in this order.
- relative freedom of women	- relative freedom of women

- meat consumption (including yak flesh)	- more frequent consumption of meat
- consumption of *chhang* (raw beer)	- more frequent consumption of chhang
- Buddhists	- Buddhists
- Tibetan dialect of Chan Kyet	- Tibetan dialect of Chang Kyet.[4]

In terms of their basic economy, Chang Pa as a whole can, depending on the altitude, be classified today into three major categories. The members of the first category live in the valleys of the high mountain zones and are a little more dependent on agriculture than on pastoralism, which, however, remains indispensable. They generally raise one crop a year and grow wheat, barley and some vegetables such as turnip, potatoes, peas and sometimes also mustard. They are mostly settled along the Indus river in villages such as Kuyul, Demchok, Kerey, Chumatang, Nyoma, Ney, Likchey, Chumoor, Korzok and Henley. The second category consists of the seminomadic and agropastoral chang-Pa, living in places like Rupshu and Kharnak. The last-category is that of the entirely nomadic Chang Pa who live only on the high plateau area of Chang Thang, in the regions of Rupshu, Kharnak and Korzok.

Whichever category they may belong to, all Chang Pa herd sheep, goat, yak and horses to varying degrees. These animals supply them with food (meat, cheese-dry **churpe**-yoghurt and butter) and also provide the ***pashmina*** (fine goat hair, commonly known as "lena") and wool which are either bartered for barley (to make *tsampa,* parched barley flour and *Chang,* a type of local bear), tea, rice, mustard oil and juggery or sold to get cash, which is then used to buy these products from nearby markets. In summer wild vegetables such as ***za-chod*** and ***pang-chod*** are collected and consumed. Meat is usually consumed dried, since animals are by and large allowed to be slaughtered in September or October every year. ***Yud*** is a very popular dietary item and is made by mixing ground ***churpe*** and jaggery with dried meat:

Before further discussion ecological parameters of the Chang-Pa life style, I would like to give the information of Drokpa of Western Tibet who are at the border of Chang-Thang of Ladakh region. The study was conducted by William H. Newell who visited Tibet in 1989 and studied 263 Tibetan ***drokpa,*** (or nomads): "These ***phala drokpa*** occupy one division **(*shiang*)** among the half million population living on the Chang-Tang (Chang-Thang) high plains, most of whose inhabitants gain their livelihood by herding yaks, sheep and goats. The ***phala*** is ***'nomad'.*** There are ten major ***Phala*** encampments and a circuit of all ten encampments could well take forty days by yak. The actual distance travelled between the permanent winter encampment and the three or four late August-to-December pastures are mostly not more than 32 km. from the permament base camp and their cycle of movement is very different from that of the Himalayan **Gaddi** shepherds of the Dhaula Dhar range in India. In Tibet, each pasture was delimited and considered capable of supporting a fixed number of animals calculated on the basis of a ***marke,*** a unit that literally refers to a weight of butter but was actually computed on the basis of the number of animals. In the 1950s one ***marke*** of pasture was suitable for thirteen yak or seventy-eight sheep or ninety-one goats, since seven goats or six sheep were calculated as the equivalent of one yak. In other words, a one ***marke*** pasture would be assigned to a family with either thirteen yak, or seventy-eight sheep,or ninety-one goats or again some specific combination of these. A pasture with a two-marke rating would support double that number and so on. Every three years the number of ***markes*** allocated would vary in accordance with whether flocks on the area had increased or decreased". Newell, William H: Nomadic Pastoralists of Tsatsey, Western Tibet and Chamba, Indian Himalayas : Some Comparative Notes; Nomadic Peoples NS (1999), Vol. 3 Issue1, Germany : 106-07.

In Ladakh like Tibetan ***drokpa*** or ***phala drokpa*** every Chang Pa is identified by the name of his family head as 'Anchoktent' etc were aloted pasture lands according to their permanent settlements. I shall now discuss two major types of resource use and ecological adaptation observed in Chang-Thang, namely agropastoralism and pastoralism.

Agropastoralism : A Case Study of Chang Pa of The Kerey and Chumoor Area: The high plateau of Kerey and Chumoor lies in the north of the Great Ladakh Range; hence rainfall is more scarce and the climate is more arid here than in the Indus valley of Ladakh. The high altitude (ranging from some 5,486 meters to 6,096 meters) is responsible for the cool climate even in summer and for the long, severe winters. Because of the cold and the aridity here in Chang-Pa can grow only one crop in a year; peas, potatoes and turnips are planned in the limited spaces of the narrow valleys called ***lungpas.*** They also engage in trade and pastoral activities, selling ***pashmina*** and wool to Ladakhis, Kashmiri and Himachali traders. From this income they buy rice, jaggery, flour and ***tsampa.*** Today these things are usually available at the nearby markets, but some decades ago when no heavy trucks or tippers were available, Ladakhis peasant-traders with their donkeys and occasionally horses provided an essential link in the system. They carried loads of flour, *tsampa,* dried apricots, mustard oil and spices on Their pack animals and exchanged these for ***pashmina*** and wool in Chang-Thang.

In the nineteenth century this trade was in the hands of individual farmers from central Ladakh, particularly from the banks of the Indus valley, who had lands suitable for agriculture and whose produce they regularly took on their donkeys up to Chang-Thang. Bartering there in return for ***pashmina,*** wool and salt, these peasants drove their donkeys down again to the valleys before snowfall. About fifty years ago Chang Pa themselves carried ***pashmina,*** wool salt and ***khuloo*** (yak wool) on their sheep and goats backs to the Leh market and exchanged these for ***tsampa,*** jaggery, flour and dry apricots. Today they are not seen much at Leh or at surrounding markets. However, they still maintain trade links with Leh butchers for the disposal of their old livestock, ***pashmina*** and yak wool[5].

In Kerey and Chumoor the economy is based on agropastoral as transhumance. Ploughing, the yalks as draught animals, generally starts in early May. The ploughing is conducted by yaks. Irrigation problems are few. It is said that formerly the lamas decided by divination on the date on which to begin irrigation and on the order of irrigation by individual households. Today, the ***goba,*** the head of a village, decides the date and irrigation is carried out jointly by all the villagers. In both Kerey and Chumoor the sowing season from May to June, depending on the weather; earlier this date was also decided by the lamas, after consulting the lunar calendar. Now it is the ***goba*** who decides the date following the traditional method of consulting the Tibetan calendar. Despite the availability of labour, agricultural activities are limited. For examples, weeding is not done and although dung is plentiful, it is not used as manure.

Much greater attention is paid to pastoral activities. In 1992 the average numbers of livestock per household in Kerey were five yaks, four *demo* and twenty sheep/goats and in Chumoor it was fifteen yaks, ten ***demo*** and forty-five sheep/goats. The richest villager had sixty yaks and ***demo,*** while the poorest had none. The population of Kerey and Chumoor has increased by about 70 per cent since 1961, the increase in the animal population in those thirty years being 67 per cent. These livestock provide milk, butter, cheese, meat, wool, and hair. Butter, which is indispensable to their daily diet, is, as far as I am aware, never sold. Many other essential items of household use, such as clothing, boots, tents, ropes, and bags are also made from these animals. Livestock also brings in cash to buy agricultural and manufactured products. The monthly income per family from livetock was estimated at Indian Rupees 3,950 in Chumoor and at about half of that (i.e. Indian Rs. 2,116.66) in Kerey. Tables 24.1 and 24.2 provide some details.

Table 24.1
Average Annual and Monthly Income in Indian (Rs.) from Livestock in Chumoor Village during 1992

Items	*Average Annual Income Rs.*	*Rs. Monthly*
1	*2*	*3*
Sheep sold to butchers	18,000.00	1500.00
Goats sold to butchers	1200.00	100.00
Pashmina	19500.00	1625.00
Wool	7200.00	600.00
Khuloo	1500.00	125.00
Total	47400.00	3950.00

Source: Study conducted by author during 1992-93.

In Chumoor more than 80 per cent of the households migrated with their animals. The rest, who were comparatively poor, had to ask someone to take care of their yaks, ***demo*** in return for payment in kind or cash. In Kerey only about 32 per cent of the households (8 of the 25 households) practised transhumance. The pattern of transhumance was, however, the same in both villages and is set out in Tables 24.3 and 24.4 and in Figure 24.1. In both village as soon as the ground is clear of snow the Chang Pa move their livestock from these winter pasture at about 4,572 metres to their spring pasture at altitudes of 4,876 metres to 5,181 metres. They stay there with the animals for nearly two months, usually till May, when they move up to the highest (summer) pastures at some 5,486 meters. After approximately four months, at the end of September when the autumn winds start to blow in the high mountains and sometimes snow falls, there Chang-Pa come down to their autumn pastures at 5,181 metres, where they stay for about two months. At the end of November when crops have been harvested, the animals are taken back to the winter pastures,

Table 24.2
Average Annual and Monthly Income in Indian Rupees (Rs) from Livestock in Kerey Village During 1992

Items	*Average Income Annual (Rs)*	*Rs. Monthly*
1	*2*	*3*
Sheep sold to butchers	7500.00	625.00
Goats sold to butchers	1200.00	100.00
Pashmina	8500.00	708.00
Wool	7200.00	600.00
Khuloo	1000.00	83.33
Total	25400.00	2116.66

Source: Study conducted by author during 1992-93.

where all the animals will graze on the barley and wheat stubble.

Table 24.3
The Annual Grazing Cycle of Kerey Herds

Valley	*Month*	*Number and types of livestock*
(1)	*(2)*	*(3)*
Chyu	January	68 yaks, 65 goats, 88 sheep
Sumdo	February	68 yaks, 65 goats, 88 sheep
Sidul	March, April and September	121 yaks, 80 goats, 151 sheep
Lunpa	May	68 yaks, 65 goats, 88 sheep
Ney	June	68 yaks, 65 goats, 88 sheep
Kangiung	July	15 yaks, 50 goats, 25 sheep
Pacha	July	53 yaks, 15 goats, 63 sheep
Machek	August	53 yaks, 15 goats
Lunpa	September to	15 yaks, 50 goats, 25 sheep
Yogma	December	
Dirigayao	November to December	53 yaks, 15 goats, 63 sheep

Source: Study conducted by the author during 1992-93.

Table 24.4
The Annual Grazing Cycle of Chumoor Herds

Valley	*Month*	*Number and types of livestock*
(1)	*(2)*	*(3)*
Lama Bum	January, Nov. to December	75 horses, 10 donkeys, 10 yaks, 700 sheep, 500 goats
Yagranchen	February to April	75 horses, 10 donkeys, 10 yaks, 700 sheep, 500 goats
Chumoor	May to August	75 horses, 10 donkeys, 10 yaks, 700 sheep, 500 goats

(Contd.)

Surroundings	September to October	75 horses, 10 donkeys, 10 yaks, 700 sheep, 500 goats

Source: Study conducted by the author during 1992-93.

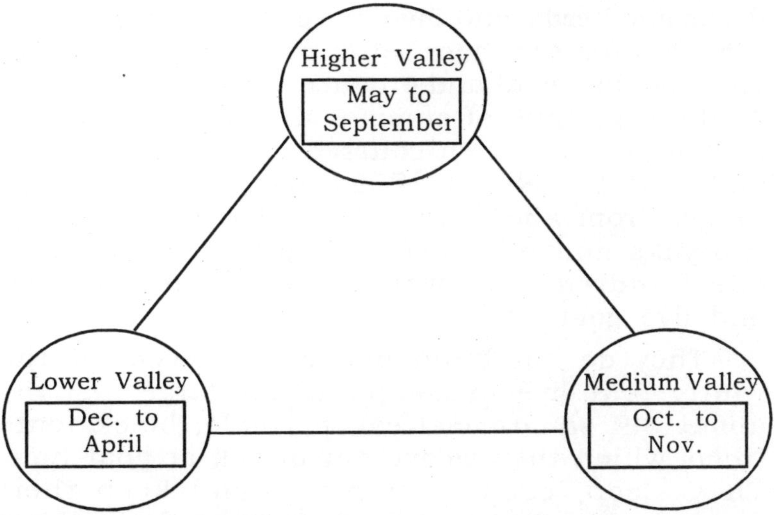

Fig. 24.1: Pattern of seagonal mobility in relation to altitude.

Source: Field study conducted by the author during 1992-93.

Pastoralism: A Case Study of the Changr-Pa of Rupshu, Kharnak and Korzok Areas.

Rupshu, Kharnak and Korzok together extend over an area of about 20,800 sq. km. It is a region of high altitude valleys lying at about 4,572 meters, 'to the west of the river Indus beyond the 5,334 meters high Thaglang pass and surrounded by mountains which rise up to heights of between 6,096 and 6,400 metres. The climate is extremely cold and dry, with clear sky in summer. As the sun sets bitingly cold winds blow and the temperature immediately sinks to 0°C; at night it further decreases to –5°C, even in the months of August and September.[6]

The Chang-Pa these areas, numbering roughly 4,000, are nomadic herds people and graze their huge flocks of *Pashmina* goats and huniya sheep throughout the year. They stay for a month or two at a time at a particular spot to graze their flocks and herds, and then move on as the advancing season promises them better pasturage. The goats are small in height and produce *pashmina* in winter. At the beginning of summer the fleece grows out or loosens; it is then coursed out from the goats and sent to Leh. In 1992 Chang-Pa herd sizes ranged from about fifty sheep, forty eight goats, two yaks and two *demo* to a maximum of about one hundred and twenty sheep, one hundred and five goats, fifteen yaks and ten demo.

They do not build house here even for the winter, but live in comparatively large (usually about 3.9 square metres), portable, black tents (*rebo*) which they weave out of yak or goat hair. They sleep, cook their meals and keep their goods inside these tents which take them about two months to make from start to finish. The yak hair tents last longer than those made of goat hair—if repaired regularly, about twelve years rather than just six. A tent is picked by fastening together the two corners of the woven cloth and fixing them on the top of upright poles and then fastering the lower corners to the ground space within the tents is enlarged if required by pulling the cloth out here and there, using extra ropes, which are led over a forked stick and then pegged down. The tents are decorated with little flags and with yak's tails fastened to the poles. In 1992 there were fabout 140 such *rebos* in kharnak and about 200 each in Rupshu and Korzok areas.

Korzok was once the headquarters of Rupshu. A house was also constructed there by Chang-Pa for their 'chief'. In 1871 Frederic Drew found about nine houses, where old and sick Chang-Pa stayed in summer while the others moved down towards the Indus. In Korzok and Rupshu today about five and ten acres respectively of land is cultivated by a few Chang-Pa, who grow barley and wheat. At a height of 4,572 metres these are probably the highest cultivated lands in Ladakh[7].

The Chang-Pa of this region have long been well known among Ladakhis as trans-Himalayan traders. Formerly they sold salt which they extracted from the Tsokar lake at the Leh market. On their return journey they filled their now empty salt bags with grain. A small pack or double bag was hung over the backs of sheep, each sheep carried about 12 kg of salt/grain, while stronger animals could carry loads of 16 kilograms.

Even today the Chang-Pa sell *pashmina* to Ladakhi traders, who work as midddlemen. The latter purchase it at low prices and sell it to Kashmiri merchants, stationed at Spituk, and Choglamsar, near Leh. These, in their turn take the *pashmina* to Kashmir where it is processed into yarn for making the world famous Kashmiri shawls. This has been the practice since the treaty of Tingmosagam in 1684, which conferred on Kashmiris the right to buy and sell *pashmina*. Till 1871 nomads from the southeast of Leh district were the great carriers of the region, transporting merchandise on their sheep and goats between central Ladakh and Gartok in Chinese Tibet and between Lahul and British India. For these service they were well paid in cash and kind. Rupshu was then a major regional extrepot for Central Asian trade (Fig.24.2) and Chang-Thang as a whole was an important centre of export and import both within the region and beyond it[8].

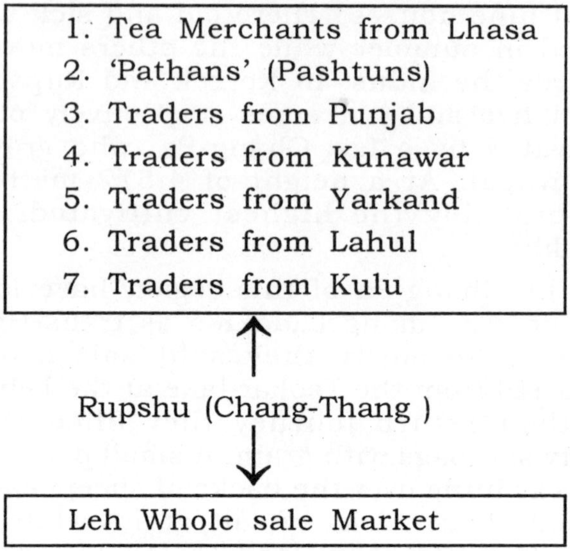

Fig. 24.2: Trading patterns in the region.

While in the beginning of the twentieth century sheep were sometimes used for transporting salt, bales of wool and borax to Leh, in the 1930s traders from the Shyam (area below Nimo) carried goods to Chang-Thang in groups of four to six, each trader having ten or fifteen donkeys. One donkey's load was 50 or 60 kg each merchant's consignment of 500—1000 kg. consisted of flour, dried apricots, and often small-amounts of tea and textiles. The tedious task of unloading at the end of each day's march and reloading the next morning needed many helps who accompanied these caravans. These set off for Chang-Thang in May. At different stages on the outward journey they deposited supplies for the return, either with their trading partners or, if these in the course of their pastoral migrations were likely to have moved on, simply concealed beneath heaps of stones at some camping ground. This system had the advantage of lightering the animals loads and also if making sure that there would be no shortfall in supplies on the way back[9].

The sheep of the Rupshu Chang-Pa still carry loads of up to 10 kg. But they carry goods mostly for their own use and not for sale-like the salt they collect from lake Tsokar. Yet the Chang-Pa of Rupshu are still a major factor in regional trade. Every year a family sells about three to four sheep or goat and wool worth some Indian Rs. 3 million is also sold annually to Lahul and Kashmiri traders. In addition, Rupshu, Kharnak and Karzok areas as a whole contribute about 52 per cent of the total. 16,000 kg. *Pashmina* produced annually in Chang-Thang and worth Indian Rs. 7 million. The government of Jammu and Kashmir of which Ladakh is currently an administrative part, has set up two goat farms (at Nimo, at the confluence of the Indus and Zanskar rivers and at Upshi on the Manali road) to boost the yield and quantity of *pashmina.* The Upshi farm has increased the average annual *pashmina* yields of a male goats from 300 gm. and that of a female from 200 gm. to 300 gm. Besides, veterinary facilities provided by experts at these farms and better grazing sites have reduced the mortality rate among kids from over 40 per cent to less than 01 per cent. These farms also supply superior bucks for breeding, so that the *pashmina* yield can be raised further.

In Rupshu, the *goba* decides each year who is responsible for grazing animals: two families are designated to look after the horses of the whole community, while one family is made responsible for the animals of the Thugze monastery (gonpa). These three families graze their own animals together with all the horses and with the gonpa's animals, whereas the other Chang-Pa graze their animals separately. This leads to a difference between the pasture areas and migration cycles of these three families and the rest of the community. Thus, in January and February, when the other Rupshu Chang-Pa graze their herds at Tasaput, near the Thugze *gonpa,* these three families graze theirs 10 km eastwords. Likewise, in May-June when the latter move to Yaguchen all the other go to the Rock Chen Rock Chun area. In August everyone goes to the Thaglang-la valley-except these three, who move to Chee, east of Thaglang-la, to Phu and further to the Zera valley. Then, when everyone moves west of the Thugze monastery to Pon-kan-Neu valley to stay there till the end of November, these three families stay near the gonpa. In December the majority graze their hards at Thaglang-la for twenty five days, leaving their tents at Pon-Kar-Nau. At the end of December they move closer to the monastery and join up there with the three families. These varying migration cycles are set forth in Table: 24.5.

While in summer the Rupshu Chang-Pa children, women and the elderly remain at the camps, young men accompany their herds. They graze their milch animals early in the morning, bring them back at about 11 a.m. for milking and then again send them to pasture. In the evening they take them in to the *rebo* earlier than the other animals. Table: 24.6 gives a rôugh, idea of the grazing schedules.

Formerly in summer the Rupshu Chang-Pa split into two camps, which went to distinct pastures, to join together again only in winter. Today no such splits take place, though every day in summer the youth of each family grazes the milch and dry animals separately as shown in Table: 24.6 and small children take the kids and lambs to separate pastures nearby.

Table 24.5

The Migration Cycles of the Rupshu Chang-pa

Valley	*Month*											
	J	*F*	*M*	*A*	*M*	*J*	*J*	*A*	*S*	*O*	*N*	*D*
Hum Go (Tasaphuk Changeri)	–	×	×	–	–	–	–	–	–	–	–	–
Tasaphuk (Chum-go)	–	–	×	×	–	–	–	–	–	–	–	–
Rock Chen Rock Chun (Yaguchen)	–	–	–	–	×	×	–	–	–	–	–	–
Thaglang-La valley (Chee)	–	–	–	–	–	–	×	×	–	–	–	–
Middle of Zera valley (east of Thanglang-la)	–	–	–	–	–	–	–	–	×	×	–	–
Pon-Kan-Nau valley (near Thugze Gonpa)	–	–	–	–	–	–	–	–	–	–	×	–
Thaglang-la valley	–	–	–	–	–	–	–	–	–	–	–	×

The name of the valleys in parenthesis refer to the grazing areas of three families, while the initials represent the twelve months; (× = period of location)

Source: Fields study was conducted by the Author during 1992-93.

Table 24.6

Grazing schedules in Rapshu during Any Normal Day

Type of livestock	*Rough distance of pasture from rebo*	*Grazing timings*
milch animals	nearby	4 a.m. to 11 a.m. (morning cycle)
milch animals	nearby	12 a.m. to 4 a.m. (afternoon cycle)
other animals	far away	4 a.m. to 5 a.m. throughout the day

Source: Fields study was conducted by the Author during 1992-93.

Changing Environment of Chang-Thang: Concluding Observations

In March 1959 upheaval broke out in Tibet against the tightening rule of the People's Republic of China and the Dalai Lama fled to Dharamsala, in India. Following this many Tibetan refugees poured into Chang-Thang area together with their herds. Initially this did not lead to serious social problems but it did lead to economic ones, especially to shortage of pasture. Two years later China attacked India via Chang-Thang and occupied a great deal of this area. This brought further pressure on grazing resources, since it led both to a reduction of about 10 per cent in the pasture on grazing resources, since it led both to a reduction of about 40 per cent. The fact that the herds of the 'Tibetan refugees' are not controlled or co-ordinated by the Chang-Pa *goba* of different localities still leads to considerable overgrazing[10].

Over the last few decades many Chang-Pa have abandoned their pastoral system and are now settled-in different valleys where they cultivate land. Some of them began smuggling Chinese goods in return for *pashmina*. In 1988 the Government of India lifted the ban on tourism in the area, and increasingly tourists pass through the Rupshu area. This has affected the local economy in many ways. Now Chang-Pa sometimes take up work as laborers, on road sides; others start small wayside teastalls or rest houses. In recent years this has led to a rapid increase in local wages and increasingly young man are unwilling to accompany the herds. But the *goba* have adapted to the new situation and allowed some families to work outside the pastoral sector.[11]

The last few decades have also seen much social change in the region as a whole. The Tibetan refugees and then the Indian army and paramilitary forces posted in the areas have had a tremendous impact on Chang-Pa society. Many Tibetan refugees have married Chang-Pa girls and thus become members of Chang-Pa society. Today they are largely involved in business and as middlemen exploiting the Chang-Pa. They purchase *pashmina* at low prices from Chang-Thang and sell it to Kashmiri traders at much higher prices. This could in future lead to social tension, especially since the Tibetans are gradually becoming richer than the Chang-Pa.

The demise of polyandry is also gradually leading to an increase in population growth. With the division of the nuclear family and increasing, sedentarisation, the livestock population is also increasing. In Rupshu, where the *goba* earlier appointed two families for looking after the community horses and one for the animals of the Thugze *gonpa,* now he has to appoint six families for doing this. It is conceivable that a time will come when the Rupshu Chang-Pa have to select two or three *gobas* to overseer all the herd management.

Chang-Pa economy and society are undergoing change in a larger political and economic setting, that is highly unpredictable, *pashmina,* not so long ago a rare product is now being produced in large quantities, not only in neighboring Himalayan region, but also in Mongolia. Wedged in between China and India, the regions is politically sensitive. Since 1990, with the growing armed conflict in Kashmir, of which Ladakh is an administrative part, the overall situation has become still more volatile.

The responses to the socio-economic and political transformations of this entire region should be focused on in future studies of these pastoral peoples.

Notes and References

1. King Singe-Namgyal : Senge Namgyal, he was the greatest Ladakhi King. He ruled Ladakh kingdom for twenty six years. He was described as the great physical powers and warlike ability. He probably came

to the throne while quite young, and when yet a young man led an expedition to the south and east against the "back pastures" of Guge and brought back from the northern slopes of *Tise* (Mount Kailasa) ponies, yaks, goats, and sheep, and filled his'own land with them. Later he made intermittent war against Central Guge, and eventually established his supremacy over that ancient kingdom. In the other direction, to the north and west, lay Baltistan, and he himself was as we have seen, a Balti on his mother's side, thus at the outset he seems to have enjoyed friendly relationship here. Finegan, Jack: 'Tibet: A Dreamt of Image', Tibet House, New Delhi; 1986: 178-79.

2. Rupshu Goba: He was treated as the King, Rupshu region of Ladakh.
3. Gara, Kange-zen and Sebde have lower social status. The Gara usually worked with iron: the Kange-zen eat the meat of the Tibetan wild ass (Kyang: Equus hemionus Kiang) and the Sebde are said to emit unpleasant smells.
4. Those settled near army or paramilitary camps also understand some Hindi, the National Language of India.
5. Rizvi, J., 'Peasant Traders of Ladakh: A study in Oral History,' *India International Centre Quarterly,* 1985, 12 (1): 14-21.
6. Drew, F., 'The Jammu and Kashmir Territories, A Geographical Account, Delhi (Reprinted); 1976.
7. *Ibid.*
8. Bhatt, M., and S. S. Gupta: 'Warmth from cold Ladakh,' *The Tribune* 9, August, 1990: 3.
9. Rizvi, J., *op. cit.*
10. Jina, Prem Singh: 'Pasture Ecology of Leh, Ladakh', in Wissenschaftsgeschichte and gegenwartige Forschungen in Northwest-Indian. Dresden, 1990: 171-81.
11. *Ibid.*

25
Threat to Black Necked Cranes in Ladakh

Black necked crane (Grus nigricolli) is one of the most endangered specie. In Ladakh region it is popularly known Cha-Thang-Thung, migrates from Siberia and other remote areas of Central Asia arriving in the beginning of summer when the ice is melting on the lakes of Chang-Thang a sub-division of Leh district lies in the north-east of Ladakh region, covers nearly 4000 sq.km in area between 34°-79′ and 33°-79′ east latitude and 78° and 79° north longitude[1] (Map 25.1).

In 2004, I was invited in an International Buddhist Conference, organised by Japanese Temple, Both Gaya. Here in the Japanese Temple I saw many beautiful paintings of Black necked cranes on the ceiling. From a Japanese scholar I asked:

"What is the significance of painting Black necked cranes here in this temple?"

"We treat Black necked as a angel or god's bird".

A Bhutanese scholar, who was sitting behind me, supported him and said:

"Black necked cranes have a sacred halo we called them 'Lhabja' the winter visitors from the Himalayan and Tibetan valleys are revered as harbingers of good fortune and prosperity."

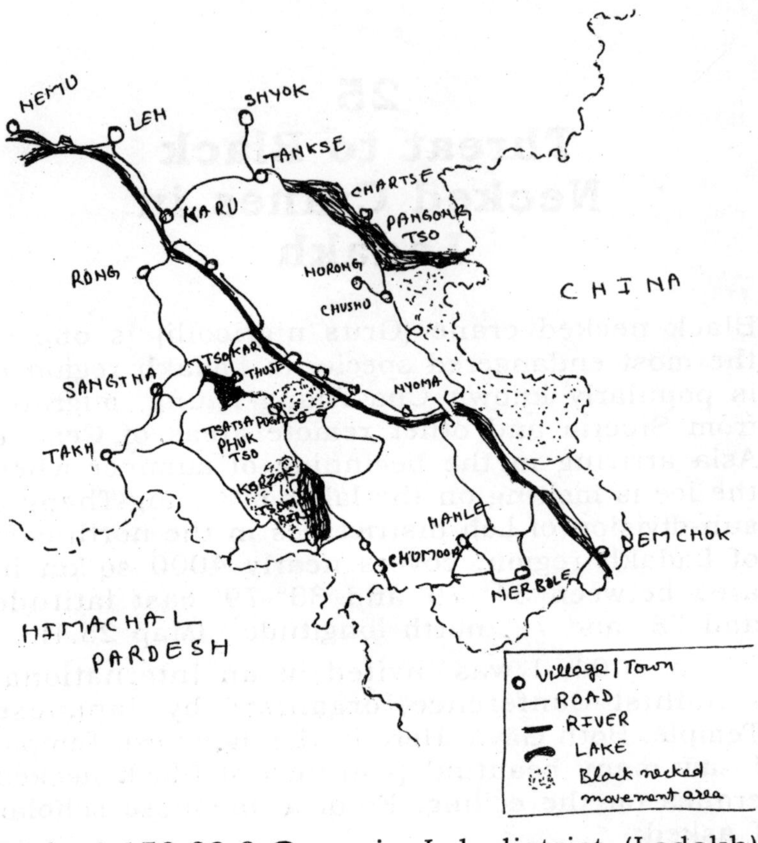

Scale 1:150,00,0 ⊕ in Leh-district (Ladakh)

Map 25.1: Black necked movement areas in Chang-Thang

In Bhutan, eastern and western parts of the valleys, local people profect the cranes not only as their religious duty but also in the hope that the winged guests would continue their annual sojourns. And happily for them, the birds have doing just that and in increasing numbers[2].

The world's black-necked crane population is just 3,000 and it is confined to a few spots in the Himalayas. In the recent study tour i.e. during 2004-2005, I have counted two or three breeding pairs in Chushul marshi land, the same numbers in Tsomoriri, and 5-6 non-breeding birds in Tso-kar and Henley areas of Chang-Thang region.

Mohd. Abass, Range Forest Officer in Leh, surprisingly saw a pair of Demoiselle crane (Anthropoides Virgo) in Chushot village, about 10 km. from Leh City, at an altitude of 3113 m on one evening in October 2003. According to him.

"He searched cranes feeding and roosting places and found them in Chushot village. At the morning they were busy feeding on grains on the agriculture field, were not very shy of human and biotic interference and were seen with local animals. He found that one of them was lingering a bit while walking. From its size, he assumed it male. Its left knee was later found to be swollen. He observed the cranes for seven days. At night they used the wet lands on the left side of the Indus River. During the day they were sighted in the agriculture fields, which had been harvested in August"[3].

It is a welcome sign if such new cranes as said Mohd. Abass. However, to protect such important species of crane we need to give good healthy environmental conditions specially we need to clean the marshi and wetlands along the Indus River banks as well as such lands of Shey village.

According to the Royal society for the Protection of Nature, there were about 175 cranes in Bhutan during 1992-93. Recent observations indicate that its numbers are rising in some parts of Bhutan, as Bhutanese loved cranes. Lam Dorje, Programme Officer RSPN says:

"The cranes have a special bond with local people in Bhutan[4]."

In Bhutan Buddhists have got reverence on these birds since early days to 1600, when a Buddhist monk spotted two cranes at the building site of a monastery. In fact the altars in Bhutanese monasteries are adorned with beautiful painting depicting scenes of cranes living in harmony with humans[5].

In Ladakh like Bhutan Ladakhis don't disturb the activities of black necked cranes. However, I have heard that during 1982-'85 some cranes were illegally killed by army personnel, but when Forest Department took action against them, such nonsense killing being stopped by army and paramilitary personnel.

Ladakhis, particularly Buddhists are non-violence in nature, they often see cranes are flying to Ladakh and before winters return to their home places. They were never awarded about their numbers and other related activities.

In olden days Ladakh was the popular trade centre, traders came here from far and wide. Some of them were very fond of crane eggs. They stayed here until winters started. Then they went to cranes, breeding places in Chang-Thang, when cranes flew back to their destination during winter, these traders searched their eggs from the banks of lakes, after the collection of their eggs they carried to Tibet and sold in Tibetan markets and sometimes they eat them on their way to Tibet. Now stray dogs reach their eggs and eat them. As a result crane population is not increasing.

Today foreign tourists flow to Tsomoriri lake during summer season receives about 1000 often in groups of 10-15. A small number may think, but enough to ruffle the sensitive avians.

The sight of these tourists dressed in bright colours and walking along the trek sometimes scares the birds. Not only this many of them go very close to these cranes and take snap with flashlights. Such activities disturb cranes. The situation may becomes serious when birdwatchers go close to roosting places and use flash cameras.

To sum up we should be well aware about the activities of black necked cranes and to do needful action. In this direction the following recommendations should be adopted.

Recommendations

1. Tourists should not be allowed to the roosting places of cranes.
2. They should not be allowed to park their taxes at the bank of Tsomoriri lake.
3. Strange and bright colour dress disturb cranes' behaviour, therefore, tourists are adviced not to wear such dress, while watching these cranes.
4. It will certainly help if there are signboards listing the do's and don't of crane watching. Such signboards are far more effective than verbal advice. If possible Wildlife Protection Department of J & K State Govt. build hideouts from where visitors can watch the cranes closely without unsettling them.
5. How nice it would be if cranes' roosting and feeding areas are protected. Besides, a Research and Nature Study Centre to be built with the local support for conservation effort.
6. Local people and tourists to be educated about the important of black necked cranes and the need to protect them.[5]

References

1. Kitchloo, A Nasier: ' Unifed Ecosystem Management Plan for the Chang-Thang wilderness areas Ladakh, August 1994 : 5.
2. Chang Soh Koon: 'Bhutan's black-necked cranes under threat' *Times of India,* September 2, 1993.
3. Mohd. Abass: 'A new crane comes to Ladakh', *Ladags Melong;* January-March 2005: 32.
4. Chng Soh Koon; *op. cit.*
5. *Ibid.*

Abbreviation

1. RSPN: Royal Society for the Protection of Nature, Non Governmental Organisation in Bhutan.

26
Politics in Kargil District of Ladakh

Hill Development Council to Kargil: When Ladakh Hill Development Council was declared to Leh district, the Kargil district Muslim dominated did not pay much attention. Possibly the leaders of this district thought to see the performance of Ladakh Autonomous Hill Development Council, Leh. Therefore, the development council for Kargil looked like a demand conceded. Thus the demand in this regards never raised, never passed. During 2003, J & K State Assembly passed a bill under which it had been rejected to grant the Kargil district a Hill Development Council. However, in June 2003, J&K State Government had decided to grant Hill Development Council to Kargil district as well as to announce election schedule for Councillors for constituting Hill council[1].

Criticism: To grant Hill Development Council to Kargil district as well as in the mean time to announce election for the same was seemed to be an hasty decision, and had the criticism the Govt. and ruling coalition faced in the house on the issue of granting more powers to Ladakh Antonomous Hill Development Council, Leh (L.A.H.D.C.- Leh). The criticisms came from the National Conference (N.C.) which had reduced the LAHDC to a District Development Board. Now the same extended powers would apply to the Kargil Council and that presumbly, would 'satisfy' the critics. Apart from the fact whether it actually would satisfy these critics, it raised a question of development and perceptions[2].

Religious Politics: In Jammu & Kashmir state it is well evident that during national conference regime, religious politics was booming very well. Kashmir valley was given maximum benefits. A Former Minister of the state actually decried the devolution of powers to the Ladakh council as 'Division' state. In practice, the powers are no more than a ministerial prerogative. The chairman of the LAHDC, who appeared to be of a cabinet minister, no more[3].

State Autonomy: The National Conference has been demanding an autonomy for the state which borders on secessionism. It wants even the jurisdiction of the Supreme Court and Election Commission curtailed in the State. Apparently, the implications of those recommendations for national unity and integrity have never crossed the minds those legislators and party. There, it become the 'Identity' and 'izzat' of people while the devolution of a few powers to a subordinate council exercises the members so much that they raise specters of division and dismemberment. This illigical thinking is a marvelous trait some politicians in this state have cultivated. They have also undone much in this state with those irrational streaks in their thoughts and acts. It is this thinking, not devolution, which may yet lead to a division of the state[4].

By Poll Election in Zanskar: The polling was held on 25th August 2005 and counting of votes was taken on August 31. In all, five candidates were in the fray for the Zanskar Assembly Constituency. However, an independent candidate Ghulam Mohammad, retired from the contest in favour of Ghulam Mohammad Raza. The National Conference candidate was Syed Abbas while the other two candidates were Mohammad Amin and Tsering Gyalpo,both independents. Mr. Raza had emerged as the consensus candidate.[5]

Voters Statistics: Zanskar Assembly constituency has 70 polling stations. It has 21,992 voters, including 11,603 female electors[6].

Mr. Raza an Influencial Leader : During election campaign Shia leader, Mr. Asghar Karbalai supported him. Mr. Abbas and Mr. Gylpo had only a few pockets of influence in the segment. Mufti Mohammad Sayeed and State Congress Persident Peerzada Mohammad Sayeed had jointly compaigned for Mr. Raza[7].

Mr. Raza won the Election: The move was seen as an effort by ruling Peoples Democratic Party (PDP) and Congress at present a combined front ahead of the change of guard in the state, so with their combined candidate Ghulam Mohammad Raza won the election by 3600 votes from his nearest contestant[8].

Conclusion

The ruling Congress and Peoples Democratic Party under the Chief Ministership of Ghulam Nabi Azad Ladakh Autonomous Hill Development Councils of Leh and Kargil will get sufficient funds for the economic development of the regions during right time. This time Ladakh Autonomous Hill Development Council, Leh has LUTF Government, but without any partial Leh district will get favourable financial help for the development projects like Kargil district.

References

1. *The Daily Excelsior*: Council for Kargil, 17 June 2003 : 6.
2. *Ibid.*
3. *Ibid.*
4. *Ibid.*
5. *Ibid.*
6. *The Daily Excelsior*: Compaigning ends for Zanskar by poll, August 24, 2005 : 3.
7. *Ibid.*
8. *Ibid.*

27

Ladakh Union Territory Front Makes

Clean Sweep and Clenched the Power

On the second week of August 2002, all the major parties from Leh district of Ladakh had joined Ladakh Union Territory Front. Before joining to LUTF M.P. Rev. Thiksey Rinpoche, Rev.Togdan Renpoche, Minister in the State Government and T. Namgyal, a member of State in the National Conference Govt. resigned from National Conference Party. Former Minister P. Namgyai of Congress also resigned from Congress Party and joined LUTF. Besides, Muslim Community of Leh district also favoured Union Territory Status to Ladakh, later Muslim Associations-Moin-ul-Islam and Immamia joined LUTF. Finally, LUTF conducted meeting in order to nominate candidates for M.L.A. seats from Leh and Nubra. Nawang Rigzin Jora and Pinto were consensus candidates for M.L.A. from Leh and Nubra Assembly seats. Subsequently both were elected unopposed from the above seats, at this movement Rigzin Jora said:

"All the political parties in Leh decided to disband their respective units and come on a common political platform by way of a new political party to put up a concerted fight and a struggle for obtaining U.T. status Ladakh. And this front has been named LUTF. Whenever required Ladakhis come together for Ladakh's common cause."[1]

Formation of Congress Party in Leh

Thupstan Chhewang, who headed LAHDC for about 09 years before switching over to the National politics being elected as Member of Parliament from 4-Ladakh Parliamentary Constituency, in last year's, i.e., 2004 election as an independent candidate the LUTF banner.

After being elected to Lok Sabha, Mr. Chhewang had resigned as LAHDC chairman. He was succeeded by Rigzin Spalbar. In summer 2005 when Thupstan Chhewang returned Leh after attending, the Parliamentary session, he found everything changed in Leh. All the councillors of Ladakh Autonomus Hill Development Council, Leh including Chief Executive Councillor, M.L.A. and Minister in State Union Cabinet Rigzin Jora joined Congress party. Tsering Samphal became the President of Congress Party at Leh unit. To know the above political changed in Leh, Thupstan Chewang stunned but didn't react, and followed the policy of 'to wait and watch the situation'.

Third Term Ladakh Autonomous Hill Development Council, Leh Election

This years on 16th October, 2005 the Third General Hill Council Election was held in Leh. The Congress, which ruled Ladakh Autonomous Hill Development Council, Leh for two terms had contested election with all councillors, the other party was LUTF. Congress party, was led by Nawang Rigzin Jora and Rigzin Spalbar, on the other side Thupstan Chhewang, Rev. Thiksey Rinpoche and Rev Togdan Renpoche led LUTF.

In this election Ladakh Union Territory swept to the Council Election by winning 24 seats out of 25 constituencies. In the 30 members Council, 26 Councillors are elected and rest are nominated. One seat which was declared elected uncontested.[2]

The Councillor seat of Chuchot has not been announced till 24 October 2005 due to some technical problem, later announced in favour of Congress.

In the third General Hill Council election 93,609 voters were eligible to elect 25 councillors and out of it 53,000 voters exercised their right to vote representing 57 per cent. Cent-percent polling was recorded at Skumpata, Ursi and Thugji Gonpa.[3]

Lower Leh constituency has the maximum number 13,772 votes, out of it 43 per cent of votes were polled. Thupstan Chhewang, who is also the Member of Parliament, contested for councillor and won the seat by defeating the sitting chief executive councillor Rigzin Spalbar by a margin of 2179 votes. Spalbar, who also contested from Kungyam constituency lost by securing 257 votes. Table: shows the details of winners.

Table 27.1

A List of Winning LUTF Candidates

Sl. No	*Name of Candidate*	*Name of Constituency*
1	*2*	*3*
1.	Mohd Khan	Turtuk
2.	Chering Tundoo	Hundar
3.	Chewang Rigzin	Disket
4.	Stangzin Delik	Tigar
5.	Chering Angchuck	Panamik
6.	Dorjey Stangzin	Tangtse
7.	Sonam Thering	Chushul
8.	Nawang Norboo	Nyoma
9.	Dorjey Mutook	Kungiam
10.	Chotar Tsering	Kurzok
11.	Geyal Wamgil	Sakti
12.	Tsering Paldan	Igoo
13.	Tundup Spalzang	Thiksey

(Contd.)

(contd.)

1	*2*	*3*
14	Tsering Dorje	Upper Leh
15.	Tsering Angdus	Saspol
16.	Dorje Numgyal	Temisgam
17.	Tsering Norbu	Khalsi
18.	Chewang Gompa	Lamayuru
19.	Phungsok Stangzin	Skrubuchan
20.	Tsering Angdu	Marchelong
21.	Tsering Tundook	Basgo
22.	Jigmet Namgyal	Phyang
23.	Thupstan Chhewang	Lower Leh
24.	Sonam Dorje	Lingshed
25.	Golh. Abbas Abidin	Chushod (Congress)

Later at a big gathering at polo-ground Leh, the winning candidates were welcomed by *Khadags*. Thousands of people were gathered to attend the oath function.

The function was among others addressed by chairman LUTF Tsering Dorje and the Member Parliament Thupstan Chhewang. Later LUTF has claimed to form council. Tsering Dorje was unanimously nominated chief executive councillor.

In conclusion I would say Leh Public had showed their faith on Thupstan Chhewang leadership, in the meanwhile they also alarmed their leaders to fight for Union Territory status to Ladakh.

References

1. LUTF makes clean sweep, Cong routed, *Daily Excelsior*, October 22, 2005, Vol. 44, pp. 1 and 4.
2. LUTF Sweeps to Power. The Kashmir Times, Vol. 62 ; October 23, 2005, pp. 1 and 4.
3. Jina Prem Singh: Ladakh Himalaya: Past and Present; Anmol Pub, New Delhi; 2006.

28
Togdan Rinpoche (Tib. rtogs ldan rin-po-che) The Head Lama of Drigung pa Order in Ladakh

Jigten Gonpo was the founder of Drigung pa order[1] a suborder of Kagyud-pa. He was the main disciple of Phakmotru-pa.[2] In 1179 Jigten Gonpo established Drigung monastery just 128 kms from Lhasa from which the sect took its name. Later Jigten Gonpo also known as Drigung Rinpoche[3]. Gradually Drigung pa order propagated throughout in Himalaya from Kumaon to Sikkim in India and Bhutan. At present His Holiness Che Chang Rinpoche the head of Drigung order, whereas in Ladakh Togdan Rinpoche is the head lama of all the monasteries in Ladakh. Here follows the details:

First Incarnation

In 1585, the first incarnation of Togdan Rinpoche was born in Tibet. At an early age he received consecration from Gyalvang rtan[4] and gave him name Togdan Phunchok Targyas[5].

Second Incarnation

Kong po od shod[6] was the second incarnation of Togdan Rinpoche was also born in Tibet. He received consecration from Dregung chos gyal Phunchok[7], who gave him new name Tashi Sonam[8]. Later he became the head of three Drigung monasteries of Kham region in Tibet.

Third Incarnation:

Lama Rinchen Wanchok[9] was the third incarnation was born in Tibet. Thereafter, he took admission in Nag shod chos kar yangspa monastery in Tibet[10]

Fourth Incarnation:

Stanzin Nangyal was born in Tibet. He was the fourth incarnation of Togdan Rinpoche, later became Khanpo of Dregong dan[11].

Fifth Incarnation:

Chos kyi lodos stanzin dadul[12] was the fifth incarnation. He received Buddhist Philosophy education under learned lamas of Tibet, later became good teacher, time and again preached lamas and public about Bhuddhism.

Sixth Incarnation:

Stanzin Chosdags, the sixth incarnation of Togdan Rinpoche. When he entered in Buddha Sangha, his name change Je Padam Gyaltsan[13] according to lama tradition. Later in 1770, he went to Naris[14] and became head lama of Sgang non monastery[15]. During king Tsewang Namgyal he visited Ladakh but soon returned to Tibet. Later became Khanpo of Gundan monastery.

Seventh Incarnation:

Nawang Gelegs[16] was born in Tibet. He was the seventh incarnation of Togdan Rinpoche, while entering in Buddha Sangha, he was given new name Skyabgan Chosnit Norbu[17]. He visited Ladakh and became Chosje of Sgang Gonpa[18].

Eighth Incarnation:

Konchok Stanzin[19], the eighth incarnation was born in Stok village[20]. He entered in Bhikshu Sangha in an early age and was given new name Skyabgon thugs je nima,[21] later became Chosje of sgong gonpa in Ladakh. He propagated Drigung pa order in Hanu, Darchik, Shara and Lamayuru areas of Ladakh.[22]

Present Incarnation: The present Togdan Rinpoche Thubstan Stanbe Gyaltsen was born in 1938 at Tangtse village in Chang-Thang region of Leh district in Ladakh. Father Tshultim and mother Lhadol decided to give him Buddhist philosophy education at an early age, therefore they sent him to monastery in Ladakh. He got education under the guidance of learned lamas in the monastery. At the age of 14 years he was sent to Tibet for higher education in Buddhist Philosophy. In 1960 he returned to Ladakh and preached Ladakhis about Buddhism. In 1972, he came in politics and contested Legislative Assembly election from Leh, but defeated from late Sonam Wangyal. However, in 1995 became M.L.C. and had became Minister in Dr. Farooq Abdullah State Govt. of National Conference. On August 2002 he resigned from the National Conference Party as well as from Dr. Farooq Abdullah Cabinet Ministry and joined newly formed LUTF party. This year in the Leh councillor's election he supported LUTF. Thus LUTF under his leadership sweep the election and won 24 seats out of 26 constituencies.

Notes and References

1. **Drigung pa order:** Tib. 'bri gung pa order. It is the suborder of the Kagyu-pa and was founded by 'Jig rten mgon po:

2. **Phakmotru-pa:** He was the founder of Phag mo gru pa suborder of Kagyu-pa. After earlier study with teacher of other orders including the Sakya-pa and the Kadam-pa, Phakmotru-pa came late in his own life to Gampo-pa and felt that only then he gained truly deep insight. In 1158, a few years after the death of Gampo pa, Phakmotru-pa founded the monastery of ***mthel*** as the head monastery of (Densa Thil) of his sect 96 km. southeast of Lhasa in the valley of the Yarlung

Tsangpo. At first the monastery consisted of only the grass hut in which Phakmotru-pa himself lived, surrounded by the huts of his followers. Later, however, with the support of a noble family named "Lang" the monastery became powerful and wealthy, and in memory of its origin and its founder the original hut of Phakumotru-pa was built into the chief monastery temple. Cf. Finegan, Jack: Tibet: A Dreamt of Image, Tibet House, New Delhi; 1986 : 95.

3. **Drigung Rinpoche:** 'Jigten Gonpo was the pupil of Phakmotru-pa. In 1179 he established his own monastery named Drigung, 128 km. northeast of Lhasa, from which the sect took its name and he himself known as Drigung Rinpoche. Cf. Finegan, Jack, *op. cit.*: 96.

4. **Gyalvang rtan :** Tib. Rgyal dbang rtan. He was a good scholar of Mahayana Buddhism.

5. **Togdan Phunchok Targyas:** Tib. rtogs ltan phum tshogs tar rgyas. According to monastic tradition any child/person when gets admission in the monastery, he gives new name with respective monastery.

6. **Kong po od shod:** Tib. Kong po 'aod shod.

7. **Dregung Chos Gyal Phunchok:** Tib. 'abri gung chos rgyal phun tshogs.

8. **Tashi Sonam:** Tib. bta shis bsod nams. This name was given under *gonpa* tradition.

9. **Rinchen Vanchok:** Tib. rin chen dbang phyug.

10. **Nag Shod Chos Kar Yangspa:** Tib. nag shod chos skar byam pa.

11. **Dregong dan:** Tib. 'abri gung gdan.

12. **Chos kyi lodus stanzin dadul:** Tib. Chos kyi blo gros bstan 'azin dgra 'adul.

13. **Je Padam Gyaltsan:** Tib. rji padam rgyal mtshen.

14. **Naris:** Tib. mng'a ris. It includes Guge, Zanskar, Ladakh as well as Purang areas.

15. **Nawang Gelegs:** He was the seventh incarnation of Togdan Ripoche and pronounce in Tibetan language as ***nrgag dbag dge legs***.

16. **Sgang-Non Monastery:** Tib.sgang sngon monastery.

17. **Skyabgon Chosnit Norbu:** Tib. Skyabs mgon chos nyit nor bu.

18. **Sgang Gonpa:** Tib. Sgang gonpa. This is one of the important Drigung Ka'gyud pa monastery in Ladakh.

19. **Konchok Stanzin:** Tib. dkon cog bstan 'azin.

20. **Stok Village:** (or Tok); Lat 34° 6′ Long, 77° 40′, Elev. 11, 228 ft.

This is a village situated about 6 km. from the left bank of the Indus River, opposite Leh. It was bestowed as a jagir upon the deposed gyalpo by Zorawar Singh in 1835, and is still held by his descendents Cf. Gazetteer of Kashmir and Ladakh First Pub. 1890; Reprinted in 1974 by Vivek Pub. House, Delhi, India : 825.

21. **Skyabgon Thugs je Nima:** Tib. skyabs mgon thugs rje nyima.

22. **Sonam Phuntsog**; Ladakh, 2000:67-68.

29

Nawang Cams Pa Stanzin (Tib. dga dbang byams pa bstan 'adzin): The Head Lama of Thiksey Monastery of Ladakh

Introduction

Thiksey Rinpoche belongs to Bilupa family[1], was born in 1943 at Chushot[2] village, near Leh[3]. His father Phunchog Paljor[4] and mother Tanpalzin[5] decided to give him primary education under the guidance of Skyabje Kushok Bakula[6]. Hence, he got initial education of Buddhist literature from him, later got Buddhist Philosophy education from Kachen Camspa Thubstan[7].

Higher Education in Tibet

In 1953, Thiksey Rinpoche went to Tibet for higher education in Buddhist Philosophy. He met Pan Chen Choskyi Vang Chuk[8] in Tashilhunpo monastery[9], then went to Draspung monastery[10] for further study. Here he met His Holiness Dalai Lama, who blessed him, later he returned to Draspung and continued his further study in Buddhist Philosophy under the guidance of Gandan Thipa Khanpo Nawang Nima, Yidjon Norbu[12] and Lama Labzang Zodpa.

China Invasion

In 1959 China attacked on Tibet. Thiksey Rin-po-che was at that time in Lhasa. Some Chinese troops reached very near to Lhasa, and opened fire. It is said that some bullets were passed through his Shantab.[13] Viewing the upset condition of Lhasa, one Lama requested him to return to Tashilhunpo monastery. Accordingly Rinpoche went to Tashilhunpo monastery. Here he studied Bhoti language and Grammar under the guidance of Kachen Lobzang Zotpa[14].

Return to Ladakh

In 1959, political situation in Tibet was worsed, Chinese army entered in all the big cities, they had destroyed Buddhist monasteries and within a short time took full control over Tibet. Therefore, viewing the turmoil situation, Rinpoche decided to return to Ladakh. At the Indo-China border important Ladakhi leaders and officers, popular among them were Kalon Phuk du and Tashi lhagya welcomed him. At Thiksey monastery, villagers and lamas of the monastery gave warm welcome. He didn't stay much in Thiksey and went to Nubra, where he gave preaching to public.

Rinpoche's Contribution:

The major contribution of Thiksey Rinpoche is to renovate/decorate temples in Thiksey monastery and to improve Buddhist monastic establishment. Here follows the details:

(1) **To Decorate Dukhang Karmo[15]:** This is the biggest Dukhang in Thiksey monastery has a capacity for about 1000 lamas, who at a time sit and offer prayers. Here, he directed to build thousand small Buddha statues during 1970. Besides, many important Buddhist wall paintings were made.

(2) **Nyung Nas Khang:** In 1981, he constructed Nyung Nas Khang. This temple has Avalokitesvara

and Bodhisattva statues. Rinpoche's teacher Kachen Lobzang Zotpa stayed here for long period.

(3) **Improvement in Thiksey Gonpa management society :** Thiksey Rinpoche got many complains that Gonpa management society of Thiksey monastery didn't supply food properly to lamas. In 1982, Rinpoche reconstruct the gonpa management, collected funds to meet the demands. He constructed dining hall and a kitchen just below the Cam-Khang.

(4) **Tree Plantation:** Thiksey monastery has barren fields. To take the proper use Thiksey Rinpoche asked his lamas to plant trees on these fields. Today Thiksey monastery gets fuel wood from there.

(5) **Chamba Statue[16]:** In 1978, Thiksey Rinpocha thought to make a huge statue of Chamba in the Thiksey monastery. He called Ladakhi Artist Nawang Tsering[17] and discussed how he could build a huge Chamba statue? Nawang Tsering replied:

"He could make a statue, but needs 40 feet high *Shug-pa* pole to support the statue."

"Its no problem, you go ahead now."

After sometime Thiksey Rinpoche went to Hanu Rong and met Lundup. He said:

"I need 40 feet high *Shug-pa* tree to make Chamba statue."

Lundup consulted his mother Gangzom and father Dondup in this regards. His parents felt happy to donate 40 feet high *Shug-pa* tree. Later Lundup returned to *Rinpoche* and said:

"We have no problem, you can cut any tree from here, some are more than 40 feet in height."

Later Thiksey lamas brought a 40 feet high *Shug-pa* pole to Thiksey monastery. In 1980, with the help of this pole Nawang Tsering made a 40 feet high clay statue of Chamba in Cham-Khang. On 27th July of the same year, His Holiness Dalai Lama inaugurated the statue, and performed rituals according to Geluk pa order of Mahayana.

Construction of Conference hall: In 1984 Thiksey Rinpoche constructed conference hall where lamas of the monastery gather and offer prayer.

Repairing Works: In 1985 Thiksey Rinpoche repaired eight Chortens below the Dukhang Karmo.

Political Career: In 1967 Thiksey Rinpoche contested election for M.L.A. from Leh Legislative Assembly constituency, he was defeated by Sonam Wangyal. In 1994, first councilors election took place for Ladakh Autonomous Hill Development Council, Leh. Thiksey contested from Thiksey constituency, but declared elected unoppose, later became Executive Councellor, but soon resigned. In 1999 he was nominated for Member of Parliament for Rajya Sabha from National Conference party. In 2002 LUTF party was formed in Leh, Thiksey Rinpoche resigned from M.P. (Rajya Sabha) as well as from the National Conference Party. On 16 October, 2005 IIIrd Concellors Election took place for Ladakh Autonomous Hill Development Council, Leh. He led LUTF, Party. Finally LUTF won 24 Councellors seats under his leadership out of 26 constituencies.

Religious Works: On 25th December in 1989, Thiksey Rinpoche started 'Sozong' tradition in the Dukang Karmo and encouraged Ladakhis to build Mani Dung cur in all Buddhist villages as well as on every inn.

In 1987 Rev. Kushok Bakula became Indian Ambassador to Mongolia, as a result he resigned from the Presidentship of Gonpa Association of Ladakh. Later Thiksey Rinpoche was appointed President of Ladakh Gonpa Association in his place. In 1991 alloted land to Thiksey monastery at Deskyitsal, Housing Colony, near Leh, likewise he helped to allot lands to other monasteries in Ladakh and encouraged religious activities in Leh, Ladakh[22]

Notes and References

1. **Bilu-pa Family:** Tib. sbi-lu- pa. It is the name of house of the concern family.

2. **Chushot:** Lat 34° 5′ Long 77° 35′ Elev. 10,500 feet. A large scattered village of over 600 houses, situated on the left bank of the Indus, opposite to, and 12 kms. from Leh. In olden days the Indus River was used to cross by a good wooden bridge, a double one. The smaller had a span of 30′ and the larger of 80′. Both were strongly made of popular spars laid touching each other. Now it has been replaced by Iron bridge.

3. **Leh:** Lat 34° 10′ Long 77° 37′ elev. 11,500′.

The district headquarter of Leh district is situated about 6 kms. from the right bank of Indus River. The Leh town lies about 1,000 feet above. The River, and occupies the slope, and surrounds the base of a low spur on the east side of the valley, Cf. Gazetteer of Kashmir and Ladakh; First Pub. 1890; Reprinted in 1974 by Vivek Pub. Delhi: 582.

4. **Phunchog Paljor** : Tib. Phun tshogs dpal 'abyor, he was the father of Thiksey Rinpoche, but soon died after the birth of Thiksey Rinpoche.

5. **Tanpalzin:** Tib. brtan dpal 'adzin she was the mother of Thiksey rinpoche, but unfortunately she also died after the birth of Thiksey Rinpoche.

6. **Skyabje Kushok Bakula:** His Holiness Bakula Rinpoche was born on the 15th day of the fourth Tibetan month in the royal palace of Matho village. His father was Nangwa Thaye and Mother

was Yeshey Wangmo. He received the Highest Degree of Buddhist Philosophy 'Geshe Lharampa' in 1940 from Tibet. He devoted his whole life for the welfare of Ladakhis and was awarded Padma Bhushan in 1988 by the Indian Government and the Government of Mangolia conferred on him the award of Polar Star.

7. **Kachen Camspha Thubstan:** Tib. dk'a chen byams pa thub hstan. He was the scholar of Buddhist Literature and Philosophy.

8. **Pan Chen Choskyi Vang Chak:** Tib. Pan chen chos kyi vang chok, he was the great Buddhist scholar in Tibet and resided in Tashilhunpo monastery.

9. **Tashilhumpo monastery:** Tib. bkra shi lhun bu monastery. This monastery was founded in 1447 by Genduntrup, Trongkha's nephew and disciple. He was the first lama to become his disciple. Later the Fifth Dalai Lama conferred upon his former teacher the abbot of the monastery, Lopsang Chokyi Gyentsen the title of Panchen, thus inaugurating the series of Panchen Lamas, for all of whom Tashilhunpo remained the official residence. Cf. Finegan, Jack: Tibet : A Dreamt of Image, Tibet House, New Delhi, 1986 : 154.

10. **Draspung monastery:** Tib. 'abras sbungs monastery, is 10 km. west of Lhasa. The valley is framed by mountains on three sides. This monastery was founded in 1416 by a personal disciple of Tsongkhapa known 'Jam dbyangs, served as the first abbot of he nonastery, and got perinirvana in 1449 at the age of 72 years. Cf. Finegan, Jack; *op. cit.*: 150.

11. **Khanpo Nawnag Nima:** Tib. mkhan po ngag dhang nyima. He was a great scholar of Buddhist Philosophy.

12. **Yidjin Norbu**: Tib yid bzhin nor bu. He also had good knowledge of Buddhist Philosophy.

13. **Shantab:** This is a part of lama dress which lama/nun/Rinpoche wears below belly like *peticote.*

14. **Kachen Lebzang Zotpo**: He was the teacher of Thiksey Rinpoche, came to Ladakh.

15. **Dukhang Karmo:** This is probably the oldest building in Thiksey monastery and was built in 1459. In the construction of this Dukhang Choje (Tib. Chos je) Jamyang Rinchen made his especial attention. This Dukhang has two big statues of Mitukpa and Maitreya of about 12 feet in height. Besides one big Chang chub chorten is placed in the middle of Dukhang. In glass almirah we can see 1000 Buddha statues each of 6' in height. The inside walls of this Dukhang is beautifully decorated by wall paintings of Buddhist deities, Bodhisattvas and Dolmas viz. Buddha, Je Tsongkhapa, Manjusri, Lhuvang gyi gyal po, Cho Atisa, Padmasambhava white Tara, Namgyal ma, Chepakmet, Dorje Sempa, Dukar, Chos je Jamyang, Chos je Jamyang Rinchen, Chagdor, Gonpo chag zee. Gonpo Peng, Milarepa, Pha bong kha lama, Khen Rinpoche, Gyava Singhe Naro, Chenrazik, Cang Sems shes rab zampo, Pon Palden, Medician Buddha, Opakmed, Chagdor Palden lhamo etc.

16. **Chamba Statue:** Tib. byams ba, Maitreya or future Buddha. He can be shown seated either in his full lotus posture or with his legs extended down to the floor. He may also be recognised by a white or golden stupa in his hair, while paintings he is flanked by his two chief disciples Avalokitesvara and Manjusri on his right and left respectively. Cf. Batchelor, Stephen: The Tibet Guide, Wisdom Pub., London, 1987 : 387.

17. **Nawang Tsering**: He was the master craft man at Central Institute of Buddhist Studies, Choglamsar, Leh-Ladakh, retired from the said post in 2005.

18. **Hanu Rong**: Tib. Ha nu rong. It is a village in Shyam side beyond kha-la-tse.

19. **Gangzom:** Tib. Gang 'adzom, mother of Lundup.

20. **Dondup:** Tib. Don grub, father of Lundup.

21. On August 2002, all political leaders in Leh district decided to float Ladakh Union Territory Front (LUTF) Party. Accordingly Ladakh political leaders from different political parties viz. National Congress, National Conference etc. Among popular leaders who joined LUTF party were Thiksey Rinpoche, Togdan Rinpoche, T. Namgyal, P. Namgyal, Rigzin Zora, Thupstan Chhewang etc.

27. **Sonam Phuntsog: 'Ladakh', 2000 : 55.**

Abbreviation: LUTF - Ladakh Union Territory Front.

LAHDC : Ladakh Autonomous Hill Development Council.

30

Tagtsang Rinpoche : A Great Siddha

The first Tagtsang Rinpoche was born in Tibet at Pot Gyalsa in 1574. It is said that when Tagtsang Rinpoche was about to take birth, his father Gonbo Tsering acknowledged many miracle powers. After sometimes local priest named him Tsewang Dondup. Gradually when he grew up his attention became deepen towards religion, like other children Dondup didn't like playing and extra curriculum activities. Whenever any monk visited to his house his heart felt pitty and ready something to give him[1].

At the age of 6 years Tsewang Dondup went to see a scholar Lama. The Lama later asked him:

"To whom are you taking education? How many vinaya rules do you follow? etc."

Baby Tsewang Dondup gave the answers wisely, by which lama got satisfaction.

At the age of seven years, Tsewang Dondup had perfect knowledge of Tibetan alphabets, he started to write letters to his kith and kin. Every thing was going smooth, but misfortune never comes alone his father fell seriously ill, he called Tsewang Dondup, and said:

"My son ! now I want to die, after my death Sakya tradition will also come to an end, therefore, I feel very sad. Oh yes! If you want, this tradition can be saved."

After the death of his father Tsewang Dondup didn't bother much and continued his education with full interest. But when he was 14 years old, suffered by boil. He was taken local deity called **Lhamo** for treatment. **Lhamo** told:

"You were born in Sakya cult, but didn't follow the vinaya rules according to Sakya, so you have to follow this tradition you can get relief from boil pain."

Tswang Dondup said:

"I don't know what are you saying? However, I tell you that till my mother is alive, I will do whatever my mother wants, after her death I will follow tradition of my own."

At the age of 20 years Tsewang Dondup completed his education, he later earned some money and went to meet Lha Tsewang Nawang Zangpo. He said:

"Guruji ! I want to achieve Buddhahood in one life, therefore, kindly give such power through which I can fulfil my desires."

"I understand you are sincere, therefore, I call you Sarkha Raschen." Lha Tsewang Nawang Zangpo said.

Later he got admission in the Lha Tsewang Nawang Zangpo's monastery. He studied there for three years, thereafter went to Dup Cang cupling and R-ding for further studies. In Staglung he studied Naro Cang-Cung and Lo-zong under the guidance of Pon Rinpoche.[2]

Tsewang Dondup after finishing his education from the above monastery returned to home. He was in simple dress, hence his relatives did not recognise him, when he introduced himself all of them felt sorry and started weeping. His mother said:

"My son ! I also couldn't recognise you."

"I was very happy in the monastery; see, how healthy ! am I like a lion ?"

After staying sometimes at home he returned to monastery. His teacher then advised him to go to Tagtsang Rong Dung for meditation. Initially Tsewang Dondup got many problems as evil spirits disturbed him for meditation. However, when Tsewang Dondup didn't get much effect and continued meditation; the evil spirits surrendered. The cave in which Tsewang Dondup was meditating from the distance looked like Lion's shape, he meditated in this cave for one year, thereafter became popular Tagtsang Raspa by virtue of cave.

Now Tagtsang Raspa went to China via Chagling and Zangpo. Here he stayed in *Photang* which looked like human hand. It was Kundu Zangpo's *Photang*. In China Tagtsang Raspa saw many religious places, thus got peace. Kundu Zangpo later said him:

"You are very brave, industrious, therefore you should go to see stog- cog, Cuniyan zalhara, Khatse Thistang, Puspahari, Ogyan, etc."

In 1612 Tagtsang Raspa went to Mount Kailash for meditation. In those days Kashmir had a few Buddhist scholars, therefore, he decided to visit Kashmir along with his four disciples. In Srinagar he visited Naropa's cave Puspahari. But unable to meet Buddhist scholars there, so returned to Zanskar. In Kashmir his three disciples fell ill and could not accompanied him in his further journey. After 25 days journey Tagtsan Raspa arrived in Zanskar. In Zanskar on the request of Lama Devang gyatso, he stayed one month in Bardan monastery. During his stay in Bardan he went for meditation and by virtue of his power all the evil spirits stopped their willful activities, thus helped in the development of monastic discipline in and outside the Bardan monastery. Later went to Zonkhul for meditation in Dupchen Naropa's cave. Here he meditated for two months[3].

When king of Ladakh Jamyang Namgyal came to know about Tagtsang Raspa, he sent his messenger with the message to visit Leh. By refusing King's request Tagtsang Raspa said:

"I will not go to Leh (Ladakh), even king of Ladakh requested. My present aim is to visit Ogyan. I may visit there afterwards."

In 1614, he arrived Garja. Tsering Palde was the king of Garja. He stayed there with him for one year, then via Srinagar went to Ogyan. After travelling 12 days towards the west of Srinagar, he arrived at the bank of Sindhu River. Here he took rest for sometime, later marched further to a village. To see him villagers asked:

"Are you Kashmiri?"

"No, I am Tibetan."

Villagers didn't inquire further, Tagtsang Raspa then travelled to Ogyan.

Near Ogyan he crossed a local river, Ogyan inhabitants saw him and surprised:

"Look ! A yogi Shambhunath has come here."

After sometime Ogyan inhabitants became friendly with him. Tagtsang Raspa according to his plan visited all the nearby Buddhist sites. Popular among them were Herukha Cuglakhang, Choling etc. Then returned to Srinagar, and once again visited Puspahari. He made Mandala and stayed here for seven days. Subsequently returned to Zanskar via Kistwar.

In Zanskar Tagtsang Raspa got the massage that Ladakh king Jamyang Namgyal died, queen Tsering Wangmo and prince Nawang Namgyal were staying in Shey palace; another queen Gyal Khatoon and prince Singhe Namgyal were staying in Bargo Palace. Later Prince Sighe Namgyal became the king of Ladakh. Now Tagtsang Raspa remembered his promise to meet Ladakh King, accordingly decided to visit Leh to meet the king of Ladakh[4].

Tagtsang Raspa from Zanskar arrived at Alchi. He saw Alchi Choskor, then came to Basgo. At Basgo palace he was given warm welcome by King Singhe Namgyal queen Gyal Khatoon and other important dignitories. He stayed a few days in Basgo then with his disciple Dukpa Shesrab arrived Gya village. Here he meditated a few months thence came to Hemis. In both the places he spent four years in meditation. Thereafter went to Karche. In this way after visiting important Buddhist places, at the age of about 47 years decided to return to Tibet. In Tibet on the request of Baksam Wangmo he had written a book on his journey to Ogyan. Thereafter, he visited Kailash Mansarovar. In the mean time he was invited by the people of Guge. On their request he constructed Cangchub Chorten in front of the Somopham lake, and three *Lhatos* of Padmasambhava near to mountain. In the mean while he got the invitation of Ladakh king Singhe Namgyal[5].

In 1621, Tagtsang Raspa came to Ti-sar with his ten disciple. He welcomed by Chos-je Mud-zin. Later Tagtsang Raspa stayed for sometime in Ti -sar. When he remembered[6] Ladakh King Singhe Namgyal's invitation he decided to go to Ladakh.

In the same year Tagtsang Raspa arrived Ladakh border at Nyoma. King Singhe Namgyal sent his ministers and other important men to welcome him. By the time Tagtsang Raspa reached at Marshelang. Therefore, welcomed them at Marshelang. This time Tagtsang Raspa didn't meet king Singhe Namgyal and instead to visit Leh, he went to Go-chang for meditation. After sometime King Singhe Namgyal came to Go-chang to see him, later he requested:

"Guruji Pranam ! My father king Jamyang Namgyal is no more. Therefore, kindly let me know, what should I do to give peace to his soul?"

"It is very sad ! However, if you make Chamba statue in memory his soul will get peace."

In 1622 King Singhe Namgyal gave order to his artists to make a big Chamba Statue. On 15th of the 9th month in1623 Tagtsang Raspa performed Rabnas prayer. On this occasion 100 lamas, 1000 high ranked officials, 80 Artists and 1200 villagers attended the function. It is said that Queen Gyal Khatun offered 3-5 kg. gold and other precious things, which later placed inside the statue[7].

Tagtsang Raspa's contribution for flourishing the Drugpa Ka'gyud order in Ladakh

Vamle Gonpa: After the completion of meditation in Igoo-chang cave above the present Hemis monastery, Tagtsang Raspa decided to progagate Durgpa Ka'gyaud order of Buddhism in Ladakh. In this connection he started construction works for a monastery at Vamle. Thereafter in the following two years, he fully devoted himself for the installation of Mani-Tùng-Chur and built 4 Dung-churs[8].

Hemis monastery : This monastery was built by Tagsang Raspa in association with King Singhe Namgyal. It took three years in the completion. Tagtsang Raspa became well known throughout in Ladakh, therefore just after the completion of monastery building 50 lamas and 100 Dup-pa were attached with this[9].

Renovation of Ce-thir Monastery: In 1644 Tagtsang Raspa arrived Ce-thir. To see the poor condition of the monastery, he directed to the concern authorities to renovate it, for this works he gave his full support[10].

Shey Tshugla - Khang : In 1647, queen Kalzang Dolma and King Deldan Namgyal met Tagtsang Raspa. He blessed them. Later advised king to construct Tshugla-Khang at Shey palace, king did the same[11].

Death of Singhe Namgyal: In 1642, Gusri Khan defeated, the Tsang ruler was killed and Fifth Dalai Lama became the religious head of the country. In the meantime Ladakh forces crossed Mayum pass and reached near Sakya monastery. However, defeated by Tsang forces, but had full possession of all Tibetan territory west of the Mayum pass. As Ladakhi forces under the direction of King Singhe Namgyal were fighting far away from their base of operation could not get proper logistic support. As a result King Singhe Namgyal fell ill, thus returned to Hnale and on 22th of 9th month in 1642 he died here[12].

Meditation of Cakrasamvara: After the death of King Singhe Namgyal Tagtsang Raspa went to Shey Palace and practiced Cakrasamvara meditation for six months. Thereafter on the request of queen Tsering, prince Nawang Namgyal became lama by the blesssing of Tagtsang Raspa and before admitting him in Hemis monastery he was re-named Jamling Tragpa according to the monastic tradition[13].

Go-chang (Tib. Go-tashang) Temple: Go-chang Temple is a few kms. above to the present establishment of Hemis monastery. In 1630, Tagtsang Raspa built main communal hall (Tib. tshogs khang Pron. tschokhang) in Go-Chang. This temple was built well before the normal time period as it has one long cave, therefore after using a few construction materials it was built easily.

To put Thiksey Monastery under the control of Drug-pa Ka'gyud order: Thiksey monastery is one of the big establishment of Geluk-pa order. King Singhe Namgyal had strong faith on Tagtsang Raspa as well upon Drugpa order. Therefore, requested:

"Guruji ! Thiksey monastery is a big monastic establishment of Geluk-pa order in Ladakh. In order to spread Drug-pa order in Ladakh, you should take your control over Thiksey monastery."

"Maharaj ! we should pay our full regard to Sakya, Geluk, Nyingma etc. order. These all are the pillars of Buddhism. To convert one tradition into another is sin, we should keep ourself away from such thinkings."

Thus, on the advise of Tagtsang Raspa, King Singhe Namgyal didn't convert the tradition of Thiksey monastery to Drug-pa order.

Death of Queen Kalzang Dolma: In 1950 King Deldan Namgyal met Tagtsang Raspa and requested:

"Guruji pranam ! Kindly give a name to my son."

"Your son's name will be Delegs Namgyal."

"Guruji ! Queen Kalzang Dolma wants to visit Kailash Mountain. Should I allow her?"

"No, this is not a right time."

Later against the Tagtsang Raspa's advise queen Kalzang Dolma went to Zanskar, unfortunately due to sever fever she did not return and died there in a Zanskari house[15].

Parinirvana of Tagtsang Raspa : In Hemis monastery, by the inspiration of Tagtsang Raspa, lama population increased considerably. When he was 80 years old he directed to make Padma Karpo statue. On this occasion he said to his assistant:

"My age is now more than eighty years, I may get Parinirvana at any time, therefore, all of you should understand your duties clearly."

In 1650 Tagtsang Raspa was not feeling well, he stopped to take part in all his religious activities. thereafter in 1651 he got Parinirvana[16].

Second Incarnation: In 1653 Choskye Dorje was born in Karja. After formal ritual ceremony he was declared the incarnation of Tagtsang Raspa. It is said when Mongol Army attacked Ladakh in 1676 he was in Zanskar. He got Parinirvana in 1716[17].

Third Incarnation: He was born in 1720. King Deskyong Namgyal of Ladakh was his father and queen Nilza-Wangmo was mother, and named him Sarkyong Namgyal. When he was about 4 or 5 years old king Deskyong Namgyal sent him to Hemis monastery. After admission in the monastery his name according to the monastic system changed into Mipham Tsewang Stanzin. He was not given any exemption in the monastery, like other monks he had to follow all monastic rules and regulations. He worked in the monastery from Gyalingpa upto Lopon. Finally, he was offered the throne of Tagtsang Raspa. Gelong Norbu was then the chagzot in the monastery. After sometimes Mipham Tsewang Stanzin, the second incarnation of Tagshang Rinpoche visited Tibet for higher studies. In Tibet he studied under 7th Dukchen Rinpoche Jangsal Pavo. In 1770 he returned to Ladakh. He brought many stupas and Thankas from Tibet. These were purified by the Dukchen Rinpoche. Thereafter, under the direction of second Tagshang Rinpoche; Gelong Tukpa Thinlas Katok Rigzin Tsewang and Norbu made strict Vinaya rules in the Hemis monastery and still followed in the monastery[19].

Inscription in the Temple of Hemis Monastery: There is a yellow temple in the Hemis monastery in which we can see the Tibetan inscription, and translated in the following way: Rigzin Tsewang Norbu is not a Amchi of Ladakh (On the request of public that they need one qualified Amchi Doctor for their patients) king Tsewang Namgyal ordered his Minister Tsewang Tondup to sent his son to Tibet for Amchi education. He accordingly sent his son to Tibet, who studied

Amchi system under the guidance of scholar Lama Nima. Later he had written a latter to his father Tsewang Tondup which is still preserved in Hemis monastery[20].

A Huge Padmasambhava Thanka: It is said that Panchen Paldan Ishes was a rich person in Ladakh. Later on his request Geshes Rinpoche had sent silk cloth from Tibet to Ladakh. Tashi Norbu was then the Chagzot of Hemis monastery and directed Jopale to make a big thanka of Padmasambhava by silk cloth. Later he made 5 storeyed huge thanka of Syantuk Padmasambhava. This is a unique piece of Buddhist painting and was made by precious stones and pearls. After sometime he made another thanka of Pehar Gyalpo. In 1798 a new Dukhang was constructed in the monastery. With the kind blessing of Tagtsang Raspa, the third incarnation Hemis Tse-chu and Chemde Angchok annual festivals were organised by the Hemis and Chemde monasteries respectively[21].

Fourth and Fifth Incarnation: The fourth incarnation of Tagtsang Raspa was born in Marshelang in Ladakh, did not last long. Later in 1870 Fifth incarnation Nawang Zampal was born. He was a good Buddhist scholar, written books and in Go-tshang practiced meditation for 12 years. Later he repaired many temples in Hemis monastery[22].

Present Tagtsan Raspa: Rev. Choskyi Nima is the present incarnation of Tagtsang Raspa. He was born in Tibet. In 1956 in his short trip in India he came Ladakh for the first time, second time he visited Ladakh in 1986 and preached Ladakhis later returned to Tibet[23].

Notes and References

1. Jamyang Gyaltsan (ed.) : The History of Ladakh Monasteries, Pub. by All Ladakh Gonpa Society, Leh-Ladakh ; 1995: 135-148.

2. *Ibid.*
3. *Ibid.*
4. *Ibid.*
5. *Ibid.*
6. *Ibid.*
7. *Ibid.*
8. *Ibid.*
9. *Ibid.*
10. *Ibid.*
11. *Ibid.*
12. *Ibid.*
13. *Ibid.*
14. *Ibid.*
15. *Ibid.*
16. *Ibid.*
17. *Ibid.*
18. *Ibid.*
19. Sonam Phuntog: 'Ladakh', 2000.
20. *Ibid.*
21. *Ibid.*
22. *Ibid.*
23. *Ibid.*

31

Sonam Norbu : First Ladakhi Who Conferred Padma Award

Introduction

Sonam Norbu was born on 27th May 1909, near Leh town at Skara village. He belonged to Nya Cu Khangpar family. Both his father Sonam Wangdus and mother Pal-don were simple persons[1].

Education: In those days education standard in Ladakh was very poor, and seriously handicapped by its geo-political situation. Ladakhis were hardly aware by education and instead to send their children to Government school, they would prefer to donate them to monasteries. Moreover, Jammu and Kashmir Government made some efforts to improve the standard of Government schools. Teachers were allowed to teach in Buddhi and Urdu medium. English language was taken as optional subject. As a result 17 per cent of the total students in Leh got admission in Govt. Schools. (Table 13.1).

Sonam Norbu was an intelligent student, therefore without bothering the poor educational standard in Leh he took admission in Leh Govt. Junior High School. In 1972, passed Junior High School. As there was no High School in Leh Tehsil, he felt sorry and met Tagtsang Raspa, expressed his feeling :

"Guruji" I have passed Junior High School. I want to study more, but don't know, how could I continue my studies?"

"You have bright future, you should continue your education and take admission in any good school in Srinagar."

Sonam Norbu felt happy and by the blessing of Tagtsang Raspa, the head Lama and Rinpoche of Hemis monastery of Ladakh; decided to go to Srinagar for higher studies. In this connection Lacumir Tsewang also gave him moral support[2].

Higher Studies: Sonam Norbu, now had confidence and went to Srinagar, later after some efforts he got admission in High School. In 1929, he passed High School from Srinagar and went Jammu for further studies. He took admission in Jammu University and performed very well. Tagtsang Raspa became very happy for his performance and awarded Rs 500/-. In the meanwhile he got selection for Engineering course in London. In 1942, passed Engineering degree from Sheffield University, London, U.K.[3].

Appointed Engineer in J & K Govt. : After passing Engineering Degree from Sheffield University, Sonam Norbu returned to Jammu. Hari Singh was then King of Jammu & Kashmir Riyashad. As soon as king came to know about the brilliant performance of Sonam Narbu, he immediately appointed him as a Civil Engineer and deputed him to construct Srinagar and Rawalpindi road.[4]

Married Life: In 1942, Sonam Norbu got job in Jammu & Kashmir Riyashad. In Ladakh his relatives were engaged to search a good girl for marriage. Finally in the same year he got married with Yancan Palzes. From her he got two daughters and a son. Later his elder daughter Deskyit Vangmo married with Kalon's son at Leh and son Sonam Wangchok became Minister in Jammu & Kashmir Government for some times.[5]

Pakistani Kabali Rebels Attack: In 1948, Pakistani Kabali rebels attacked India. They occupied Skardu and entered further in Indian territory upto Kashmir and in Ladakh near Leh. Col. Prithivi Chand and Sonam Norbu together made strategy to defend Ladakh. Sonam Norbu himself took the responsibility to construct airstrip at Leh, so that Indian Army could land in Leh. Col. Prithivi Chand made plan to attack Pakistani rebels from different directions. Construction works for Leh Airport was started at war level. Finally Airstrip at Leh was ready for Air Force plane landing within a record time of 3 weeks in 1948.

Road Construction Between Sonamarg and Leh: In 1958, Jammu & Kashmir Government gave a responsibility to Sonam Norbu to construct Sonamarg to Leh, 340 kms. motor road. It was a uphill task, but under the skillfull guidance of Sonam Narbu who was promoted as Superintendent Engineer completed the road construction work with in a year i.e., by 1959 the road was ready for traffic. As a result of this remarkable work, he was awarded Padma Shri. Thereafter, he was appointed Deputy Commissioner of Ladakh and worked on this post from 1965 to till 1967[6].

Diplomatic Assignment in Mongolia : He was the first Ladakhi to get diplomatic Assignment as Indian charged' affairs in Mongolia in 1967, later became Ambassador to Mongolia[7].

Minister in Jammu & Kashmir Govt.: He was the first Ladakhis to become Minister with Cabinet rank in the State Government as a Minister for Ladakh Affairs in 1975. Subsequently in 1977, became P.W.D. Minister[8].

Conclusion: Sonam Norbu was a great Engineer. He was responsible to build many roads, bridges and buildings. Thus by doing so he did remarkable job in the infrastructural development of Ladakh. Finally he was recognised as a Ladakh builder and died in 1980.

Table : 31.1

The number of students in Ladakh Govt. School during 1900 A.D.

Sl.No.	Name of region	No. of student	% of the total
1.	Kargil	48	58.5
2.	Skardu	20	4.4
3.	Leh	14	17.1
	Ladakh	82	100.00

Source: Compiled from Census India and Gazetteer of Kashmir and Ladakh, Vivek Pub., 1974.

Glossary

1. Skara : Tib. ska - ra, a village near Leh.
2. nga cu khang par: Tib. nya cu khang par.
3. Sonam Vangdus: Tib. bsod nams dbang 'adus.
4. Paldon : Tib. dpal sgron.
5. Tagtsan Raspa: Tib stag tshang ras pa
6. Hari Singh: Tib. Hari Sing, Maharaja of Jammu & Kashmir Riyashad.
7. Yancan Palzes: Tib. dbangs can dpal mdzes.
8. Diskyit Vangmo: Tib. bde skyid dbang mo.
9. Kalon : Tib bk'a blon ; Prime Minister in king regime.
10. Sonam Wangchok : Tib. bsod nams dbang phyug.

Notes and References

1. Sonam Phuntsog : 'Ladakh' 2000 : 80.
2. *Ibid.*
3. *Ibid.*
4. *Ibid.*
5. *Ibid.*
6. *Ibid.*
7. *Ibid.*
8. *Ibid.*

32

Lama Cang Sems Shesrab Zangpo: The Founder of Thiksey Monastery of Ladakh

Introduction

Lama Cang Sems Shesrab Zangpo[1] was a great Buddhist scholar of Thiksey village. He was born in 1380. In his early age he became lama and got primary education of Buddhism in the nearby monastery under the guidance of lamas. Later on, the advice of Father Tashi[2] and mother Palzon[3] he was sent to Tibet for Higher education on Buddhism and Philosophy. In Tibet he met Je-Tsong-Kha and later became his disciple. Under his guidance he learnt Buddhist Philosophy and Tantra. When Lama Cang Sems Shesrab Zangpo completed his education in Tibet, returned to Ladakh on the advice of his Guru Tsong-Khapa[4] for the propagation of Geluk-pa order.

To Propagate Geluk pa order in Ladakh: In Ladakh Lama Cang Sems Shesrab Zangpo first met king Dragpa Bumde, but could not get suitable respect by the king, therefore went to Nubra with his assistant as to know that king's brother Dragpa Bum was there; possibly with his recommendation king of Ladakh would help him in the propagation of Geluk-pa order in Ladakh.

In Nubra, Lama Cang Sems Shesrab Zangpo and his assistant met Dragpa Bum, who warmly welcomed them. Later Lama Cang Sems Shesrab Zangpo expressed his views before Dragpa Bum that:

"Maharaj! by the blessing of Tsong-Khapa, the founder of Geluk-pa order and my teacher decided to propagate his sect at the banks of Indus River or in Ladakh. In this connection I met king Dragpa Bumde, but he didn't pay much attention on my talks, therefore I alongwith my assistant came out from his palace. I don't know how I could fulfil the desires of my Guru? If possible please help me."

Dragpa Bum listened him carefully and after thinking a few minutes replied:

"You should meet him once again, my brother is a kind hearted man, he must failed to understand you, or you were unable to present the desires of your teacher in a proper way or he would be upset when you met him. Therefore, I advice you to first present the Amitayus statue, thereafter tell him the details why have you visited Ladakh? And so on so for."

Lama Gang Sems Shesrab Zangpo understand the situation and departured to Shey palace. This time he very well brief the gatekeeper, who accordingly informed in details about the purpose of meeting of Lama Cang Sems Shesrab Zangpo. King Dragpa Bumde listened all patiently, later allowed Cang Sems Shesrab Zangpo and warmly welcomed him and his attendent at the palace. After presenting the Amitayas statue to king Bumde, Lama Cang Sems said:

"Maharaj! This precious statue is miraculously made by the blood of Tsogkhapa, who later gave it to me to present you."

"Thank you very much. How nice it would be, if you will stay in Ladakh, construct gonpa anywhere in Ladakh, help human being. In this regards whatever help from my side will be required please don't hesitate, I will endeavour to provide you."

Lama Cang Sems Shesrab Zangpo thanked king Dragpa Bumde for his kind co-operation, later along with his assistant came out from the palace and went towards Tagmo village[5] in search of proper place for the construction of monastery. He took night halt at Tagmo village. At the next day morning after prayer he "along with his assistant went towards the village site, near a hillock of the village he took a sample of soil, by ritual performance tested it, and said:

"After the examination of soil, I feel Tagmo village is suitable for the monastery."

"As you wish guruji."

Therefore, with the kind co-operation of King Dragspa Bumde and villagers Lama Cang Sems Shesrab Zangpo constructed a temple at Tagmo village. He and his assistant stayed there for a few years then went to Nubra valley and founded Diskyit[6] and Inja[7] monasteries.

The role of Tashi Od de: Tashi Ode[8] was the king of Guge[9]. As soon he came to know about the religious activities of Lama Cang Sems Shesrab Zangpo in Ladakh, he felt very happy, called his two sons at his palace and said:

"Dear sons, do you know about Lama Cang Sems Shesrab Zangpo?

"No."

"Then listen carefully, Lama Cang Sems Shesrab Zangpa is a disciple of Tsongkhapa, at present he is in Ladakh and according to the desires of his great teacher Tsongkhapa, propagating his sect in Ladakh. Therefore, my dear sons you may also help him in spreading Buddhism."

"As you wish father."

Later with the permission of Od de his both sons became lamas and came in Zanskar. They met King Rinchen Palde[10] and queen Zompas[11]; subsequently requested:

"Maharaj! We came here to propagate Buddhism, if your Highness give us support we would like to establish Buddhist monastery in Zanskar."

"We are pleased to know your feeling, you are allowed to build monastery anywhere in Zanskar."

Thereafter both the sons of king Tashi Od de with the support of Zanskar king and local people constructed Tshazar Gonpa.

Thiksey Monastery: In Nubra valley Cang Sems Shesrab Zangpo got good support from King Dragpa Bum and Nubra people. Soon after he succeeded to get confidence of Nubrapas, many of them became his followers. He stayed in Nubra for a few years, alongwith his assistant and followers he propagated Geluk pa order in Nubra. Later he returned to Tagmo gonpa. In Tagmo he didn't get good response from the villagers. He reviewed monastic activities, but felt sorry to know that according to the expectation, the number of lamas in the Tagmo monastery didn't increase. Later, went for meditation.When came out from the temple, he brought *chotpa* or *'prasad'* to offer to birds, thus went to the adjoining hillock. At the top he placed the *'prasad'* and hid nearby later saw:

"Two crows first sat near *'prasad'* then carried it away to the Thiksey hillock."

He surprised to see this incident and returned to Tagmo monastery. After sometime his main disciple Paldah Shelrab came in his room. He said:

"Paldan, today I saw an interesting incident."

"Guruji! please tell me what was that?"

"Listen, when I placed *'prasad'* on a rock, two crows flew up and picked up it to Thiksey hillock."

"Guruji, what is new in it ?"

"You will not understand, now let us go to Thiksey hillock to "see the position of *'prasad'*.

"O.K."

Both went to Thiksey hillock, soon after they reached there and astonished to see:

"The *'prasad'* was placed on a stone without harming it."

Cang Sems Shesrab Zangpo said:

"Paldan, Now you understand."

"No, Guruji."

"The *'prasad'* was carried here by the two envoys of our supreme Guru Tsongkhapa. This indicates that this place is good for the monastery. Therefore, we should construct a new monastery here. And you will take this responsibility."

"All right Guruji."

"I hope, you will not face any problem, by the blessing of Guruji monastery will have bright future, now we can fulfil the desires of our Guruji and will able to propagate Geluk pa order in Ladakh."

Thereafter both returned to Tagmo temple. After sometimes Lama Cang Sems Shesrab Zangpo called Paldan Shesrab at his room and said:

Paldan, now time has come, you have to go to Thiksey and construct temple on the hillock. I hope villagers and administration of Ladakh kingdom will help you in this auspicious work."

"All right Guruji, as you wish."

Paldan Shesrab alongwith some lamas of the Stagmo monastery went to Thiksey. They contacted villagers for help. By the blessing of Tsongkhapa nobody denied for the religious works. Very soon they were able to construct a temple, gradually villagers started to donate their children to the Thiksey temple to become monks. When the number of monks had been increasing, they constructed rooms for them near the temple. Gradually, Dukhang, and other temples were constructed. Now Lama Chang Sems Shesrab Zangpo shifted to Thiksey. By the time Thiksey temple had been developed into the shape of Thiksey monastery. It had many lamas. Therefore, Cang Sems Shesrab Zangpo decided to make proper schedule for the monastic activities in the Thiksey monastary as well as he had established monastic discipline.

Journey to Zanskar: When all monastic activities in the monastery was performed according to his planning and time table, Cang Sems Shesrab Zangpo decided that he should not remain in Thiksey monastery for long period, and to propagate Geluk pa order in the other parts of Ladakh. Therefore, he gave his all responsibilities of Thiksey monastery to Paldan Shesrab and went to Zanskar. After sometime he arrived in Zanskar and stayed in Phugtal monastery[12]. He took a long meeting with lamas and administrators of Phugtal monastery. After the long discussion he came to know that Phugtal monastery was needed his assistance. Thence, he stayed in the monastery and according to the Vinaya rules and regulations he improved the vinayaic rules and stricted the monastic discipline. As a result lama population increased considerably within a short period. To witness self sustain development of Phugtal monastery, Cang Sems Shesrab Zangpa moved to other monasteries in Zanskar, for example, Stong de[13] and Karsha[14] where he strictly implimented the Vinaya rules and asked senior lamas of the respective monastery to follow monastic discipline. Besides, he preached lamas and encouraged them to engage themselves in and outside the monastery works.

To decorate Zanskar monasteries by paintings: Cang Sems Shesrab Zangpo when arrived in Zanskar, he saw maximum monasteries were either without painting works or were being deteriorated. Therefore, to beautify these monasteries, he invited Pon Paldan Shesrab and Shesrab Lotus from Thiksey, who later under his direction decorated the temples of Phugtal, Stongde and Karsha monasteries.

Contribution of Dode Rinchen: In Zanskar Lama Dode Rinchen was very much impressed by the Cang Sems Shesrab Zangpo's scholarly speech and became his disciple, later under the direction of his guru he constructed Sani monastery in Zanskar, thereafter visited to Nubra, Spiti etc. to propagate Geluk-pa tradition of Buddhism.

Parinirvana of Cang Sems Shesrab Zangpo: On his last days of his life Cang Sems Shesrab Zangpo concentrated Zanskar for his religious works. At last this great scholar and disciple of Tsongkhapa got parinirvana on 28th May 1457[15].

Conclusion: Lama Cang Sems Shesrab Zangpo, came in Ladakh from Tibet to propagate Geluk-pa order on the advice of his teacher Tsong-khapa. In Ladakh he established Geluk pa monasteries, strengthened monastic discipline.

Notes and References

1. **Cang Sems Shesrab Zangpo:*****Tib. byang-sems-shes-rab-bzang-po.*** He was the main disciple of Tsong-Khapa of Geluk pa order.
2. **Tashi:** ***Tib. bkra shis,*** **he was the father of** Cang Sems Shesrab Zangpo.
3. **Palzon:** ***Tib. dpal adzon.*** She was the mother of Cang Sems Shesrab Zangpo.
4. **Tsong-Khapa:** ***Tib. Tsong-kha-pa.*** He was born in the district of Tsong kha (Tsongkha), meaning, Onion Valley, in the vicinity of Lake Kokonor (Qinghai Hu) in Amdo (Northeastern

Tibet), where in 1578 the sku bum (Pron Kumbum) monastery was founded at his birth place. At a very early age he received a consecration from ***Rol pa'i rdo rje*** (Pron. Rolpe Dorje), who was the Fourth Gyelwa' Karmapa, and was a boy of eight he received a further consecration and an introduction to the disciplinary rule of Vinaya, and to the Tanatra, from a great spiritual friend Don grub rinchen, who also gave him the monastic name of ***blo-bzahg grags pa.*** At the age of sixteen Tsongkhapa went to central Tibet and for many years studied with famous teacher Nyingma-pa, Shalu-pa, Jong-pa, Kaya-pa, Phakmotru-pa, Shalu-pa, and Kadam-pa. Lama Buma-pa brought Tsongkhapa into mystic communication with Boddhisattva Manjusri (Manjushri), to whom Tsongkhapa turned for guidance at various points in his life. He himself was the incarnation of Manjusri. Cf Finegan, Jack; Tibet: A Dreamt of Image; Tibet House; 1986: 100-10.

5. **Tagmo Village: *Tib. stog-mo.*** It is on the left of Leh-Manali Highway or at the north-east of Thiksey monastery, about 5 km. from Thiksey village.

6. **Diskyit:** Lat 34° 33′
   Long 77° 36′
   Elevation: 9,950 feet.

   Tib. bde skyid. It is on the left bank of the Shyok River, opposite its junction with Nubra River. It is one of the largest village in Nubra valley and is the headquarter of Nubra subsector of Leh district. During nineteen century A.D. It had fifty eight houses out of which fifty three payed taxes to the concerned Government. There were very few artisans and handicraft workers viz in between 5 to 10 only. The livestock population was also not very large, i.e. 5.3 horned cattle, and over a thousand sheep and goats. The cultivated lands of the village lie on a sloping bank, rising rather steeply out of the plain. Many apriot trees grew among the houses, large enough to afford a shade under which a tent could be pitched. Here much of the plain in encrusted with soda. On the top of the mountain, a big monastery of Geluk pa order is situated. This monastery is partially administered by Thiksey monastery in Leh. Cf. Gazetteer of Kashmir and Ladakh; First pub. 1890; Reprinted in 1974 by Vivek Pub. House, Delhi, India: 289-90.

7. **Inja: *Tib. dben s'ai.*** Here on the mountain slope a monastery of Geluk-pa order tradition is situated. It is about 6 km. from the Panamik village in Nubra valley.
8. **Tashi Od-de: *Tib. bka shi'od lde.*** He was the king of Guge province.
9. **Guge:** It is a province in western Tibet, ***kyid Nyima Gon*** had divided his kingdom into his three sons: Pelgyigon, Trashgon and Detsugon. Detsugon received the kingdom of Guge province and became the first king.
10. **Rinchen-Palde: *Tib. rin chen dpal lde.*** In olden days Ladakh had many princely states. Therefore Zanskar during 15th century was ruled by Rinchen-Palde.
11. **Zompas: *Tib. Dzon pas.*** She was the queen of Zanskar during fifteenth century A.D.
12. **Phugtal monastery: *Tib. phug-dal.*** This beautiful monastery has a huge cave high up in the sheer mountain face of a lateral gorge through which a major tributary of the southern Lungnak River flows. Perhaps the most isolated monastic establishment of Zanskar. This monastery was founded by ***'Phags-pa Shes-rab'*** the great translator of Zanskar. He was

the teacher mdo-sde rin-chen who was responsible to flourish Geluk-pa order of Buddhism in Zanskar alongwith, ***Shes-rab-bzang-po.*** Cf. Thuspstan Paldan: Buddhist monasteries and Royal Castles in Ladakh; 1976 : 24.

13. **Stong-de:** ***Tib. stong-sde.*** This monastery lies 18 km. to the north of Padum on the road leading to Zangla, the second largest monastic establishment in Zanskar of Geluk-pa order. This monastery was founded by the famous Siddha Marpa. Therefore, sometimes this monastery is known as **Mar-pa-Ling.**

14. **Karsha:** ***Tib. dkar-sha.*** Pron. Karsha. This monastery is one of the largest monastic establishment of Zanskar, resided nearly 150 monks, built along the steep gradient of the mountain side above the Stod River. It was founded by phags-pa shes-rap, the great translator of Zanskar of Geluk-pa order.

15. Sonam Phuntsong; Ladakh; 2000: 52.

Bibliography

Jina, Prem Singh (1981): Ladakh Aur Paryatan In: All India Conference, CIBS; Leh-Ladakh.

——; (1983): Seet Kal me Leh Ghati; Sheeraja-65, J&K Cultural Academy Pub. Jammu (Hindi), March.

——; (1983): Santi Stupa Ladakh Ke, Yojana, Jammu, March : 15-16.

——; 1983: Baudh Bhikshu of Ladakh, In: All India Conference on 'Buddhist and Jaina Monasticism' Deptt of Buddhist Studies, Delhi Univ. 5th Sept.

——; 1984: Leh Kitana Praceen Kitana Aadhunik; Navaneet, Hindi Digest, Bombay.

——; 1984: Karl Mark and Bodhisattva Ka Parath, Proceed All India Conference, Ladakh Prabha (2): 65-69.

——; 1984: Foreign tourists and their import on Ladakh, In: All India Conference Central Institute of Buddhist Studies, Choglamsar, Leh-Ladakh.

——; 1984: 'Ladakh me Ring cell ka Mahatava', *Sheeraja*- 71, June-Sept.: 23-25.

——; 1984: The Foreign tourists traffic in Ladakh; *Himalayan Research and Development* (Problem Oriented Studies), Vol. 3 (i), Nainital, June.

——; 1984: Buddhism in Ladakh and World Peace, In: Xth International Buddhist Conference,

On; *'Buddhism and World Peace'*, Indosan Nipponji, Bodh Gaya, Dec. 8-9.

——;1985: The Bhotios: A Socio Economic and Cultural Study In: All India Conference, CIBS, Leh-Ladakh.

——;1985: Ladakh Ki Sanskriti Ke Upvan me Stok Rajvans', *Sanskriti,* April, Vol. 27, No. 2 : 11-12.

——; 1986: 'Buddha kaleen yug me cikitsa; padayati', *Vigyan Pragati,* Delhi, Feb: 53.

——; 1986: 'Economic and Cultural Relations between Ladakh and Lahul and Spiti, In: First All India Conference, Boudh Darshan Mahavidhyalaya, Keylong (H.P.).

——; 1986: 'A brief Introduction of Ladakhi Gonpas', In : All India Conference, Kashmir University, Srinagar, J&K State.

——;1986: Pasturelands Zanskar and its effects on Ecology', In: 1st National Conference, Desert Dev. Agency, Leh-Ladakh.

——;1986: Pasturelands of Leh and its effects on Ecology, In: First National Conference, Indian Army, Trishul Natural Conservation, Leh-Ladakh.

——; 1987: Rashtarapal paricheda Aek Dristi, In: All India Conference, CIBS, Leh- Ladakh.

——;1987: Desvi Satabadi me Kashmir me Bodh Dharam Aur Ushka Ladakh Ki Sanskriti Par Prabhav; In: All India Conference, CIBS, Leh-Ladakh.

——;1986: A survey of Buddhist Community in Ladakh Himalaya, In: 12th International Buddhist Conference on 'Buddhism and Social Harmony' Japanese Temple, Bodh Gaya.

——;1987: 'Pasture Ecology of Leh-Ladakh', In: International Conference on Ladakh Studies, Dresdan, Germany.

——;1988: 'Bodh Dham Leh-Ladakh', *Hindu Cetana,* Vol. 7, No. 21-23, June.

——;1988: 'Ladakh me Bodh Raja' *Hindu Cetana,* Vol.10: 19-20

——; 1988: Asangha and his Contribution, In: All India Conference, Leh-Ladakh, CIBS Proceed Ladakh Prabha[6]: 97-98.

——;1988: 'Monasteries in the Economy of Leh-Ladakh' In: All India Conference, CIBS, Leh-Ladakh.

——;1989: 'Ladakh Ki Mahila Prasashak: Wangmo', *Hamara Sahiya;* Jammu 104-06.

——;1989: Losar in Himalaya; In: All India Conference, Shimla.

——;1989: 'Eco-Environmental Study of Tourists Industry in Ladakh Himalaya' In: All India Conference, Kashmir University, Srinagar, J&K State.

——;1990 'Buddhism, and Human values in the History of Conference on Buddhism, Japanese Temple," Bodh Gaya.

——;1990: 'Pashmina Economy in Ladakh', *Yojana,* Delhi, Dec. 16-13.

——;1991: 'Ladakh me Bodh Kala Ka Udbhav, Avam Vikash' *Sheeraja,* Vol. 1. March: 12-14.

——; 1991: 'Ladakh: History and Growth of Education' *Himalaya Today,* Sept. No.Vl Vol. Ill, No. 2: 16-18.

——;1992: 'Ladakh Shirobhusa-Perakh' *Sheeraja,* Feb-March, Vol. 6, Jammu: 20-23.

——;1993: 'Ladakh Vadiya Sanyantra-Daman' *Sheeraja,* Vol. 4, Oct-Nov.: 27-29.

——;1993: 'Dasvi Satabadi Purva Lahul me Bodh Dharam Evam Sanskriti' *Janjati Mela Smarika:* 32-63.

——;1993: 'Tourism and Environment' In: International Conference on Ladakh Studies, IALS, Leh-Ladakh August.

——;1993: 'Buddhism in Ladakh and its Approach to Material World' In: International Buddhist Conference, Japanese Temple, Bodh Gaya, Dec. 8-10.

——;1993: 'Impact of Tourism on Ladakhi Society and Culture' In : All India Conference, Jawahar Lal Nehru Univ., Delhi.

——;1994: 'Tourist Industry in Ladakh Himalaya *Himalaya Today,* Jan-March, Vol. 2: 20.

——;1994: 'Kesar: A Great Epic' *Sheeraja,* Vol. 11 June-July, Jammu.

——;1994: 'Ladakh me Losar' *Sheeraja,* Aug-Sept. Vol. 3:22-29.

——;1994: 'Bikshumi Sangha Avam Ladakh Me Usaki Stithi' In: All India Conference; Keylong, H.P.: 50-52.

——;1994: 'Tibetan Me Musalmano ka Aagaman, *Neeshant'* March-Sept. Aligarh Muslim Univ. Pub. Vol. 3-12: 29-30.

——;1994 : 'Spiti Ka Sanskritik Itihas' *Janjati Utsav,* Keylong: 70-72.

——;1994: 'Tourism in Ladakh Himalaya' Indus Pub. Co. New Delhi.

——;1995: 'Some Famous Explorers to Ladakh' Indus Pub. Co. New Delhi.

——;1995: 'Phyang Monastery of Ladakh' Indus Pub. Co. New Delhi.

——;1995: 'High Pasture lands of Ladakh' Indus Pub.Co. New Delhi.

——;1996: 'Lahul Va Spiti Me Bodh Dharam' Somshi, June-Sept.

——;1995: 'Buddhism in Ladakh' *Yug Udbodhan,* Vol. 9, Sept. 14-16.

——;1996: 'Ladakhi Gonpa Me Bhiksu, Ki Pravesh Vidhi' *Yug Udbodhan,* Vol. 2; No.6, New Delh: 9.

——;1996: 'Tabo Monastery: A Unique Monument in Spiti Valley' *Yug Udbodhan,* Vol. 2, No. 11, New Delhi: 13.

——;1996: 'Hemis: The Biggest Monastery of Ladakh' *Yug Udbodhan,* Vol. 2, No.4, New Delhi: 15.

——;1996: 'Ladakh: The Land and the people' Indus Pub. Co. New Delhi.

——;1997(ed.) 'Recent Researchers on the Himalaya' Indus Pub. Co. New Delhi.

——;1997: 'Dasvi Sathi Avan Lahul' Somshi, July-Oct.

——;1997: 'Travel Accounts of the Chinese pilgrims in the Himalaya' In: *'Recent Researchers on the Himalaya'* : 35-42.

——;1997: 'A.H. Franke's contribution in the cultural History of Ladakh' In: *Recent Researchers on the Himalaya:* 43-52.

——;1997: Nawang Tsering' A Brilliant Sulptor of Ladakh, In: *Recent Researchers on the Himalaya:* 61-64.

——;1997 : Bhotia of Nepal: A Socio-Economic and Cultural Study, In: *Recent Researchers on the Himalaya:* 74-77.

——;1997; 'Lamayuru Monastery of Ladakh', In: *Recent Researcher's on the Himalaya:* 82-86.

——;1997: 'Modernisation and Buddhism in Ladakh' In: *Recent Researchers on the Himalaya:* 106-13.

——;1997: 'Impact of Tourism on the Ecological Setup of Ladakh Himalaya' In: *Recent Researchers on the Himalaya:* 122-25.

——;1997: 'Utility of Nemo-Padum Road for the Economic Development of Zangskar', In: *Recent Researchers on the Himalaya:* 126-28.

——;1997: 'Turmoil and Success in Ladakhi politics' In: *Recent Researchers on the Himalaya'.* 216-19.

——;1998: Ladakh Bodh Vivah Geet, Sheeraja, Feb-March, Vol. 6: 21-26.

——;1998: 'Tibetan Manuscripts and Inscriptions of Ladakh Himalaya' Satguru Pub., New Delhi.

——;1998: 'Buddhism in Ladakh and Ushka Parath' In: XXIII International Buddhist Conference, Indosan Nipponji, Bodh Gaya, 8-9, Dec.

——;1999: 'Boddhism and non-violence' In: XXIV International Buddhist Conference, Indosan Nipponji, Bodh Gaya, 8-9 Dec.

——;1999: 'Ladakh' In: Dhara Se Gagan Tak' Vijay Kumar Tiwar (ed.).

——;1999: 'Ladakh Mera Anubhav, *Anjuri.*

——;1999: 'The Chang-pa of the Ladakh Himalaya: Some Observation on their economy and environment' Nomadic Peoples, NS (1999), Vol. 3. Issue No. 1. Universitatzu , Albertus Magnus-Platz, Koln, Germany: 94-105.

——;1999: 'History of education and growth in Ladakh': The International Conference on Ladakh Studies' IALS, Leh, Aug.

——;1999: 'Some monasteries of Drigung pa Order in Central Ladakh' Satguru Pub., New Delhi.

——;1999: 'Changing Face of Ladakh Himalaya' Om. Pub. New Delhi.

——;1999: 'Lamayuru Monastery of Ladakh Himalaya' Om Pub., New Delhi.

——;2000: *Ladakh Past and Present* Gyan Pub., New Delhi.

——;2000 (ed.): 'Eco-Environment study of Chang-Thang Cold Arid zone of Ladakh; A case study of Tsomoriri Lake region' (Abstraet) In: National Workshop on Conservation of High Altitude Wetlands in Ladakh Region, W.W.F.; 20-30 July.

——;2000: 'The Role of Green Tourism in Ladakh' In: *Ladakh Past and Present:* 99-102.

——;2000: 'Tourist Attractions of Ladakh' In: *Ladakh Past and Present:* 89-98.

——;2000: 'Some Muslim Monuments': A case study of Leh district', In: *Ladakh Past and Present* : 107: 110.

——;2000: 'Cultural History of Mangtro Monastery of Ladakh' In: *Ladakh Past and Present* : 111-122.

——;2000: 'Murals of mGon-pa in Gon-khang of Phyang Monastery of Ladakh' In: *Ladakh Past and Persent* 127-138.'

——;2000: 'The Social Economy of Buddhist Monasteries' in Ladakh' In: *'Ladakh Past and Present':* 159-168.

——;2000: 'Changing Horizon of Ladakhi Politics' of In: *'Ladakh Past and Persent* : 169-180.

——;2001: (ed.): 'Religious History of Ladakh' Satguru Pub, New Delhi.

——;2001: 'Ladakh Ki Kala Avam Sanskriti' Indira Gandhi National Center for Arts, New Delhi.

——;2001: 'Varshavas Ka Mahatava' In: (All India Conference, C.I.B.S., Leh-Ladakh.

——;2001: 'Ladakh Ke Pramukh Bodh Vihar' *Sindhu Darshan,* Vol. 3: 20-25.

——;2002 (ed.): 'Development of Ladakh: Recent Researchers; Gyan Pub., New Delhi.

——;2002: 'A Look at Bhoto Society in Ladakh' In: *Development of Ladakh: Recent Researchers, :* 31-36.

——;2002: 'Bhoti and Arabic Influence upon Dok' culture of Ladakh, In: *Development of Ladakh: Recent Reseachers:* 41-44.

——;2002: 'Buddhist monasteries in Ladakh' In: Development of Ladakh : Recent Reseachers: 59-64.

——;2002: 'Hemis Tsechu and Ladakh' In : *Development of Ladakh : Recent Researchers:* 65-68.

——;2002: 'Chortens of Ladakh' In: *Development of Ladakh : Recent Researchers:* 69-76.

——;2002: 'Famous mGon-po dkar-brgyed in Nubra Valley of Ladakh' In: *Development of Ladakh: Recent Researchers:* 77-80.

——;2002: 'Monasteries of Ladakh : A case study of Tashi-Ga-Tsal Monastery of Ladakh' In: *Development of Ladakh : Recent Researchers:* 81-90.

——;2002: 'Painting in Phyang Monastery of Ladakh' In: *Development of Ladakh : Recent Researchers:* 91-104.

——;2002: and T. Tundup Gojing Pa, 2002: 'Buddhist Art in Ladakh, A case study of sumda valley' In: *Development of Ladakh: Recent Researchers:* 105-128.

——;2002: 'Sindhu Abhiyan (Sindhu Darshan)' In: *Development of Ladakh: Recent Researchers:* 129-138.

——;2002: 'Tourism and changing environment of Ladakh' In: *Development of Ladakh: Recent Researchers:* 139-152.

——;2002: 'Dok -Pa: An Aryan Raee of Ladakh' In: *Development of Ladakh: Recent Researchers:* 181-88.

——;2002: Tsering Sonam : 'Historical, Background of Ayou kalon of Ladakh' In: *Development of Laddk: Recent Researchers:* 211-214.

——;2002: Grazing Fee and Begari System in Ladakh, In: *Development of Ladakh : Recent Researchers:* 217: 220.

——;2002: 'Ancient Trade Route' Via Balu-mkar to Central Asia, In : *Development of Ladakh: Recent Researchers:* 221-224.

——;2002: 'Some Rock, stone and wooden sculptures of Ladakh' In: *Development of Ladakh : Recent Researchers:* 225-232.

——;2002: Konchok Namgyal Ladakh, Before and During the Indo-Pak War 1947, In: *Development of Ladakh : Recent Researchers:* 230-40.

——;2002: Thinles Yangzor 2002, Origin and Growth of Ladakhi Medicine (Amchi) System; In: *Development of Ladakh : Recent Researchers* : 241-58.

——;2002: 'Morup Namgyal' : A famous Ladakh Artist, In: *Development of Ladakh: Recent Reseachers* : 259-62.

——;2002: 'Rinpoches of Ladakh' In: *Development of Ladakh: Recent Researchers:* 263-66.

——;2002: 'Lamas of Ladakh' In: *Development of Ladakh : Recent Researcher.* 267-278.

——;2002: 'Ge-Sar Epic of Ladakh' In: *Development of Ladakh; Recent Researchers.* 271-278.

——;2003: A.H. Franke: [First collection of Tibetan Historical Inscriptions on Rock and Stone from Ladakh, Himalaya, Satguru. Pub. New Delhi.

——;2003: 'History of Education in Ladakh before Independance' In: All India Conference, CIBS, Leh-Ladakh.

——;2003: Hemis Bodh Vihar: A Sansipth Praicaya; *Sindhu Darshan*, Vol.: 21-23.

——;2004: 'Ladakh Abhushan: Perag'; *Sindhu Darshan*, Vol. 5. F.R.L. Leh.

——;2004: Varshavash (A reference of Bodh Bhiksus in Ladakh), In : All India Conference, CIBS, Leh-Ladakh.

——;2004: 'Buddhism to Human Rights and Status of women' In: International Buddhist Conference, Japanese Temple, Bodh Gaya.

——;2004: 'Kesar', Sakshi. Pub. New Delhi.

——;2004: 'Buddhism for Twenty First Century, In: International Seminar on Buddhism for twenty first century ; 25-29 Aug, C.I.S.B. Leh-Ladakh.

——;2005 'Ladakh Sthit Thiksey Bodh Vihar me prachin co-mo Lhakhang Ka Adhyan' In: All India Conference; C.I.B.S. 10-14 Aug.

——;2006 'Ladakh Himalaya' 'Past and Present' Anmol Pub., New Delhi.

——;2005: 'Ladakh, Profile' Gyan Pub., New Delhi.

——;2006: 'Thiksey Monastery of Ladakh Himalaya' Satguru Pub., New Delhi.

——;2006: Char Brahma Vihar; In : All India Conference, C.I.B.S., Leh-Ladakh.

——& Jigmet Omachikpa : 'Tourist Resources of Ladakh : A Study of Gur Phug Monastery; Anmol Pub., New Delhi (In Press).

Index

C

L

M

N

Q

R

T

V